Shaping
Constitutional
Values

Jerry

Your scholarship and friendship have meant a lot to me. Thanks for providing important insights to this book. Thanks also for your back cover comments

Neal

INTERPRETING AMERICAN POLITICS
Michael Nelson, Series Editor

The Logic of Lawmaking:
A Spatial Theory Approach
Gerald S. Strom

The Institutional Presidency
John P. Burke

Regulatory Politics in Transition
Marc Allen Eisner

Executive Privilege: The Dilemma of
Secrecy and Democratic Accountability
Mark J. Rozell

With Reverence and Contempt: How Americans
Think about Their President
Thomas S. Langston

The Two Majorities: The Issue Context
of Modern American Politics
Byron E. Shafer and William J. M. Claggett

The Selling of Supreme Court Nominees
John Anthony Maltese

The Foundation of Merit:
Public Service in American Democracy
Patricia Wallace Ingraham

Shaping Constitutional Values:
Elected Government, the Supreme
Court, and the Abortion Debate
Neal Devins

Shaping Constitutional Values

*Elected Government,
the Supreme Court, and
the Abortion Debate*

NEAL DEVINS

THE JOHNS HOPKINS UNIVERSITY PRESS
BALTIMORE AND LONDON

© 1996 The Johns Hopkins University Press
All rights reserved. Published 1996
Printed in the United States of America on acid-free paper
05   04   03   02   01   00   99   98   97   96   5   4   3   2   1

The Johns Hopkins University Press
2715 North Charles Street, Baltimore, Maryland 21218-4319
The Johns Hopkins Press Ltd., London

ISBN 0-8018-5284-6   ISBN 0-8018-5285-4 (pbk.)

Library of Congress Cataloging-in-Publication Data will be found at
the end of this book.
A catalog record for this book is available from the British Library.

For my grandmother, Ann Weitzman,
with love and gratitude

Contents

Foreword

EVERY FOUR YEARS, AT APPROXIMATELY noon on 20 January, the president speaks the following words from Article II section 1 of the Constitution: "I do solemnly swear (or affirm) that I will faithfully execute the Office of the President of the United States, and will to the best of my Ability, preserve, protect and defend the Constitution of the United States." (It is by custom that presidents since George Washington have added the phrase "so help me God.") Members of Congress take a similar oath to uphold the Constitution when they begin their terms, as do other government officials and employees.

Why, then, is it so widely believed that the Supreme Court is the ultimate arbiter of what the Constitution means? Not because of Chief Justice John Marshall, who in declaring in *Marbury* v. *Madison* (1803) that courts are empowered to say "what the law is" did not intend to deny the right or the responsibility of the elected branches of government to make similar determinations. Not because of Abraham Lincoln, who stated in his first inaugural address (1861) that "if the policy of the government . . . is to be irrevocably fixed by decisions of the Supreme Court . . . the people will have ceased to be their own rulers." And certainly not because of Franklin D. Roosevelt, who in 1937 tried to pack the Supreme Court with six additional justices when it ruled against his New Deal agenda.

According to Neal Devins, the Supreme Court's claim to be the "supreme" expositor of the Constitution can be traced only to the Warren Court's decision in *Cooper* v. *Aaron* (1958). Yet even in the wake of that ruling the reality of constitutional interpretation is different. "Constitutional decision-making cannot be traced solely to the efforts of nine justices, or a majority of nine," Devins argues. "Other parts of government interpret the Constitution and influence the judiciary." Indeed, because of the limitations that Article III of the Constitution places on judicial jurisdiction, "elected government often is the ultimate, indeed the only, interpreter of the Constitution." By elected government Devins means not just Congress and the president but also the governments of the states.

By considering elected government–Supreme Court dialogues on equality, separation of powers, federalism, and religion, Devins demonstrates the pervasive role that elected officials play in shaping constitutional norms. In a detailed case study of the law and politics of abortion, he shows that *Roe* v. *Wade*, the 1973 Supreme Court decision that shrouded a woman's right to have an abortion in the garb of constitutional protection, began a constitutional controversy rather than settling one. Between 1973 and 1989, forty-eight states passed 306 statutes to limit the right to choose abortion. Congress passed the Hyde Amendment, which reduced the number of abortions paid for by the federal Medicaid program from more than a quarter-million a year to virtually none. Presidents Ronald Reagan and George Bush appointed hundreds of pro-life judges to the federal courts and barred abortion counseling at federally funded clinics. In 1989 and 1992, responding to these political pressures, the Supreme Court modified the *Roe* decision in the cases of *Webster* v. *Reproductive Health Services* and *Planned Parenthood* v. *Casey,* respectively. Bill Clinton was elected president in 1992 with a pledge to make abortion "safe, legal, and rare."

Devins's point is not the Supreme Court is unimportant in constitutional policymaking—far from it. It is, rather, that "by focusing almost exclusively on Court decisions, the constitutional law class hardly ever considers elected government." Yet elected officials not only take oaths to uphold the Constitution, they also act on the basis of those oaths. On the abortion issue, Devins concludes, elected government has served the country well.

Michael Nelson

Preface

THE IDEA OF WRITING A BOOK ON what the abortion dispute teaches us about constitutional decision-making occurred to me in the fall of 1991. At that time, Louis Fisher and I were completing work on *Political Dynamics of Constitutional Law*, a book that canvasses the role of nonjudicial influences in several landmark Supreme Court decisions. After examining two dozen subjects in *Political Dynamics*, I was ready to see what could be learned by examining the pervasiveness and impact of interchanges between the courts and elected government through an in-depth treatment of one subject. I was especially interested in seeing whether the lessons from such a focused study would bolster or contradict impressions that I had previously formed about the scope and sweep of nonjudicial influences.

Two interrelated questions are examined in this study: (1) does elected government respect the Court as a co-equal branch of the federal government? and (2) does the Court respect elected-government efforts to shape constitutional disputes? In asking these questions, this book sheds light on several other matters, including the extraordinary range of powers and techniques available to elected government in shaping constitutional values; the role Supreme Court decision-making plays in elected-government responses to Court action; the costs single-issue politics impose on political institutions; the Supreme Court's sensitivity to political reprisals; and the role of public opinion in shaping judicial doctrine.

Why then focus on abortion? After all, elected-government interpretation figures prominently in all areas of constitutional decision-making. Abortion nonetheless is indisputably the perfect candidate for a comprehensive treatment of the role played by nonjudicial forces in the shaping of constitutional values. In the more than twenty years since *Roe* v. *Wade*, elected government has pursued a staggering number of abortion-related initiatives. The culmination of these initiatives is *Planned Parenthood* v. *Casey*, a 1992 Supreme Court decision that moderated *Roe* and quieted the abortion dispute. With the abortion issue now quieted (if not fully settled) an assessment about the style and impact of Court–elected government dialogues can take into account how elected government and the courts have shaped each other.

This study is not simply well-timed, for studies subsequent to this will have the even greater advantage of twenty-twenty hindsight. Remarkable as it may sound, the questions explored in this book have not been considered elsewhere. With one exception, other books on this subject have sought either to juggle abortion politics with other concerns or have limited their sights to a select number of topics in abortion politics. Only the political scientists Barbara Craig and David O'Brien, in their 1993 *Abortion and American Politics*, have provided a near-comprehensive accounting of federal and state abortion politics. Craig and O'Brien, however, draw no conclusions about what abortion politics reveals about American political institutions (or, conversely, what American political institutions tell us about abortion politics). The authors' sole objective—which they accomplish with distinction—is to demonstrate that political actors, as well as courts, shape abortion rights.

A principal purpose of this book is to provide guidance both on how to measure the quality and impact of elected-branch constitutional interpretation and on how to assess the factors that affect elected-government responses to Court action. These objectives extend well beyond the abortion dispute. They inform this book's ultimate quest of assessing whether interchanges between the Court and elected government are as constructive as they are inevitable.

Acknowledgments

A GREAT MANY PEOPLE CONTRIBUTED TO the thinking, researching, writing, and editing of this book. My friend and sometimes collaborator Louis Fisher deserves credit for piquing my interest in elected-branch constitutional interpretation. Over the past fifteen years, Lou has been an invaluable commentator on my work, including a draft manuscript of this book. David Garrow, Michael Nelson, David O'Brien, Jeremy Rabkin, Henry Tom, and an anonymous reviewer also provided invaluable commentary on my draft manuscript.

Michael Nelson and Henry Tom deserve special thanks for other reasons. Mike suggested to me that I do a book on elected government constitutional interpretation and backed up that suggestion with a book contract. Henry, from the beginning of this project, played an instrumental role in keeping me focused on and committed to this project.

Several students at the College of William and Mary School of Law read the draft manuscript and offered important substantive and stylistic suggestions. These students include Donna Buddenhagen, Jason Kelly, Doug Onley, and Chris Shea. Other William and Mary students played an instrumental role in the researching of this book. These students include Katherine Ennis, Paula Hannaford, Matt Ide, Jason Kelly, Megan Kelly, Jeanne Locascio, Tracy Nelson, Phil Runkel, Susan Seiger, Ann Shepherd, Brad Wagshull, and especially Wendy Watson. I am also indebted to Kenny Greenspan and especially Jason Kelly for assisting me in proofreading the final manuscript as well as preparing the book's index. Finally, Keith Finch coauthored chapter 5 of this book, a chapter that grew out of a yet-unfinished joint law review project.

Thanks are also owed to Miriam Kleiger for her excellent copyediting of the manuscript and to Della Harris, Sarah Crotty, and Sherry Thomas for word-processing support. Finally, I am indebted to the College of William and Mary School of Law. Over the past several years, the law school has provided me with summer research support and reduced teaching loads to facilitate the completion of this and other research projects.

It is a bit staggering to realize how many people have played a direct role in the writing of this book, mostly giving of their time and good will for little or no compensation. Beyond the individuals mentioned above, I also owe an enormous debt to my family for being interested in my work and accepting of my unusual work habits. In particular, my wife, Deborah Vick, along with Moby, Pookie, Rocky, and Scout (who lay at my feet throughout the writing of this book), have put up with and cared for me during this endeavor.

1 / Introduction

IMAGINE THE RIGHTS OF WOMEN without *Roe* v. *Wade;* the rights of racial minorities without *Brown* v. *Board of Education;* or the rights of criminal defendants without *Miranda* v. *Arizona.* For those who see the courts "as powerful, vigorous, and potent proponents of change,"[1] that world would be horrific. Indeed, the political furor over Clarence Thomas, Robert Bork, and other Supreme Court nominees is largely informed by the belief that Supreme Court justices wield enormous political power. This belief also explains, as Justice Antonin Scalia complained, why the justices are subject to "carts full of mail from the public, and streets full of demonstrators, urging us—their unelected and life-tenured judges . . . —to follow the popular will."[2]

This portrayal of the Court as a player, shaping policy through decisions having a nationwide impact, is hardly surprising. Nevertheless, starting with Ronald Reagan's 1986 elevation of William Rehnquist to chief justice, a vigorous debate has emerged over the potency of judicial decision-making. Flying in the face of longstanding attacks against an "imperial judiciary" by conservative critics of the Court, left-leaning political scientists and constitutional lawyers began depicting court-ordered reform as a "hollow hope." For this new wave of Court critics, meaningful reform is accomplished through social movements and elected-branch initiatives.

Epitomizing this ongoing debate over the reach and wisdom of judicial policy-making is *Roe* v. *Wade.* For conservative critics, such as Judge Robert Bork, *Roe* is "the greatest example and symbol of the judicial usurpation of democratic prerogatives in this century."[3] In sharp contrast, liberal critics, such as the political scientist Gerald Rosenberg, contend that the Court was "far less responsible for the changes that occurred than most people think" and that the growth of "right-to-life" forces in the wake of *Roe* suggests "that one result of litigation to produce significant social reform is to strengthen the opponents of such change."[4] Within the Court itself, the political wisdom of *Roe* also has been debated. Most strikingly, two avid pro-choicers are the principal combatants in this dispute—the Clinton appointee Ruth Bader Ginsburg, and *Roe*'s recently retired author, Harry Blackmun.

BLACKMUN VERSUS GINSBURG

Roe v. *Wade* was designed to help put an end to the abortion dispute. Justice Harry Blackmun put forth a trimester test governing state authority over the abortion decision, both to make clear what the Court intended and to forestall future governmental efforts to sidestep the Court's decision. Specifically, the trimester test rejected state regulation of abortion during the first trimester of a pregnancy, approved reasonable state regulation during the second trimester, and authorized the prohibition of third-trimester abortions. Over objections by Justice Potter Stewart that the trimester standard was "inflexibly 'legislative,'"[5] Blackmun nonetheless persisted in his efforts to clarify the reaches and limits of governmental authority in this area. While recognizing that his specification of a woman's unqualified right to abortion in the first trimester of her pregnancy was "arbitrary," Blackmun perceived that such judicial policy-making was "not to be avoided."[6] Indeed, Blackmun implored his colleagues to decide *Roe* "no later than the week of January 15 to tie in with the convening of most state legislatures," and proposed issuing a press statement to accompany the decision (something that had never been done before and ultimately was not done here) to keep the press from "going all the way off the deep end" in reporting the news of the decision.[7]

Blackmun's efforts here reveal that politics played a large role in both the content and the packaging of *Roe*. When the decision was announced, however, Blackmun started his opinion by observing that the judicial task was "to resolve the issue of constitutional measurement, free of emotion and predilection."[8] Blackmun's vision, announced in a subsequent abortion case, was that "as judges . . . we are sworn to uphold the law even when its content gives rise to a bitter dispute."[9] Portraying the Court as being above the political fray, the supreme pursuer of constitutional truth in our three-branch system, Blackmun apparently sought to strengthen the Court's legitimacy and, in so doing, ensure that *Roe* was widely followed. Along the same lines, when the Rehnquist Court fell one vote short of overruling *Roe* in its 1992 *Planned Parenthood* v. *Casey* decision, Blackmun again professed his belief in judicial supremacy. Attacking "all who have tried to turn this Court into yet another political branch" (a not-so-cryptic reference to Presidents Reagan and Bush), Blackmun saw the future of *Roe* as riding on the 1992 presidential election. "I am 83 years old," wrote Blackmun. "I cannot remain on this Court forever, and when I do step down, the confirmation process for my successor may well focus on the issue before us today. That, I regret, may be exactly where the choice between the two worlds may be made."[10] With the election of a pro-choice candidate, Bill Clinton, Blackmun got his wish. On 14 June 1993, Clinton nominated Ruth Bader Ginsburg to succeed Byron White, one of *Roe*'s original dissenters and a long-standing opponent of abortion rights. Ginsburg, a longtime federal court of appeals judge, had also served as an advocate of women's rights both as a law professor and as a lawyer for the American Civil Liberties Union.

The Ginsburg appointment, however, is tinged with irony for staunch defenders of the power of the judiciary to settle emotionally divisive issues through decisions such as *Roe*. Unlike Blackmun, Ginsburg has emphasized that judges "play an *interdependent* part in our democracy. They do not alone shape legal doctrine but . . . they participate in a dialogue with other organs of government, and with the people as well."[11] Indeed, Ginsburg went so far as to suggest, in December 1992, that *Roe* had "prolonged divisiveness and deferred stable settlement of the [abortion] issue" by short-circuiting legislative reform efforts in the early 1970s.[12] On another occasion, Ginsburg attacked *Roe* as "heavy-handed judicial intervention" and said that it "ventured too far in the change it ordered."[13]

Ginsburg's challenge to Blackmun's view of the Court's role and the consequential nature of judicial decision-making almost proved her undoing. Clinton initially passed over Ginsburg precisely because, by questioning the propriety and workability of *Roe*, she challenged a sacred cow of the new administration. In the end, although openly disagreeing with her assessment of *Roe*'s impact, Clinton came around to Ginsburg because she was pro-choice "and that was, to me, the important thing."[14]

THE FACTS ON ABORTION

Twenty-three years after *Roe*, the abortion wars—albeit diminished—still rage on, and Blackmun's belief that *Roe* might settle the issue seems to have been—to put it mildly—hopelessly naïve. What Blackmun didn't take into account was the inevitable backlash from elected government at both the state and federal levels. Whatever respect is accorded Supreme Court decisions, the Court clearly does not have the last word on highly charged issues. Indeed, with *Planned Parenthood* v. *Casey*, the Supreme Court has replaced Blackmun's rigid trimester test with an "undue burden" standard that returns some of abortion regulation to elected government.

That Blackmun is wrong, of course, does not necessarily mean that Ginsburg is right. Ostensibly arguing that constitutional decision-making is a dialogue involving all of government, "with the people as well," Ginsburg nonetheless suggests that judicial participation in the abortion dispute was bound to be counterproductive for the cause of women's rights. Although particularly harsh on *Roe*'s draconian standard, on the grounds that it made a constructive dialogue impossible, Ginsburg's observations that legislative bodies were well on their way to validating abortion rights and that *Roe* spurred on the right-to-life movement extend well beyond the particulars of *Roe*'s resolution.

Ginsburg's contention is certainly in vogue among progressive Court critics. The *New Republic*'s Michael Kinsley and the University of Chicago's Cass Sunstein have argued that "*Roe* may have taken national policy too abruptly to a point toward which it was groping more slowly, and in the process may have prevented state legislatures from working out long-lasting solutions based upon broad public consensus."[15] Gerald Rosenberg takes this claim one step further. *Roe* v. *Wade*, rather than being characterized as a watershed, is seen as counterproductive, solidifying a "widespread, vocal, and effective" pro-choice lobby and accomplishing little else.[16] But in the end, while certainly closer to the truth than Harry Blackmun's judicial supremacy model, these claims concerning *Roe*'s limits are ultimately unsatisfactory.

Roe, as will be demonstrated in this book, is consequential in several ways. While abortion rates did not change dramatically after the decision, abortions became safer, more affordable, and more available. Moreover, as the historian David Garrow and the law professor Kathleen Sullivan have observed, "many of the political dynamics," especially the emergence of powerful right-to-life forces, "that Ginsburg and others believe commenced only in the wake of *Roe* . . . were very much present on the national political scene for almost three full years prior to" the decision.[17] Widespread support for abortion rights at the time of *Roe* (roughly two-thirds of Americans opposed abortion bans in a 1972 poll) was neutralized by "imperfections in the political marketplace," in the form of intense pro-life lobbying, which "thwart[ed] the vindication of majority preferences."[18] In plain terms, there is little reason to think that the pre-*Roe* liberalization movement would have avalanched into sweeping abortion reform throughout the nation.

Roe, finally, prompted a constructive constitutional dialogue between the courts, elected government, and the public. It is incorrect to characterize post-

Roe responses as an unduly mean-spirited and disruptive attempt to both over-rule *Roe* and shake the Court's institutional foundations. State challenges to *Roe*, many of which were rejected before 1989, typically involved waiting periods, spousal and parental consent, and other restrictions not explicitly addressed by the Court. Congressional and executive-branch actions to restrict *Roe*, all of which were validated by the Supreme Court, never directly attacked the 1973 ruling. Rather than a prohibition of judicial review of abortion-related matters or a specification—through either legislation or a constitutional amendment—that human life begins at conception, there was a pursuit of funding bans and regulations prohibiting direct or indirect support of abortion rights. Because of these persistent and wide-ranging entreaties by the state and federal government (including Supreme Court appointments), the Court moderated *Roe* in *Planned Parenthood* v. *Casey*. Of equal significance, while *Roe* invalidated forty-six state laws, the Court's loosening of *Roe* in *Casey* did not prompt a new round of antiabortion legislation and regulation. Instead, elected government has been content with the pre-*Casey* status quo, which was dramatically affected by *Roe* and its progeny. Abortion disputes continue, but they focus on ancillary concerns such as funding, clinic access, and health care.

This interaction between the Court, elected government, and the American people is an extraordinarily important feature of the abortion landscape. For this reason, Robert Dahl goes too far in suggesting that the Court's constitutional decisions eventually follow "the policy views dominant among the lawmaking majorities of the United States."[19] While it may be true, as Robert McClosky noted in his seminal study of the Supreme Court, "that the Court has seldom lagged far behind or forged far ahead of America,"[20] it is also true that—just as the Court is shaped by its social environment—the Court plays a significant role in the shaping of American mores.

That *Roe* ignited a constructive constitutional dialogue is easily overlooked. Indeed, no other study of abortion politics has come close to making this claim. The reason is that the abortion dispute is portrayed as "a clash of absolutes."[21] Specifically, pro-choice and pro-life positions are "morally and politically irreconcilable. The conflict between them is rooted in different beliefs about whether the fetus is a person, whether the right to life extends to the obligation of women to realize the human potential of a dependent fetus, and whether women have freedom of choice with regard to their bodies even if the life of an innocent person is at stake."[22] These irreconcilable positions, moreover, are considered ill-suited to judicial or political resolution. The winner-take-all nature of judicial solutions, as Michael Kinsley wrote, "has made extremists and hypocrites of us all—pro-choicers enshrining trimesters in the Constitution, pro-lifers using an ostensible concern for the mother's health to restrict the mother's freedom of choice."[23] Political approaches have been equally savaged. According to the political scientist Amy Gutmann: "Rarely have so many public officials worked so hard to say so little about an issue on the minds of so many citizens."[24]

It is for these very reasons, however, that interchanges between the Court and elected government on abortion have been somewhat successful. To begin with, this "constitutional dialogue" must be judged in context. Abortion does not lend itself to universal solutions, so some conflict is inevitable. Witness, for example, the squabbling between pro-choice and pro-life members of Congress over abortion coverage in health care reform. In July 1994, seventy-two House members announced that abortion coverage was a prerequisite for their support; thirty-five members responded by threatening to oppose any bill that provided such coverage. There is no way around this; interchanges between the Court and elected government therefore should not be condemned for failing to do what cannot be done. Instead, reflecting the impossibility of choosing one side or the other in the abortion dispute, constitutional dialogues between the courts and elected government offer a mechanism to forge middle-ground solutions in a dynamic environment that does not shut out either side of the debate. This process was at work in *Planned Parenthood* v. *Casey,* a decision that stands as a testament to the power both of elected government to shape the Court and of the Court to shape elected government. The accompanying demise of some of *Roe* v. *Wade,* a decision rooted in judicial supremacy which prompted severe elected-branch reprisals, is the other side of this dynamic process.

Admittedly, for pro-life advocates who see abortion as the taking of innocent human life and pro-choice interests who see any governmental intrusion upon a woman's right to choose as an improper constraint on liberty, this paean to middle-ground solutions is hardly satisfactory. Nonetheless, abortion is too emotionally divisive for absolutist positions—even if morally correct—to be politically workable. Just as *Roe* prompted furious reprisals by elected government, congressional efforts to fend off Reagan and Bush administration antiabortion initiatives suggest that the Court's overturning of *Roe* would have prompted an elected-government counterrevolution.

THE POLITICS OF CONSTITUTIONAL INTERPRETATION

The abortion dispute is truly extraordinary. Almost every governmental actor and every governmental power has figured prominently in this controversy. In *Roe*'s wake, tens of thousands of legislative proposals and administrative initiatives at both the federal and state levels have emerged. Irrespective of one's views of elected government's efforts, the abortion dispute provides a revealing glimpse into the workings of American political institutions. Although elected-branch interpretation figures prominently in all areas of constitutional decision-making, abortion is the perfect candidate for a comprehensive examination of the role nonjudicial forces play in shaping constitutional values.

Abortion's special status, however, does not mean that participation by elected government in other areas of constitutional decision-making is of lesser consequence. Congress, the White House, governmental agencies, and the states all play critical, interdependent roles in interpreting Supreme Court decisions and the Constitution itself. Every day, congressional staffers, legislators, attorneys in the Department of Justice, and agency officials actively engage in the business of constitutional interpretation. Before a case comes to court, once a case is in court, and after adjudication, elected government shapes both the content and the consequences of judicial rulings. In many instances, elected officials, not judges, speak the first and last word on matters of profound constitutional significance. What distinguishes abortion is the volume and persistence of elected-government efforts.

Most landmark Supreme Court decisions, as this book will demonstrate, cannot be understood without paying attention to the politics surrounding them. First, justices pay attention to a case's social and political context when crafting their decisions. Second, political responses to a decision often serve as a benchmark for measuring the correctness of Supreme Court fact finding. Third, political judgments shape Court doctrine, especially decisions concerning the constitutional grounds on which to base legislative or administrative initiatives. Fourth, the willingness of governmental actors to support or resist judicial decision-making contributes to the ultimate meaning of Court action. And fifth, once the Supreme Court has decided a case, a constitutional dialogue takes place between the Court and elected government, often resulting in a later decision more to the liking of political actors.

The chapters that follow reinforce the above propositions and offer additional insights into the appropriateness and impact of elected-branch interpretations. The questions examined in this book include whether and when the elected branches take seriously their responsibility to interpret the Constitution; whether elected-branch efforts to limit the force of judicial decision-making undermine the federal judiciary's status as a co-equal branch of government; whether Court decisions are instrumental or ancillary to the achievement of the social policy objectives associated with these decisions; how the structure and procedures of the legislative and executive branches affect elected-branch interpretation; whether the judiciary gives due regard to elected-government attitudes and interpretations; and finally, how the executive, legislative, and judicial branches should share the task of constitutional interpretation.

For the most part, these matters will be examined through a detailed review of congressional, executive, and state participation in the abortion dispute. To put that dispute into a broader context, the next three chapters of this book provide an overview of constitutional politics. Chapter 2 debunks the myth that the Supreme Court is the ultimate constitutional interpreter and its decisions are the last word on constitutional controversies. This viewpoint is without any historical basis, honored more in the breach than in the observation. These repeated breaches, moreover, highlight the critical role played by elected government in shaping constitutional values. Chapter 3 specifies the various powers used by elected government when interceding in constitutional disputes and reveals that every attribute of governmental authority can be and has been used to impact constitutional decision-making. Chapter 4 makes concrete the lessons of chapters 2 and 3 through a series of mini-case studies on a wide variety of constitutional disputes involving federal and state actors.

This overview of nonjudicial constitutional interpretation sets the stage for an in-depth examination of the abortion dispute. This examination will proceed in two phases. Separate chapters on Congress, the executive, and the states illustrate the pervasiveness of nonjudicial influences and the need to view constitutional interpretation as a dialectic involving all of government. The book's last three chapters serve up broader lessons about the abortion dispute and its implications for constitutional interpretation. Chapters 8 and 9 speak exclusively to the abortion dispute and what it teaches us about American politics. Unlike authors who view the abortion controversy as "a disappointing reflection of the American governmental and political process,"[25] these chapters sound a somewhat upbeat message. Specifically, while abortion-related decision-making often has come at a high institutional cost, constitutional interpretation typically is viewed as a vital part of legislative and executive deliberations regarding abortion-related initiatives. Moreover, elected-branch reprisals have never called into question the integrity of the judicial branch. Indeed, the reluctance of state legislators to reenter the abortion fray, in the wake of the Supreme Court's loosening of *Roe* in *Casey*, reveals that Court decisions serve as a sounding board against which elected government measures its responses.

The question of whether exchanges between the judiciary and elected government make for better constitutional interpretation is the subject of the last chapter, which focuses on the Court's 1992 *Planned Parenthood* v. *Casey* decision and its noneventful aftermath, and extols the virtues of this dialectic process. This chapter also takes issue with political scientists and constitutional theorists who attack the Court for "following the election returns." The Court shapes and is shaped by political and social influences. This dynamic process makes the Constitution more vital and durable. It also makes it incumbent upon each of us either to participate in constitutional decision-making or to suffer the consequences of a stagnant constitutional order.

2 / Judicial Review or Judicial Supremacy?

Is THE SUPREME COURT THE ULTIMATE constitutional arbiter? In a 1987 survey, six out of ten respondents said yes. Newspaper coverage of this survey noted that those six were "correct."[1]

During the Reagan administration, Attorney General Edwin Meese sparked controversy by arguing that Supreme Court decisions are not "binding on all persons and parts of government henceforth and forevermore." For the *New Republic*'s Michael Kinsley, the speech was "a jurisprudential stink bomb." Anthony Lewis of the *New York Times* described the speech as "invit[ing] anarchy." Laurence Tribe warned that the Meese position "represents a grave threat to the rule of law." Even Eugene C. Thomas, then president of the American Bar Association, castigated Meese, noting that "public officials and private citizens alike are not free simply to disregard" that Supreme Court decisions are the law of the land.[2]

The reaction to the Meese speech and the reporting of the survey both reflect the view that Supreme Court interpretations control the Constitution's application. This belief—that the Supreme Court has the "last word" in constitutional disputes—accords with much of the Court's writing on this question. In establishing the judiciary's authority to declare acts of Congress unconstitutional in his 1803 *Marbury* v. *Madison* decision, Chief Justice John Marshall declared that it is "emphatically the province and duty of the judicial department to say what the law is."[3] By 1857, the Court was sufficiently confident in its "high and independent character" that Associate Justice John Catron informed President-elect James Buchanan that, in the matter of *Dred Scott*, the Court would "decide and settle a controversy which has so long and seriously agitated the country."[4] One hundred years later, the Court conveyed a similar message in a quite different context. Responding to efforts by Arkansas governor Orval Faubus to stop court-ordered desegregation in Little

Rock, the Court proclaimed that *Marbury* "declared the basic principle that the federal judiciary is supreme in the exposition of the law of the Constitution."[5] The Court's vision of itself "as ultimate interpreter of the Constitution" persists today. In its 1992 decision reaffirming abortion rights—*Planned Parenthood* v. *Casey*—the Court claimed the authority to resolve the abortion dispute, invoking "the Nation's commitment to the rule of law" and declaring that "the Court's interpretation of the Constitution calls the contending sides of a national controversy to end their national division by accepting a common mandate rooted in the Constitution."[6]

The belief that Supreme Court decisions are the "last word" in constitutional disputes is overly parochial, ultimately shortsighted, and factually inaccurate. Other parts of government often disagree with the Court and express that disagreement through open challenges to the Court's constitutional reasoning. In fact, the Constitution specifies that executive and legislative officers, as well as judges, "shall be bound by Oath or Affirmation to support this Constitution."

MARBURY V. *MADISON*

John Marshall's rhetorical flourish in *Marbury,* the declaration that courts "say what the law is," is the supposed foundation of judicial supremacy. However, the facts and holding of *Marbury* demonstrate just the opposite: politics and constitutional decision-making are inextricably linked to each other.

The issue before the Court in *Marbury* was the propriety of Secretary of State James Madison's refusal to deliver a justice-of-the-peace commission to William Marbury. In resolving this dispute, the Court declared for the first time that an act of Congress was unconstitutional, thereby establishing judicial review—that is, the judiciary's power to declare unconstitutional an act of Congress, the president, or a state government. When the case was decided, however, the Court's justification for judicial review was hardly noticed. Instead, the controversy surrounding *Marbury* centered on Marshall's assertions that a conscientious executive branch would have delivered to Marbury his commission and that an order directed against the secretary of state was a proper remedy.

Marshall deliberately chose the *Marbury* case to establish judicial review. To understand that choice, consideration must be given to the historical background and the political influences originating in the legislative and executive branches. Marbury's eleventh-hour appointment was part of Federalist party efforts to transform the judiciary into a Federalist stronghold in the wake of John Adams's defeat by Thomas Jefferson. Through the Judiciary Act of 1801, the lame duck Federalist Congress and president created a host of new judicial offices and then rushed party loyalists through the appointment and confirmation process. Federalists viewed the Judiciary Act as a bulwark against their political opponents; Jeffersonians (forerunners of the Democratic party) saw the act as a partisan effort to subvert their well-earned victory in 1800.

Marbury thus became a symbol of the political battle between Federalists and Jeffersonians, with the principal warriors being John Marshall, a Federalist (who as secretary of state under Adams had neglected to deliver Marbury's commission and then as chief justice was set to rule on the legal significance of his negligence), and President Thomas Jefferson (who refused to deliver Marbury's commission). Indeed, Jefferson, viewing *Marbury* as a Federalist powergrab, had directed Madison to ignore a previous show-cause order from the Court, thereby forcing the Court to decide the case without the benefit of the executive's arguments. This opprobrium of the *Marbury* proceedings helped convince Marshall that Jefferson would ignore any order that the Court might issue. Furthermore, as Supreme Court justice Harold Burton recognized, "if the Court asserted such power over the Legislative and Executive Branches of the Government, this assertion would provide Congress with the necessary basis for the impeachment of the offending Justices and for their removal from office."[7] Marshall took the impeachment threat seriously, writing that it would be better for the elected branches to reverse a Court opinion by statute than to impeach Supreme Court justices. For Marshall, "a reversal of those legal opinions deemed unsound by the legislature would certainly better comport with the mildness of our character than [would] a removal of the Judge who has rendered them unknowing of his fault."[8]

Marshall's challenge, therefore, was to craft an opinion that would both support judicial power over the elected branches (to prevent the Court, and with it, the Federalists, from appearing impotent) and avoid a head-to-head confrontation between the judiciary and the executive (a battle that the Court would lose so badly that it would be rendered impotent). The solution was to first acknowledge the merits of Marbury's challenge but then conclude that the Court was without jurisdiction to resolve the dispute. Along the way, the Court was also able to establish judicial review, holding unconstitutional the statute that granted it jurisdiction in the *Marbury* dispute.

Chief Justice Marshall's tactics in *Marbury* reveal that Supreme Court decision-making cannot be divorced from its political context. Indeed, *Marbury v. Madison*'s fame as the beacon of constitutional law, and John Marshall's status—in the words of Chief Justice Earl Warren—as *the* "expounder of the Constitution,"[9] derives from the political practicality of Marshall and his opinion in *Marbury*, not the brilliance of Marshall's explication of the justifications for judicial review. Moreover, it is significant that Marshall never again declared an act of Congress unconstitutional, although he remained on the Court until 1835. Instead, he regularly *upheld* statutes that expanded congressional power.

FROM MARSHALL TO TANEY

John Marshall undoubtedly would be surprised that his declaration, in *Marbury*, that courts "say what the law is" was subsequently understood to mean that the "federal judiciary is supreme" in expounding the Constitution's meaning. *Marbury*, while establishing judicial review, does not come close to suggesting that elected government also cannot interpret the Constitution or that elected government must treat Supreme Court decisions as definitive. Indeed, at the time of *Marbury*, constitutional decision-making was dominated by the elected branches. Without a body of Supreme Court decisions to look to, Congress and the president had no choice but to engage in definitive constitutional interpretations. In 1789, for example, James Madison spoke of the duty of Congress "to take care that the powers of the Constitution be preserved entire to every department of Government" and said that Congress should "expound the Constitution, so far as it relates to the division of power between the President and the Senate."[10]

The power of the president to engage in constitutional interpretation was made clear by Thomas Jefferson. Asserting that judicial supremacy would transform the Constitution into "a mere thing of wax" that the courts "may twist and shape into any form they please,"[11] Jefferson, in 1801, declared the Alien and Sedition Act (which criminalized speech critical of the government) a constitutional "nullity" and pardoned everyone prosecuted under it. Ironically, Jefferson had earlier endorsed the Bill of Rights attachment to the Constitution because a legal check on repressive legislation would be placed "into the hands of the judiciary."[12] The courts' failure to void the Alien and Sedition Act helped to convince Jefferson that concerns over individual rights obligated the executive to play an active role in constitutional interpretation. Forty years later, Congress followed suit, declaring the Alien and Sedition Act "unconstitutional, null, and void" and reimbursing anyone fined under it.[13] Through these legislative and executive interpretations, the Supreme Court eventually declared that the act had been invalidated by "the court of history."[14]

A more dramatic example of the elected branches controlling constitutional decision-making occurred in 1832, when President Andrew Jackson vetoed legislation rechartering the Bank of the United States. The fact that a unanimous Supreme Court had approved the Bank's chartering in *McCulloch* v. *Maryland* was irrelevant: "The opinion of the judges," proclaimed Jackson, "has no more authority over Congress than the opinion of the Congress has over the judges, and on that point the President is independent of both." "Each public official who takes an oath to support the Constitution swears that he will support it as he understands it, and not as it is understood by others."[15] For this reason, Jackson—albeit in another context—is reputed to have said, "John Marshall has made his decision, let him enforce it."

McCulloch v. *Maryland*'s inability to seal the constitutional fate of the rechartered bank was overshadowed by the Court's contemporaneous failure to resolve the slavery dispute in *Dred Scott* v. *Sandford*. Congress, unable to achieve a workable political balance through its parceling out of "free" and "slave" states, sought refuge in the courts. The White House also sought to pass the buck to the courts, with James Buchanan promising the nation in his inaugural address that the slavery issue would be "speedily and finally settled" by the Court. Two days later, the Supreme Court issued its "definitive" ruling on the constitutionality of the Missouri Compromise in *Dred Scott*. For only the second time in its history (*Marbury* being the first), the Court declared an act of Congress unconstitutional. Through the voice of its chief justice, Roger B. Taney, the Court prohibited Congress from preventing the spread of slavery into the Western Territories because the right to own a slave was "distinctly and expressly affirmed in the Constitution."[16] Rather than definitively settle the slavery dispute, however, the Court deepened the schism that ultimately resulted in civil war.

THE LINCOLN-DOUGLAS DEBATE

Dred Scott's status as the "last word" on slavery was immediately called into question, most notably by Republican senatorial candidate Abraham Lincoln. In a series of debates with Stephen Douglas, Lincoln both challenged the binding effect of *Dred Scott* and defended the constitutional authority of the elected branches to challenge Supreme Court decision-making.

Lincoln, claiming that the *Dred Scott* decision could not stand in the face of the Declaration of Independence's embrace of inalienable human rights, spoke of the need "to reverse that decision." Reminding his listeners that Jackson's bank veto revealed "that the Supreme Court had no right to lay down a rule to govern a co-ordinate branch of the government, the members of which had sworn to support the Constitution," Lincoln emphasized that "somebody has to reverse that *Dred Scott* decision, since it is made, and we mean to reverse it, and we mean to do it peaceably."[17]

Stephen Douglas feigned surprise at Lincoln's claim, remarking, "I have never heard before of an appeal being taken from the Supreme Court to the Congress of the United States to reverse its decision."[18] For Douglas, constitutional design and political necessity demanded "that I take the decisions of the Supreme Court as the law of the land." The Constitution itself established that "the right and province of expounding the Constitution, and construing the law, is vested in the judiciary."[19] "Whoever resists the final decision of the highest judicial tribunal," according to Douglas, "aims a deadly blow to our whole Republican system of government—a blow which if successful would place all our rights and liberties at the mercy of passion, anarchy, and violence."[20]

Douglas's absolutism made it impossible for him to recognize the subtlety in Lincoln's approach. For Lincoln, court decisions were necessarily binding on the parties themselves and were "also entitled to very high respect and consideration . . . by all other departments of the government" *but* could not undermine democratic institutions by binding elected government to judicially imposed policy-making.[21] Lincoln viewed constitutional decision-making as a dynamic process involving all branches of government at both the federal and state levels. Like Douglas's, his argument was supported both by the Constitution and by policy concerns. Lincoln's constitutional argument was simply that "each member [of Congress] had sworn to support the Constitution as he understood it." He also challenged the practicality of judicial supremacy, remarking that judges have "the same passions for party, for power, and the privilege of their corps" as other men, and therefore "their power is the more dangerous as they are in office for life, and not responsible, as other functionaries are, to the elective control."[22]

Lincoln outlined the costs of judicial supremacy in his first inaugural address: "The candid citizen must confess that if the policy of the government . . . is to be irrevocably fixed by decisions of the Supreme Court . . . the people will have ceased to be their own rulers."[23] For Lincoln, the Constitution limited and empowered all three branches of government. A century later, Alexander Bickel echoed Lincoln's concern, arguing that the Constitution limits "the courts as well [as legislatures], and it may be equally absurd, therefore, to allow courts [rather than legislators] to set the limits. It is, indeed, more absurd because courts are not subject to electoral control."[24]

NEW DEAL CHALLENGES TO JUDICIAL SUPREMACY

The Supreme Court again found itself under sharp attack during the so-called *Lochner* era, a period from 1905 to 1937 in which the Court, in striking down about two hundred social and economic laws, both narrowly construed the authority of Congress and the states to regulate commerce and broadly construed the due process rights of employers. The Court's actions were universally condemned as a symbol of unprincipled judicial overreaching, and the *Lochner* era helped prompt President Franklin Delano Roosevelt's plan to enlarge the Court (from nine to fifteen justices) and pack it with jurists sympathetic to his New Deal reforms.

The case from which the era took its name was *Lochner* v. *New York*, a 1905 decision invalidating a New York law limiting bakery workers to sixty hours a week or ten hours a day. In it, the Court concluded that, rather than serve public health objectives, the law created "meddlesome" and "unreasonable" interferences with an individual's right to enter into contracts. By empowering itself to strike down laws that it deemed to be "arbitrary," "capricious," or "unreasonable," the Court functioned as a self-appointed czar over social and economic legislation.[25]

Another example of the *Lochner* Court's willingness to turn over the legislative applecart is *Hammer* v. *Dagenhart*, a 1918 decision invalidating legislation that prohibited the shipment across state lines of goods produced by children in a specified age range. In determining that this legislation was within its authority to regulate interstate commerce, the House Labor Committee had concluded that "the entire problem has become an interstate problem rather than a problem of isolated States and is a problem which must be faced and solved only by a power stronger than any State."[26] The Supreme Court disagreed, concluding that Congress's commerce power was limited to controlling the actual movement of goods across state lines and did not extend to regulating the means of production of such goods. Otherwise, said the Court, "all freedom of commerce will be at an end, and the power of the States over local matters may be eliminated and thus our system of government be practically destroyed."[27]

Congress strongly disapproved of *Hammer*. Days after the decision, Congress was again at work on child labor legislation. Although Senator Thomas Hardwick warned that "the power of Congress [in this field] was denied *in toto* by the highest court of our land,"[28] this invocation of judicial finality was rejected by Congress. Although rejecting efforts to reenact the 1916 statute and thus control child labor by means of the congressional commerce power, Congress turned to its taxing power and, in 1919, imposed a 10-percent tax on the net profits of any manufacturer employing children below specified ages. The Court rejected this indirect attack on *Hammer,* castigating Congress for thinking that it "must be blind not to see that the so-called tax [was] imposed" not to raise revenues but "to stop the employment of children."[29]

Congress responded to this setback by approving a constitutional amendment giving it the power to regulate child labor. Without ratification by the requisite three-fourths of the states the amendment floundered, and in 1938 Congress returned to the original 1916 bill that the *Hammer* Court had struck down. This direct attack on the Court's reasoning in *Hammer* succeeded, and a unanimous Supreme Court approved child labor legislation in 1941. This remarkable change in the Court's reasoning is attributable to FDR's efforts to win popular and judicial support of his New Deal programs.

The Court's infusion of laissez-faire economics into the Due Process Clause, and its constraining interpretation of the commerce authority of Congress, undermined much of the social and economic legislation passed under the New Deal. After the Court ruled in 1935 that the Commerce Clause did not give Congress authority under the National Industrial Recovery Act to create industrial codes to regulate economic activities, Roosevelt launched a counterattack. Following his landslide reelection victory in 1936, he proposed that for every Supreme Court justice over seventy years of age, he be authorized to appoint an additional justice until the Court's size grew from nine to fifteen justices. Roosevelt spoke of the need to create a "liberal-minded judiciary" and complained of the Court's "horse-and-buggy age" approach to the Commerce Clause. He said it was inappropriate for the Court to act "as a policy-making body."[30] Likening the three branches of the national government to "a three horse team," he noted that two of the horses were "pulling in unison; the third [was] not." Roosevelt said he needed to "take action to save the Constitution from the Court and the Court from itself."[31]

Roosevelt's court-packing plan did not sit well with either the Court or Congress. Responding to Roosevelt's suggestion that the nine justices couldn't keep up with the Court's workload, Chief Justice Charles Evans Hughes informed Congress that the "Court is fully abreast of its work" and that Roosevelt's court-packing plan was not only poor public policy but also very likely unconstitutional.[32] Congressional opposition was stronger; the Senate Judiciary Committee savaged the proposal, "declar[ing] that we would rather have an independent Court, a fearless Court, a Court that will dare to announce its honest opinions in what it believes . . . than a Court that, out of fear or sense of obligation to the appointing power, or factional passion, approves any measure we enact." Irrespective of what the Court might decide, "we are not the judges of the judges. We are not above the Constitution," the committee wrote. Not only must the FDR plan be turned down, it said, but the plan "should be so emphatically rejected that its parallel will never again be presented to the free representatives of the free people of America."[33]

Congress's harsh words for the FDR plan, however, did not strengthen the Court's resolve to withstand New Deal initiatives. Instead, the Court buckled to popular opinion thanks to Roosevelt's victory in all but two states in 1936, as well as to populist attacks on the Court, such as Drew Pearson and Robert Allen's 1936 book *The Nine Old Men*. Shortly after the defeat of the court-packing plan, the Court announced several decisions accepting of New Deal programs. In explaining this transformation, Justice Owen Roberts recognized the extraordinary importance of public opinion in undoing the *Lochner* era: "Looking back, it is difficult to see how the Court could have resisted the popular urge for uniform standards throughout the country—for what in effect was a unified economy."[34]

From Earl Warren to Warren Earl Burger

The failure of the court-packing plan did not end elected-branch reprisals against the Court. Dissatisfaction with decisions made by the Court under chief justices Earl Warren and Warren Earl Burger resulted in a spate of legislative proposals to strip the federal courts, including the Supreme Court, of jurisdiction in a number of controversial areas. Those proposals were rooted in Article III of the Constitution, which recognizes Congress's powers to "order and establish" lower federal courts and to make "exceptions" and "regulations" to the Supreme Court's appellate jurisdiction.

Prior to 1953, Congress did not see its jurisdictional power as a mechanism to statutorily undermine unpopular Supreme Court rulings. When federal court jurisdiction was limited—for example, in the Reconstruction Era—this limitation was a preemptive strike to protect legislative priorities by foreclosing judicial action. The Warren Court changed all that. By playing an affirmative countermajoritarian role, the Warren Court seemed quite willing to upset legislative preferences and open itself to political reprisals. Between 1953 and 1968, more than sixty bills were introduced in Congress to limit the jurisdiction of the federal courts over school desegregation, national security, criminal confessions, and a variety of other subjects.

Typical of these efforts was Senator William Jenner's response to Supreme Court decisions protecting the First Amendment rights of communists. Outraged by these decisions, Jenner introduced a bill to withhold the Supreme Court's appellate jurisdiction on these and related matters. In defending his proposal, Jenner said that withholding jurisdiction was a more effective check than the "slow and uncertain" route of constitutional amendment.[35] Attorney General William Rogers, however, found the bill a dangerous threat to judicial autonomy. For Rogers, "the natural consequence of such an enactment [was] that the courts would operate under the constant apprehension that if they rendered unpopular decisions, jurisdiction would be further curtailed."[36] Jenner answered Rogers's charge, claiming that, rather than "threaten the independence of the judiciary," his bill "threatens the imbalance which has been created by decisions of the Supreme Court in recent years. It threatens the power to legislate which the Supreme Court has arrogated to itself during those years."[37] The Jenner proposal and other proposals of this era were eventually defeated, but not without substantial debate as to the scope and meaning of the Article III Exceptions Clause.

The proliferation of court-stripping proposals during the Warren era is not surprising. Nor is it surprising that in the late 1970s a second wave of court-stripping proposals attacking the Burger Court emerged. With decisions protecting abortion rights and requiring school busing, the Burger Court continued what the Warren Court had begun—a transformation of the federal judiciary. As described by the law professor Abram Chayes, federal courts, rather than resolving private disputes between private individuals, were then "asked to deal with grievances over the administration of some public . . . program and to vindicate the public policies embodied in the governing statutes or constitutional provisions. As a result, courts [were] inevitably cast in an affirmative, political . . . role."[38]

Conservatives in Congress and the Reagan administration expressed dissatisfaction with this increasingly intrusive judicial role. The Republican party continually attacked the judiciary, arguing that "it is not a judicial function to reorder the economic, political, and social priorities of our nation. The intrusion of the courts into such areas undermines the stature of the judiciary and erodes respect for the rule of law."[39] Reagan's first attorney general, William French Smith, likewise rebuked the judiciary, charging that "not only are unelected jurists with life tenure less attuned to the popular will than regularly elected officials, but judicial policy making also is inevitably inadequate or imperfect policy making."[40] The question remained whether this dissatisfaction would translate into administration support of court-stripping measures.

Edwin Meese answered that question during his 1984 confirmation hearing for the post of attorney general. Meese characterized court-stripping proposals as both "unwise" and constitutionally "impermissible" and claimed that "if confirmed . . . [he] would recommend a veto" of such legislation.[41] It is revealing that an administration so critical of the Supreme Court would reject the efforts of its conservative bedfellows to exercise democratic control of a judiciary "run amok." Apparently, the Reagan administration thought it at least imprudent (and quite possibly wrong) to attack the integrity of the judicial branch in this manner.

MEESE AND BEYOND

Whatever points Meese may have earned by opposing court-stripping proposals were more than offset by his defense of elected-branch challenges to Supreme Court decision-making in a 1986 speech at the Tulane Law School. It did not matter that Meese pointed to Abraham Lincoln, the Supreme Court justice Felix Frankfurter, and the constitutional historian Charles Warren in explaining why the Constitution itself is distinct from and superior to "what the Supreme Court says about the Constitution."[42] It did not matter that, in addition to Lincoln's actions, the actions of Jefferson, Jackson, and Roosevelt make clear that Supreme Court decision-making is subject to elected-branch review. Despite grounding his argument on what would seem a secure foundation, Meese was subject to an avalanche of criticism from journalists and legal academics.

What prompted these attacks? Was it a belief in judicial supremacy that would have lumped together the Meese speech with Jefferson's repudiation of court-approved sedition laws and Lincoln's attacks on *Dred Scott*? Hardly. What made the Meese speech blasphemous was Meese's politics, specifically, Meese's opposition to Court rulings on abortion, affirmative action, and school prayer. In an editorial titled "Why Give That Speech?" the *Washington Post* made clear that, although Meese's central claim about the propriety of elected-branch constitutional interpretation was "self-evident," the attorney general's remarks were "very troublesome" because of his "subtle, unspoken" message.[43]

Two comments in the speech convinced the attorney general's critics that Meese's intentions were unsavory. First, Meese directly challenged one of the icons of the Warren era, *Cooper* v. *Aaron*, in which the Supreme Court pronounced that it was the "supreme" expositor of the Constitution. Meese said that *Cooper*'s self-aggrandizing declaration of judicial supremacy "would have shocked men like John Marshall and Joseph Story."[44] That *Cooper* responded to the efforts of the state of Arkansas to resist *Brown* v. *Board of Education* did not matter to Meese, but it mattered a great deal to his critics. Meese's critics also pounced on his defense of Daniel Manion, a then-controversial appeals court nominee who, while a state legislator, had sponsored legislation encouraging the posting of the Ten Commandments in public schools to express his disapproval of a Supreme Court decision prohibiting such mandatory postings. For Meese, "the nominee was acting on the principle Lincoln well understood—that legislators have an independent duty to consider the constitutionality of proposed legislation." Meese's critics were sufficiently vociferous to prompt the attorney general to clarify his position by asserting, among other things, that "it would be highly irresponsible for [government officials] not to conform their behavior to [Supreme Court] precedent."[45]

The Meese flap spilled over into 1986 and 1987 Supreme Court confirmation hearings. In 1986, Senator Arlen Specter asked chief justice designate William Rehnquist whether the Supreme Court "is the final arbiter, the final decision-maker of what the Constitution means." Rehnquist thought the question so obvious that a one-word answer would suffice: "Unquestionably."[46] According to Rehnquist: "We rightfully think of our courts as the final voice in the interpretation of our Constitution, and therefore tend to think of constitutional law in terms of cases decided by the courts."[47] One year later, Supreme Court nominee Anthony Kennedy took a different tack in answering the same question from Specter. Noting that "I can think of instances, or I can accept the proposition that a chief executive or a Congress might not accept as doctrine the law of the Supreme Court," Kennedy hypothesized a situation in which the Supreme Court overruled its earlier decision according constitutional protection to newspapers, and asked rhetorically: "Could you, as a legislator, say I think that decision is constitutionally wrong and I want to have legislation to change it? I think you could, and I think you should."[48]

By 1993, the last-word debate had abated. Ruth Bader Ginsburg hardly raised an eyebrow when she wrote that "judges play an interdependent part in our democracy . . . [,] participating in a dialogue with other organs of government."[49] At her confirmation hearings, these remarks were hardly a bone of contention. If anything, Judge Ginsburg was praised for her repudiation of judicial finality, with the Senate Judiciary Committee favorably quoting her call for interactive constitutional decision-making.[50]

CONCLUSION

Justice Robert Jackson turned a neat phrase when he claimed that decisions by the Supreme Court "are not final because we are infallible but we are infallible only because we are final."[51] This bit of humble pie, as it turns out, is a gross exaggeration. Judicial supremacy is a myth honored more in the breach than in the observation.

From John Marshall to Ruth Bader Ginsburg, Supreme Court justices have recognized the interdependent nature of constitutional decision-making. Presidents, including Jefferson, Jackson, Lincoln, Roosevelt, and Reagan, also have challenged the finality of court decision-making. Congress likewise has entered the fray, sometimes challenging Court decision-making and at other times considering draconian court-packing and court-stripping proposals.

Judicial supremacy, admittedly, is a useful rhetorical device. The forcefulness of *Cooper* v. *Aaron* is a reflection of the Court's claim of constitutional finality. The attacks on Attorney General Meese's embrace of elected-branch interpretation also were buttressed by judicial supremacy claims. In both instances, however, judicial supremacy was invoked defensively to deter elected-branch reprisals. Correlatively, when placed in its full context, Charles Evans Hughes's brazen declaration that "we are under a Constitution, but the Constitution is what the judges say it is" was designed to prevent challenges to the "independence and esteem of the judiciary" by keeping out of court and placing in a commission "directly accountable" to the people highly politicized disputes over abuses by railroads.[52]

Too much should not be read into the above demystification of judicial supremacy. The persistent failure of court-stripping proposals, the decimation of FDR's court-packing proposals, and Congress's choice to utilize its taxing power rather than directly challenge *Hammer* by again using its commerce power demonstrates that elected government is loath to launch a frontal assault on judicial authority. Nonetheless, constitutional decision-making cannot be traced solely to the efforts of nine justices, or a majority of nine. Other parts of government interpret the Constitution and influence the judiciary. Volleys between the elected branches and the courts take place on a regular basis. The balance of this book will examine these exchanges, initially through a thumbnail sketch of elected-government interpretation and then through a detailed study of the abortion dispute.

3 / Constitutional Interpretation by Elected Government

CONGRESS, THE WHITE HOUSE, governmental agencies, and the states all play critical, interdependent roles in interpreting Supreme Court decisions and the Constitution itself. The sweep and influence of these interpretations are broad and pervasive. Any case that goes before the Court must involve preexisting laws or regulations, which are often influenced by legislative or executive constitutional interpretations. And once a case is in court, the states, the Justice Department, and congressional coalitions—sometimes as parties to the case and sometimes as amici ("friends of the court")—inform the judiciary of their views. After a case is adjudicated, elected government may seek to expand or limit the holding through a number of techniques, including interpretation of the ruling, refusal to enforce it, or nullification of the ruling through constitutional amendment.

Elected-government influences extend well beyond particular adjudicated disputes. Not only the number of justices who sit on the Supreme Court but also the Court's appellate jurisdiction—as Chapter 2's discussion of court-packing and court-stripping proposals showed—are subject to elected-branch tinkering. Moreover, membership in the Supreme Court and the lower federal courts requires presidential nomination and Senate confirmation. Finally, when the Court is without jurisdiction to decide a constitutional dispute, the resolution of that dispute is left entirely to elected government.

JURISDICTIONAL HURDLES: PASSIVE VIRTUES
OR SUBTLE VICES

When John Marshall declared in *Marbury* that it is the Court's "province and duty . . . to say what the law is," he established a principle subsequently interpreted to mean that "there is no [discretionary] escape from the judicial obligation" to decide cases properly before the Court.[1] Remarkably, Marshall had concluded that the Supreme Court was without jurisdiction in *Marbury* by making strained interpretations of both statutory and constitutional language. Marshall's bit of mischief reveals that the Court sometimes will pass the buck on controversial constitutional questions by concluding that a matter is not properly before them. Whether that conclusion is rooted in a principled interpretation of their jurisdictional authority under Article III of the Constitution or whether it is a political tactic to avoid a dispute the justices would prefer not to handle, it is clear that the Court's willingness to dispose of cases on jurisdictional grounds leaves a great many constitutional questions solely in the hands of elected government.

The Constitution, by specifying that the "judicial power" extends only to "cases" or "controversies," guards against abstract judicial declarations of policy. The question of distinguishing a concrete dispute from a hypothetical claim remains. Towards this end, the Court insists that litigants must have a personal stake (i.e., standing) in the controversy and that their claims must be presented in an adversarial context (i.e., that there be adverseness). Beyond these threshold requirements, the Court recognizes that the Constitution itself commits some matters to another branch for resolution, and that other matters are non-justiciable "political questions" for pragmatic reasons, such as "unusual need for unquestioning adherence to a political decision already made," "the potentiality of embarrassment from multifarious pronouncements," and the impossibility of achieving judicial resolution "without expressing lack of the respect due coordinate branches" of government.[2]

Political question and justiciability barriers have been used to foreclose judicial resolution of several significant constitutional disputes. When Senator Barry Goldwater (R-Ariz.) challenged President Carter's termination of a Taiwan defense treaty, the Court, referring both to political question and justiciability limitations, referred the dispute back to the executive and legislative branches, "each of which has resources available to protect and assert its interests, resources not available to private litigants outside the judicial forum."[3] Furthermore, challenges to the constitutionality of the Vietnam War, the U.S.

recognition of the Vatican as a separate state, the manner in which the Senate conducts impeachment trials, and President Reagan's sending military advisers to El Salvador were all dismissed on the grounds that they were political questions. Article III justiciability requirements have had a more profound impact, leading to the Court's decision not to consider Planned Parenthood's attack on anticontraception statutes, the NAACP's challenge to the awarding by the IRS of tax exemptions to racially imbalanced private schools, and an unsuccessful law school applicant's challenge to an affirmative action plan.

Judges, especially Supreme Court justices, are adept at manipulating these threshold requirements. When judges are unprepared to resolve a dispute, these barriers are a principal "avenue of escape"; when judges are prepared to settle a dispute, these requirements "will not stand in [the] way."[4] For Alexander Bickel, arguing that "no good society can be unprincipled; and no viable society can be principle-ridden,"[5] the strategic use of threshold requirements is a necessary device to enable an unelected judiciary to avoid debilitating conflicts and thereby protect its institutional capital. For Gerald Gunther, however, avoiding adjudication through unprincipled reasoning both "damage[s] . . . legitimate areas of principle" and invites "free-wheeling interventionism."[6]

Whether this avoidance of otherwise justiciable controversies for pragmatic reasons is a subtle virtue or a passive vice, it continues. The Constitution, moreover, presupposes that the courts will steer clear of disputes that do not satisfy Article III case or controversy demands. The end result is that elected government often is the ultimate, indeed the only, interpreter of the Constitution.

APPOINTMENTS AND CONFIRMATIONS

Elected government's most direct link to judicial decision-making is the overtly political process of selecting and approving federal judges. Article II of the Constitution authorizes the president to nominate federal court judges "with the Advice and Consent of the Senate." This selection process enables the president and the Senate to advance their respective judicial philosophies (or at least, to defend against unacceptable judicial philosophies).

A quick review of judicial appointments makes clear that the Supreme Court's constitutional decision-making is very much correlated to this political nomination-confirmation process. In 1870 a seven-member Court, along strictly partisan lines, invalidated legislation seeking to discharge Civil War debts by treating paper money as legal tender; all four Democratic judges were in the majority and all three Republicans were in dissent. Fifteen months later, after Republican president Ulysses Grant filled two Supreme Court vacancies, the Court immediately overturned its decision, now declaring the Legal Tender Act constitutional. A similar feat was accomplished by FDR's New Deal appointees. These justices assured the death of the *Lochner* era by, among other things, reversing the Court's 1918 declaration that Congress cannot regulate child labor under its commerce power.

Far more dramatic was President Dwight Eisenhower's appointment of Earl Warren as chief justice in 1953. Without Warren, the Court might well have upheld segregated education in the *Brown* decision. The Supreme Court had been set to decide *Brown* in its 1952 term with Chief Justice Fred Vinson at the Court's helm. After briefs were filed (including an important brief filed by the Justice Department in the last month of the Truman administration which argued that racial segregation undermined America's stature as leader of the free world) and oral arguments were heard, the Court redocketed *Brown* so that it also could decide the constitutionality of segregated education in the "federal city"—Washington, D.C. At this time, the justices were divided—their December 1952 conference suggested a 5-to-4 opinion in favor of upholding segregated education. As Justice William O. Douglas wrote in his autobiography: "It was clear that if a decision had been reached in the 1952 Term, we would have had five saying that separate but equal schools were constitutional, that separate but unequal schools were not constitutional, and that the remedy was to give the states time to make the two systems of schools equal."[7] While Douglas's claim is subject to question, there is little doubt that the Vinson Court would have exacerbated the conflict over segregated schools by issuing a sharply divided opinion. In 1953, however, Vinson died and Warren became chief justice—an occurrence prompting Associate Justice Felix Frankfurter to exclaim, "This is the first solid piece of evidence I've ever had that there really is a God."[8] With Warren now at the helm, the Court—although still sharply divided—was able to unanimously agree upon a brief declaration that "separate educational facilities are inherently unequal."[9]

The direction of Court decision-making was also altered by the confirmation of Warren Burger to succeed Earl Warren as chief justice. In 1971, the Burger Court limited Warren Court rulings protecting individuals from being stripped of their citizenship, prompting Justice Hugo Black to complain (in dissent) that the equal protection guarantee "should not be blown around by every passing political wind that changes the composition of this Court."[10] Likewise, in 1974 Justice Potter Stewart, noting that two recent Nixon appointees provided the crucial votes in overturning a 1972 decision, remarked,

"A basic change in the law upon a ground no firmer than a change in our membership invites the popular misconception that this institution is little different from the two political branches of the government."[11]

Justice Stewart's lament is, to put it mildly, ill-informed. Supreme Court appointments are inherently political because Supreme Court decision-making, and with it, the Court itself, is part of the policy-making process. The above inventory makes clear that the White House and Senate have good reason to pay attention to the likely voting patterns of judicial nominees. Admittedly, it is nearly impossible to predict with certainty how a nominee will behave once given the life tenure of a federal judgeship. Some behave in unexpected ways once put on the Court—Earl Warren, Harry Blackmun, and David Souter being three prominent examples. Most appointees, however, follow the lead of the president who appointed them. For example, Carter administration judges, "many of whom have been described as lawyers willing to use the courts to overcome social ills,"[12] are far more liberal than Reagan appointees, who were screened to make sure that they were *unwilling* to "create new constitutional 'rights' out of thin air, usurp legislative and executive functions, or otherwise give short shrift to the will of 'we the people' as expressed in" the Constitutional text.[13]

The role of ideology in the president's judicial selections, particularly in recent years, has resulted in vigorous Senate review of judicial nominees, especially nominees to the Supreme Court. Of the 145 presidential nominations to the Supreme Court, 27 have been rejected by the Senate. This rejection rate, close to 20 percent, is higher than the rejection rate for any other post requiring Senate confirmation. Aside from exercising its veto power by turning down nominees, the Senate also shapes the judicial selection process by "advising" the president on whom he should and should not nominate. Benjamin Cardozo's 1932 nomination to the Court, for example, was the direct result of insistent lobbying by Senator William Borah, whose support on unrelated matters was desperately needed by President Herbert Hoover. Stephen Breyer's 1994 nomination by Bill Clinton came in the wake of growing Senate opposition to Clinton's apparent first choice, Secretary of the Interior Bruce Babbit.

The Senate also seeks to shape judicial decision-making through its jawboning of nominees throughout the confirmation process. "Members of the Judiciary Committee," according to a 1994 study by Stephen Wermiel, "have learned to shape the constitutional dialogue in the confirmation hearings to make clear to nominees that a willingness to profess belief in some threshold constitutional values is a prerequisite for the job."[14] Beginning with the 1981 nomination of Sandra Day O'Connor, "these threshold values have included a commitment to the existence of unenumerated rights protected by the Constitution, including the right to privacy, and respect for *stare decisis.*"[15] This strategy may well have succeeded, for O'Connor, along with Anthony Kennedy and David Souter, reaffirmed "the central holding of *Roe*" in a decisive joint opinion issued in *Planned Parenthood* v. *Casey.*

The battles over Supreme Court nominations reveal that the president and the Senate both recognize that the best way to shape outputs (Court rulings) is to control inputs (i.e., to control who sits on the Court). This principle also applies to other positions where presidential nomination and Senate confirmation are required, such as lower court judgeships and high-ranking executive-branch positions. For reasons of comity and disinterest, however, the Senate rarely intercedes in these critical appointments.

CONGRESS AND THE CONSTITUTION

Congressional influence over constitutional interpretation through the confirmation of judges and executive-branch officials is only the tip of an iceberg. Congress participates in constitutional decision-making at all phases of the lawmaking process, from the enactment of legislation and approval of constitutional amendments to the oversight of governmental departments and agencies. In recent decades, Congress also has participated in litigation both in its own name and through briefs filed by individual members.

The pervasiveness and significance of constitutional interpretation, combined with the Supreme Court's increasing willingness to defer to elected government, has led numerous interest groups to declare their principal allegiance to the Congress, not the courts. According to the American Civil Liberties Union, "Congress is increasingly asked to look at these [constitutional] issues because there is nobody else. It is now the court of last resort."[16] In a similar vein, the National Abortion Rights Action League has declared: "Clearly Congress is our Court of Last Resort. All hope of protecting our constitutional right to choose depends upon our elected representation in Congress responding to the will of the American people."[17] Legal academics have also joined in this call for congressional constitutional interpretation. For example, Robin West argues that, from "a purely pragmatic perspective, Congress [should be] freer to envision, and then to realize, a more egalitarian social order, and a freer individual and collective life" because progressive goals are "hindered, not furthered by [judicially crafted] constitutionally imposed constraints on our options."[18]

This growing call for congressional preeminence in constitutional interpretation, especially from liberal interest groups and scholars, signals a dramatic shift in perceptions. In 1979, the legal theorist Owen Fiss wrote that legislators "are not ideologically committed or institutionally suited to the search for the meaning of constitutional values, but instead see their primary function in terms of registering the actual, occurrent preferences of the people—what they want and what they believe should be done."[19] In 1983 a federal appeals court judge and former congressman, Abner Mikva, blasted Congress for its "superficial and, for the most part, self-serving constitutional debate."[20] Noting that "Congress is a reactive body unable to enact legislation until the problem at hand reaches crisis proportions" and that "the constitutional principles involved in a bill, unlike its merits, are generally abstract, unpopular, and fail to capture the imagination of either the media or the public," Mikva perceived that "regardless of the rhetoric that emanates from Congress, the legislature has . . . left constitutional judgments to the judiciary."[21] The legal theorist Paul Brest echoed these sentiments in his 1986 broadside on the "capacity and commitment" of Congress "to engage in constitutional interpretation," concluding that "until and unless Congress develops trustworthy procedures for determining constitutional issues, it must abstain from contradicting judge-made decisions."[22]

The ascendancy of Congress as supreme constitutional interpreter—in the eyes of interest groups at least—has little to do with changes in legislative review of constitutional issues and a lot to do with the Rehnquist Court's reluctance to expand (or even maintain) the boundaries of constitutional protections. This *realpolitik* explanation, moreover, suggests that earlier attacks on Congress were overstated, for they were premised on the notion that the courts were a more vigorous guardian of the Constitution than was the Congress. The truth lies somewhere in between. Congress, as Louis Fisher of the Congressional Research Service put it, "can perform an essential, broad, and ongoing role in shaping the meaning of the Constitution"; but it is a coordinate role, part of a "continuing colloquy" between courts and Congress "in which constitutional principle is 'evolved conversationally not perfected unilaterally.'"[23] The reality of congressional constitutional interpretation supports this proposition. Before, during, and after adjudication, the courts and Congress engage in a constitutional dialogue with each other as well as with the executive branch.

Before legislation is enacted, Congress often undertakes a constitutional review of the measure. This review may occur in a number of different ways. First, committee and subcommittee staff members as well as House or Senate members themselves may assess the bill's constitutionality. Second, a number of congressional offices may be called upon to assist in this review. The Congressional Research Service, the offices of legislative counsel to the House and to the Senate, and the General Accounting Office all can assist in reviewing constitutional questions. Third, through formalized legislative hearings and informal requests, constitutional scholars, Justice Department officials and other government officials, and interest groups share their views of a measure's constitutionality with members and their staffs.

Congressional consideration of constitutional questions in lawmaking, as well as congressional oversight, often hinges on which committee the matter is before. In 1963, for example, the Senate leadership insisted that the Commerce Committee take charge of landmark civil rights legislation out of fear that the more conservative Judiciary Committee would undermine civil rights reform. Differences between committees remain. A 1993 study found that the lawyer-dominated "[House] Judiciary Committee treats the Constitution and the courts with a great deal of respect, almost bordering on reverence," whereas the House Energy and Commerce Committee "rarely pays much attention to the constitutional ramifications of its decisions" and views "the federal courts as just one more political actor playing in the game of hardball politics."[24] The relative cautiousness of the House Judiciary Committee played a pivotal role in the Supreme Court's approval of the 1964 Civil Rights Act's prohibition of discrimination by restaurants, hotels, and other public accommodations. In the wake of hearings raising grave doubts about whether Congress had the authority to ground this public accommodations provision in the Fourteenth Amendment's equal protection guarantee, Congress invoked its commerce power as an alternative basis for this provision. Because the statute was framed this way, the Supreme Court was able to uphold the measure on commerce grounds without ever having to consider the Fourteenth Amendment issue. Had Congress relied exclusively on its authority to enforce the Fourteenth Amendment's equal protection guarantee, the case, of course, would not have been decided on commerce grounds and might well have come out the other way.

Aside from framing issues for judicial resolution, Congress and its members also participate in the litigation process. Sometimes the Supreme Court invites the House, the Senate, or individual members of Congress to present an amicus curiae (friend of the court) brief and participate in oral arguments. Amicus curiae briefs, most notably in abortion and separation-of-powers disputes, also have been filed at the initiative of the Senate, the House, and their individual members. For example, a coalition of more than two hundred members of Congress filed an amicus brief in *Harris* v. *McRae*, defending the right of Congress to fund or to refrain from funding abortions as it sees fit.

On rare occasions, individual members file lawsuits challenging the constitutionality of congressional or White House action. Although the courts typically refuse to resolve these disputes on justiciability or jurisdictional grounds, some members have succeeded in challenging the constitutionality of governmental conduct. Senator Edward Kennedy (D-Mass.), for example, successfully challenged President Nixon's use of the "pocket veto" during a 1972 recess. Representative Mike Synar (D-Okla.) also was successful in his 1986 challenge to the Gramm-Rudman Deficit Control Act.

Congress also participates as a party to litigation when the Justice Department refuses to defend a statute's constitutionality. In cases involving the constitutionality of the bankruptcy court and the legislative veto, for example, congressional and executive-branch interests collided. In both cases, congressional and Justice Department lawyers fought each other at oral argument and through briefs filed before the Supreme Court. To ensure that its interests would be well protected in these and other disputes, the Senate established an Office of Senate Legal Counsel in 1978. In the House, the office of the Clerk of the House handles member and institutional litigation.

Once the Supreme Court decides a case, Congress may make use of a wide variety of powers to signal its approval or disapproval of the decision. Congress, for example, regularly reverses Court rulings that interpret a statute. This process, called statutory reversal, frequently involves issues of constitutional significance, including race and sex discrimination. In 1991, for example, Congress passed a civil rights bill that overturned or modified nine Supreme Court rulings, five of them from 1989, two from 1991, and one each from 1986 and 1987.

On constitutional questions, a response by Congress to a Court decision is rarely so confrontational. Congress hardly ever pursues alternatives such as stripping the Court of jurisdiction or reenacting a statute that the Court has struck down (as it eventually did with child labor legislation). Another mechanism that infrequently comes into play is the constitutional amendment process. Requiring two-thirds approval from both houses of Congress and ratification by three-fourths of the states, the amendment process rarely proves successful. Constitutional amendment proposals are significant for other reasons, however. In some instances, they drive the legislative process. Following the Supreme Court's ruling that flag burning is protected speech and not subject to criminal sanction, Democratic leaders in the House and Senate successfully sought to stave off a constitutional amendment proposal by vigorously supporting a constitutionally suspect flag desecration statute, the Flag Protection Act of 1989. Hoping that the issue would "go away" over time, House Constitution Subcommittee chair Don Edwards (D-Calif.) remarked that "if something has to be done, it would be a statute, and hopefully, that will cool the fires."[25]

Constitutional amendment proposals also may drive judicial decision-making. In response to the Court's failure to invalidate gender-based decision-making, Congress approved and sent to the states for ratification a proposed Equal Rights Amendment (ERA) prohibiting the abridgement of "equality of rights . . . on account of sex." These efforts prompted the Court to reconsider its approach to gender decision-making, and in the early 1970s Supreme Court decision-making became "fully compatible with arguments made by leading mainstream ERA proponents in such documents as congressional committee reports and hearings records on the ERA, and in testimony in the Congressional Record by leading ERA sponsors."[26] Ironically, the ultimate defeat of the ERA is sometimes attributed to the Court's general adoption of the amendment's principles.[27]

Another area where Congress has been successful is in countering Supreme Court decision-making that does not protect rights that Congress thinks should be protected. Two recent examples in the religious liberty context stand out. After the Supreme Court upheld, in *Goldman* v. *Weinberger*, an air force regulation forbidding an Orthodox Jew's wearing of a yarmulke indoors while on duty, Congress enacted legislation overturning this regulation.[28] More strikingly, Congress significantly expanded religious liberty protections through its 1994 Religious Freedom Restoration Act. The bill was a direct outgrowth of the Supreme Court's 1990 decision in *Employment Division of Oregon* v. *Smith*, which held that generally applicable laws that adversely affect but do not single out religious exercise are not subject to federal court challenge. Finding that "government should not burden religious exercise without compelling justification" and that "in *Employment Division of Oregon v. Smith*, the Supreme Court virtually eliminated the requirement that the government justify burdens in religious exercise by laws neutral towards religion," Congress specified that government may not "burden a person's exercise of religion" except in compelling circumstances, "even if the burden results from a rule of general applicability."[29]

Congressional responses to Supreme Court decisions are not always hostile. Sometimes Congress affirmatively assists in the implementation of a Court decision. For example, in response to southern resistance, Congress took bold steps to make *Brown* v. *Board of Education* a reality. In 1964 it prohibited segregated school systems from receiving federal aid and authorized the Department of Justice to file desegregation lawsuits. These federal efforts proved critical in ending dual school systems. More actual desegregation took place the year after these legislative programs took effect than in the decade following *Brown.*

Congress, finally, may also enact legislation at the Court's behest. In 1978 the Court, while upholding the constitutionality of third-party searches of newspapers in *Zurcher* v. *Stanford Daily,* invited legislative efforts to establish "nonconstitutional protections against possible abuses of the search warrant procedure."[30] Congress accepted this invitation. Concluding that "the search warrant procedure in itself does not sufficiently protect the press and other innocent parties" and that the *Zurcher* decision had "thrown into doubt" "a longstanding principle of constitutional jurisprudence,"[31] Congress prohibited such newspaper searches in 1980.[32]

EXECUTIVE-BRANCH INTERPRETATIONS

Executive power in constitutional decision-making is extraordinarily broad. The executive appoints Supreme Court justices, recommends legislation and constitutional amendments, exercises the veto power, promulgates regulations, and uses its bully pulpit. In each of these ways, the executive interprets the Constitution and shapes constitutional values. Indeed, through its day-to-day administration of the law and management of the federal government, there is little doubt that the executive branch interprets the Constitution more often than the courts. "Whenever a federal law enforcement officer decides whether there is probable cause for an arrest, the executive branch has interpreted the Fourth Amendment; whenever federal employees are disciplined for statements they made, the executive branch has interpreted the First Amendment."[33]

The pervasiveness of executive-branch interpretation of the Constitution is underscored by the critical albeit limited role that the president and his staff play in executive-branch interpretation. The promulgation of regulations, the administration of federal programs, communications with Congress, litigation before the courts, and the resolution of intra-executive disputes are the near-exclusive province of executive departments and agencies. For a variety of reasons, White House control over agency and department heads is limited. In some instances, the president's power to appoint and remove agency heads is severely constrained by statute, and his authority to affect policy-making is thereby limited. Many of these "independent agencies," including the Federal

Communications Commission, the National Labor Relations Board, and the Equal Employment Opportunity Commission, actively engage in constitutional interpretation. In other instances, where the president can fire agency heads, these departments and agencies nonetheless view themselves as quasi-independent. Witness these comments by post-Watergate attorneys general Edward Levi (1974–76), Griffin Bell (1977–80), and William Barr (1991–92) at their confirmation hearings. Levi spoke of his intention to "give my independent judgment"; Bell spoke of the need to "professionalize" and "depoliticize" the Department of Justice; and Barr emphasized that "when an issue is brought to me, the first thing I do analytically is say, 'let's take the politics out of it.'"[34] This tradition of independence is especially pronounced at the two Justice Department offices most involved in constitutional interpretation disputes, the Office of Legal Counsel (which, among other things, advises the attorney general on pending legislation and the legality of presidential initiatives) and the Office of the Solicitor General (which is the government's lawyer before the Supreme Court). To combat this independence, the White House Counsel's Office has emerged as the president's lawyer, providing him "access to legal advice that is not filtered through the institutional biases or political preoccupations of the Justice Department."[35] For example, when President Gerald Ford directed air strikes against Cambodian forces in response to their seizure of the *Mayaguez*, a U.S. ship, Ford relied exclusively on counsel Philip Buchen's interpretation of the War Powers Resolution and the president's constitutional authority as commander-in-chief.

Constitutional interpretation by the executive pervades executive-branch operations. Efforts to shape congressional and judicial decision-making as well as regulation all involve executive-branch interpretations of the Constitution. As was true with Congress, this process occurs before, during, and after adjudication.

Before adjudication, executive-branch action affects the content of legislation and regulations, thereby framing the constitutional questions before the courts. With respect to lawmaking, the Constitution guarantees the executive a large role in legislative decision-making, requiring the president to recommend measures he judges necessary and expedient. Presidents have made frequent use of this power, sending proposals to Congress on busing, abortion, flag burning, and school prayer.

The executive also participates in the lawmaking process by sharing with Congress its views on the constitutionality of proposed legislation. When Congress debated the 1964 Civil Rights Act's public accommodations provision, Attorney General Robert Kennedy cautioned Congress against relying on its power to enforce the Fourteenth Amendment because "we might very well have some difficulty on its constitutionality"; instead, he encouraged Congress to also make use of its commerce power because "the commerce clause will obtain a remedy and there won't be a problem about the constitutionality."[36] A much different message was sent in 1989 by William Barr, then in charge of the Justice Department's Office of Legal Counsel, when Congress was choosing whether to respond to the Court's flag desecration decision with a statutory response or with a constitutional amendment. In an argument that was unsuccessful in Congress but ultimately validated by the Court, Barr claimed that "it cannot be seriously maintained that a statute [the Flag Protection Act of 1989] aimed at protecting the flag would be constitutional."[37]

Executive lawmaking authority, finally, includes the president's veto power. When the president concludes that an act of Congress is unconstitutional, the last word on that dispute typically rests with the executive (unless two-thirds of both the House and Senate vote to overturn the veto). For example, President Ronald Reagan strongly and successfully opposed legislative efforts to require broadcasters to provide equal time to parties on both sides of an issue (the fairness doctrine) and unhesitatingly followed a Justice Department recommendation that he veto the fairness bill as "antagonistic to the Freedom of Expression guaranteed by the First Amendment." "In any other medium besides broadcasting," Reagan contended, "such federal policing of the editorial judgment of journalists would be unthinkable."[38] More strikingly, President George Bush helped maintain strict abortion-funding restrictions by successfully vetoing five bills that allowed some federal funding of abortion. Even the threat of a veto is often sufficient reason for Congress to revise or remove contested language in a bill. In 1988, for example, Reagan again staved off legislative efforts to impose "equal time" requirements on broadcasters by demanding that Congress remove fairness provisions contained in a proposal for an omnibus appropriations bill.

Curiously, the president sometimes signals his constitutional objections to legislation by making "signing statements" in conjunction with his ratification of congressional action. When George Bush signed flag protection legislation, he expressed "serious doubt that it can withstand Supreme Court review."[39] Ronald Reagan was equally troubled about "violation[s] of the system of separation of powers carefully crafted by the framers of the Constitution" when he signed the Gramm-Rudman Deficit Control Act.[40] In both instances, constitutional objections were pushed aside because the president embraced these measures' underlying policies. Along the same lines, signing statements sometimes claim that bill provisions won't be enforced because the president thinks they are unconstitutional. Ronald Reagan, George Bush, and Bill Clinton, for example, have all contended that they would not comply with legislative veto provisions allowing Congress to overturn executive-branch action without having to enact legislation.

Beyond its lawmaking authority, the executive frames constitutional disputes through its regulatory authority. Executive agencies wield enormous power through the process of issuing rules and regulations. Although rulemaking is supposed to implement congressional intent, there is sufficient ambiguity in many statutes for executive officials to push in one direction or another depending on their policy preferences and constitutional beliefs. Congress, of course, can overturn these agency interpretations through legislation (subject to presidential veto). The courts, too, can strike down executive rule-making as inconsistent with congressional intent. Recent Supreme Court decision-making, however, severely limits such challenges. For example, in *Rust* v. *Sullivan,* the Court refused to overturn Reagan administration regulations interpreting legislation to prohibit federally funded abortion counseling because of the substantial deference it felt was owed to executive-branch statutory interpretations.[41] When Congress subsequently sought to overturn these regulations through legislation, President Bush successfully vetoed the bill.

Rule-making also calls on agencies and departments to determine whether their regulations are consistent with constitutional demands. When the Reagan administration proposed its abortion-counseling rule, for example, First Amendment concerns played a prominent role in the rule's promulgation. Likewise, when the Carter administration launched affirmative action initiatives in the Small Business Administration, the Department of Labor, and other agencies, the administration considered possible equal protection challenges to these requirements.

Beyond its role in setting the stage for constitutional litigation through its participation in the lawmaking and regulatory processes, the executive regularly litigates constitutional disputes both as a party and as an amicus. The decision to support or oppose Supreme Court review, as well as the preparation of briefs and oral arguments, is entrusted to the solicitor general, who is the only litigant who has a right to participate in Supreme Court litigation without first seeking the Court's permission. The solicitor general is also viewed as an officer of the Court as well as an advocate. According to the Carter Justice Department, the solicitor general "protects the Court's docket by screening the Government's cases and relieving the Court of the burden of reviewing unmeritorious claims."[42] The Court helps to perpetuate this gatekeeper image, granting review (certiorari) in roughly 70 percent of the cases presented to it by the solicitor general.[43] More significant, the Court often leans heavily on the solicitor general's arguments in its decision-making. The solicitor general's brief in *Brown*, for example, played an instrumental role in convincing the Court of the political unacceptability of segregation. Furthermore, the "undue burden" standard now utilized in abortion decisions derived from a 1983 brief by the solicitor general.[44]

Government arguments before the Supreme Court, however, are not the exclusive province of the solicitor general. In rare instances, the White House will direct filings by the solicitor general. Modern accounts of such intervention include the following: Dwight Eisenhower's drafting of portions of the government's brief in *Brown* v. *Board of Education*;[45] the Kennedy administration's order to Solicitor General Archibald Cox to challenge private discrimination as unconstitutional state action;[46] the Nixon administration's intervention in the solicitor general's filing in the *Pentagon Papers* case (involving the press's First Amendment right to publish confidential military documents) and its involvement in school desegregation and antitrust matters;[47] the Carter White House's reversal of the solicitor general's preliminary position in *Regents* v. *Bakke*,[48] an affirmative action case; the Reagan administration's insistence that the solicitor general file an amicus brief calling for the overturning of *Roe* v. *Wade* in *Thornburgh* v. *College of Obstetricians*;[49] George Bush's order to the solicitor general to reverse a position already taken before the Supreme Court and to support increased state aid to black public colleges to remedy discrimination;[50] and Bill Clinton's direct rebuke of the solicitor general's brief in *Knox* v. *United States*, a child pornography case.[51]

In other instances, the solicitor general is not the sole governmental voice before the Court. When an independent agency is a party to a dispute, for example, the agency is sometimes allowed to file a brief or argue before the Court. As a result, there are several instances where a federal agency and the solicitor general have openly disagreed with each other before the Supreme Court. Consider the following two cases involving the Federal Communications Commission (FCC): In *Federal Communications Commission* v. *Pacifica Foundation*, the FCC successfully argued that certain words could be kept off the airwaves for most broadcasting hours and thereby withstood the solicitor general's challenge to the FCC orders, which characterized them as overbroad because the commission did not consider "the context in which the offending words were used."[52] In *Metro Broadcasting* v. *Federal Communications Commission*, the commission and the solicitor general locked horns over race preferences, with the commission arguing that preferences served "the compelling governmental interest in promoting diversity in broadcast programming and remedying discrimination," and the solicitor characterizing preferences as "precisely the type of racial stereotyping that is anathema to basic constitutional principles."[53]

Executive-branch participation in constitutional adjudication does not end when the Supreme Court hands down its ruling. The executive may seek to affect further court action through judicial appointments, judicial reorganization plans (court packing), and court-stripping proposals. The executive can also seek to overturn Court action through constitutional amendment proposals. Over the past decade, for example, the White House strongly supported constitutional amendment proposals to overturn *Roe* v. *Wade* (on abortion) and *Texas* v. *Johnson* (on flag desecration).

Executive-branch responses to court constitutional decision-making is typically less adversarial than an outright call for repeal. For the most part, the executive works around the Court by recommending and vetoing legislation and through its power to interpret Court decisions when promulgating regulations. Abortion is a prime example. Dissatisfied with *Roe* v. *Wade*, Presidents Reagan and Bush launched numerous statutory and regulatory initiatives and used their veto authority to block the enactment of legislation approving abortion funding by either the federal government or the District of Columbia. President Clinton, in contrast, signaled his approval of *Roe* by embracing a pro-choice statutory and regulatory agenda that, among other things, sought to limit the effect of Supreme Court rulings that had narrowed abortion rights.

STATE INTERPRETATIONS

Constitutional decision-making involves much more than the three branches of the federal government. State judges and officials take an oath "to support and defend the Constitution," and put this oath into effect through interpretations of both the U.S. Constitution and their state constitution. In many instances, these independent state interpretations provide broader individual rights protections than those mandated by the Supreme Court. However, the most visible state responses to Supreme Court decision-making were the southern states' massive resistance to *Brown* and the efforts of numerous states to undercut *Roe* through the enactment of restrictive abortion regulations.

State efforts to derail *Brown* are a hideous reminder of the pervasiveness of segregation in Jim Crow states. Just three years after *Brown*, 136 laws designed to preserve segregation had been enacted, including anti-NAACP laws, laws establishing segregation committees, amendments to or repeals of compulsory public school attendance statutes, authorizations of school closures, laws encouraging segregated private schools, and measures withholding state aid to desegregated schools. "Ambitious politicians, to put it mildly, perceived few incentives to advocate compromise."[54] Orval Faubus, governor of Arkansas, was lauded for resisting *Brown* and forcing President Eisenhower to send federal troops to open Little Rock's schools to black children; Faubus won a landslide reelection in 1958. Alabama's George Wallace was equally adamant, declaring in his 1963 inaugural address, "I draw the line in the dust and toss the gauntlet before the feet of tyranny, and I say segregation now, segregation tomorrow, segregation forever."[55]

The South's campaign against *Brown* can only be understood as open defiance. In contrast, most state efforts to limit *Roe* raised issues that the Court had not explicitly considered. Spousal consent, parental consent and notification, waiting periods, informed consent requirements, and the like had not been formally considered in *Roe*. From 1973 to 1989, nearly all of these efforts failed, but the steady stream of legislation (306 antiabortion measures were passed during this period) kept the abortion issue before the Supreme Court and provided the Court with countless opportunities to expand state authority in this area.

In sharp contrast to state legislative campaigns against *Brown* and *Roe*, state courts have played a leadership role in expanding constitutional protections. So long as state courts base their decisions on "bona fide separate, adequate, and independent grounds," the Supreme Court will not stand in the way of state court efforts to expand individual rights protections.[56] In short, the last word on state constitutional law rests with state courts.

The Supreme Court approves of and sometimes encourages this practice. Each state, according to the Court, has the "sovereign right to adopt in its own constitution individual liberties more expansive than those conferred by the Federal Constitution."[57] Indeed, disappointed Supreme Court justices often remind their state counterparts that state courts may reach an opposite result under state constitutional law. As Chief Justice Warren Burger once remarked: "For all we know, the state courts would find this statute invalid under the State Constitution."[58]

Although most state court judges are appointed, several states allow for popular election or removal of state judges. For this reason, state courts can be an important part of the constitutional dialogue that takes place between the Supreme Court and elected officials. Take the case of California, whose judges are subject to popular election. In one decision, the California Supreme Court did not even see the need to explain the source of their authority: they simply "pause[d] to reaffirm the independent nature of the California Constitution and our responsibility to separately define and protect the rights of California citizens despite conflicting decisions of the United States Supreme Court interpreting the federal Constitution."[59] Indeed, the California Constitution provides that the "rights guaranteed by this Constitution are not dependent on those guaranteed by the United States Constitution."[60]

Exemplifying the many ways in which state constitutions provide broader protection than the federal Constitution are state court rulings on abortion. State court involvement here is not surprising: ten state constitutions contain explicit privacy provisions, and several others contain clauses that have been interpreted to protect the right to privacy. Other areas where state courts have been particularly active include the exclusionary rule and school finance.[61]

Holdings such as these are likely to become increasingly commonplace. The Rehnquist Court's reluctance to expand constitutional protections already has caused interest groups to turn their attention to state courts and state legislatures. This flurry of activity on abortion and other questions which is going on in state government and state courts therefore is more than a harbinger of things to come; it is proof of the fundamental role played by the states in shaping constitutional values.

CONCLUSION

The Supreme Court is but one of several governmental actors that interpret the Constitution. Congress, the White House, governmental agencies, and the states all play critical interdependent roles in shaping constitutional values. The sweep and influence of their interactions are broad and pervasive. Indeed, unlike the influence of the courts, whose role in constitutional decision-making is confined to resolving "cases or controversies," elected-government influences occur before, during, and after litigation. Moreover, because elected government resolves constitutional conflicts not subject to judicial action and appoints and confirms judges, some matters of profound constitutional significance are its exclusive province.

These limitations on judicial authority do not undermine the Court's profound role in constitutional decision-making. "Nonetheless," as Justice Robert Jackson put it, "the Constitution-makers left the Court in vital respects a dependent body."[62] How sensitive the Court is to this "dependency" on elected government, and how willing elected government is to make use of its powers over the Court, are a principal concern of the chapters that follow.

4 / Constitutional Dialogues Case Studies

CONSTITUTIONAL DECISION-MAKING neither begins nor ends with a court decision. The shaping of constitutional values is a dynamic process that involves all parts of elected government in an ongoing dialogue. To understand the pervasiveness of this dialogue, it is necessary to get beyond a simple specification of the numerous ways in which elected government helps shape constitutional meaning. The richness of constitutional dialogues between the courts and elected government, instead, is best revealed through case studies that highlight the volleys that take place between elected government and the courts over a number of years. Since these interchanges involve several governmental actors as well as a range of governmental powers, the sweep, scope, and fluidity of constitutional decision-making is most vividly seen through case studies. This chapter is a step in that direction. Through mini–case studies of equality, federalism, separation of powers, and religion issues, this chapter demonstrates that constitutional decision-making involves all of government and takes place over many phases. It adds an exclamation mark to what has come before—the debunking of judicial finality and the delineation of elected government's broad powers of constitutional interpretation.

EQUALITY: SCHOOL DESEGREGATION

Supreme Court efforts to end racial isolation in education exemplify the reaches and limits of the judiciary's ability to transform society. *Brown* v. *Board of Education*'s declaration that "separate educational facilities are inherently unequal" is universally applauded.[1] Robert Bork, for example, describes *Brown* as "the defining event of modern American constitutional law" and "the greatest moral triumph constitutional law had ever produced."[2] The elected branches, moreover, eventually rallied behind *Brown,* making tangible the *Brown* mandate through a series of 1960s legislative and regulatory initiatives. In sharp contrast, the approval of mandatory busing remedies in *Swann* v. *Charlotte-Mecklenburg County Board of Education* is one of the Court's most criticized rulings. Alexander Bickel, for example, characterized court-ordered busing as sheer folly, arguing that "no policy that a court can order, and a school board, a city or even a state has the capacity to put into effect, will in fact result in the foreseeable future in racially balanced public schools. Only a reordering of the environment . . . might have an appreciable impact."[3] The elected branches also attacked the Court here, enacting legislation and adopting enforcement schemes designed to undermine mandatory busing remedies. The quite different responses to *Brown* and *Swann* offer telling evidence of the elected branches' role in Supreme Court decision-making.

From Brown *to Busing*

Between 1954 and 1964, *Brown*'s promise of equal educational opportunity was rendered meaningless by southern resistance. By 1964 there was a growing recognition on Capitol Hill that "we must simply face the fact that the decisions of the Supreme Court are not being carried out . . . and unless we are to make a mockery of [them] . . . Congress must act to put the strength of the National Government behind [them]."[4] The solution was the 1964 Civil Rights Act, which, among other things, authorized Justice Department participation in school desegregation litigation (Title IV) and demanded that federal grant recipients be nondiscriminatory (Title VI).[5]

More significant, the implementation of the Elementary and Secondary Education Act of 1965 (ESEA),[6] coupled with the issuance and enforcement of guidelines for Title VI of the Civil Rights Act of 1964, marked a significant shift in federal power over state education systems. With Title VI's nondiscrimination requirement, Congress became willing to pump out billions of dollars of aid for the compensatory education of educationally deprived children. This money supplied sufficient incentive for many school systems to comply with the nondiscrimination standards of the Office for Civil Rights (OCR). Between 1963 and 1968, the percentage of black children in all-black schools in the South dropped from 98 percent to 25 percent.[7]

However, the elected branches' endorsement of *Brown*'s simple nondiscrimination demand was, from the start, tempered by opposition to forced busing. A provision of the ESEA prohibits the use of federal funds for "the assignment or transportation of students . . . in order to overcome racial imbalance."[8] With the election of Richard Nixon in 1968, the White House also signaled its opposition to mandatory reassignments. Nixon's presidential campaign prominently featured a "Southern Strategy" in which candidate Nixon promised to ease the pressure being applied to southern school districts to end segregative practices.

It was against this backdrop that the Supreme Court, in *Swann* v. *Charlotte-Mecklenburg*, announced that court-ordered busing was an appropriate technique to remedy unconstitutional segregation.[9] Immediately after *Swann*, several members of Congress issued strong statements rebuking the Court. More significantly, President Nixon delivered a national address on the evils of busing and submitted legislation that, among other things, would have had Congress designate a hierarchy of remedies in school desegregation lawsuits, ranging from more preferred to less preferred (busing would only have been used as a limited remedy of "last resort" for school segregation, and then "only under strict limitations").[10]

The constitutionality of Nixon's proposal and the power of Congress to restrict the use of the busing remedy for violations of the constitutional rights of black schoolchildren were a matter of heated debate in 1972. Congress ultimately rejected the Nixon plan, claiming that the Court's status as a co-equal branch warranted legislative respect for its constitutional holdings. In its place, Congress enacted restrictions both on federal financial support of mandatory busing and on federal advocacy of busing "unless constitutionally required."[11] Congress's hesitancy here is revealing. Although it may well be able to limit the Court's remedial authority under its powers to enforce the Fourteenth Amendment and to make exceptions to Court jurisdiction, Congress generally views those devices as too intrusive. Consequently, legislative responses to judicial excess often take the form of restrictions on funding.

The Politics of Busing

Congressional opposition to busing persisted throughout the 1970s. With the election of pro-busing candidate Jimmy Carter, however, executive-branch rule-making was utilized to support student reassignments. Take the case of the Emergency School Aid Act (ESAA) of 1972,[12] which provided federal support to school districts implementing a school desegregation plan. Although originally devised as part of Nixon's strategy to recognize the "special needs" of southern systems subject to desegregation orders, ESAA—especially in the hands of the Carter administration—proved an extraordinarily effective device to advance school desegregation. Specifically, by conditioning ESAA eligibility on school district compliance with strict nondiscrimination standards, the

ESAA "carrot" prompted massive pupil reassignment. For example, during a particular two-year period, 244,000 schoolchildren were reassigned out of racially isolated classrooms.

The 1980 election of Ronald Reagan dramatically changed the face of school desegregation politics. The Reagan administration, by deemphasizing the federal role and refusing to pursue mandatory busing, rejected the desegregation techniques championed by the Carter administration. President Reagan called forced busing "reverse segregation," and his assistant attorney general for civil rights, William Bradford Reynolds, expressed concern that busing remedies "are threatening to dilute the essential consensus that racial discrimination is wrong and should not be tolerated in any form."[13] The Reagan administration also took its case to Congress. Through his "New Federalism in Education" campaign, Reagan successfully implored Congress to repeal the ESAA program along with more than two dozen separate education programs and authorized these programs' various activities in a new education block grant.[14] Under the block grant, states would receive lump sum federal support and then establish their own priorities. Not surprisingly, having been given the freedom to spend federal dollars on instructional equipment (a usage reported by 90 percent of school districts responding to one survey), school systems have not used this money for activities previously supported by the ESAA (a usage reported by only 6 percent of the responding districts).[15]

Reagan and Beyond

Despite academic studies indicating that the level of segregation grew significantly between 1988 and 1991 (so that the number of black children attending predominantly minority schools is the highest it has been since 1968), Congress and the White House, since the mid-1980s, have displayed little interest in school desegregation. Courts, too, seem ready to get out of this business. The Rehnquist Court, for example, has made clear that federal courts should be willing to terminate desegregation orders, placing increasing emphasis on judicial restraint and extolling the virtues of local school board control in "allow[ing] citizens to participate in decisionmaking, and allow[ing] innovation so that school programs can fit local needs."[16] Right or wrong, the courts and elected government are no longer at war with each other over this issue. The story of school desegregation is one in which, after the Court's monumental decision in *Brown,* Congress and the executive have framed the debate. First, the elected branches, by giving meaning to the *Brown* mandate through mid-1960s reforms, helped to propel increasing judicial scrutiny in

Swann. Second, after two decades of attacking mandatory reassignments (and appointing Supreme Court justices), the Court has ceded to elected-branch desires and returned much of school desegregation to the control of state and local government.

This give-and-take process reveals the extraordinary importance of social and political pressures in shaping Court doctrine. A similar tale will unfold in the abortion context, where the Supreme Court's eventual loosening of *Roe* v. *Wade*—in *Planned Parenthood* v. *Casey*—was intended to stabilize, if not re-solve, the abortion dispute. As with school desegregation, moreover, this con-stitutional dialogue took place over an extended period of time, with elected government sometimes facilitating and at other times hindering the implemen-tation of Court decisions.

FEDERALISM: THE SAGA OF MINIMUM WAGES

Beginning with the decision of the First Congress to establish a National Bank, all parts of government, federal and state, have hotly debated the constitu-tional parameters defining the distribution of power between them. Starting with Andrew Jackson's declaration that the bank was unconstitutional, despite a unanimous Supreme Court decision to the contrary, the last word on federal-state relations has been spoken by the elected branches at least as often as by the courts. Indeed, following FDR's efforts to curb *Lochner*-era abuses of doctrine through court-packing proposals and judicial appointments, the courts have been extraordinarily reluctant to intervene in federalism disputes. For exam-ple, when Congress chose to ground the 1964 Civil Rights Act's public accom-modation provisions in its commerce power, the only meaningful considera-tion of the outer reaches of this power took place on Capitol Hill and not at the Supreme Court.

One notable exception to the Court's yea-saying approach to Commerce Clause initiatives is federal action that regulates the "states as states." In its 1976 *National League* v. *Usery* decision, after forty years of unquestioning allegiance to Congress's invocation of its commerce power, the Court invalidated 1974 legislation extending minimum wage and maximum hour protections to most state employees. Writing for a five-member majority that included fellow Nixon appointees Warren Burger, Harry Blackmun, and Lewis Powell, William Rehn-quist, then an associate justice, declared the 1974 measure unconstitutional because, in conflict with the Tenth Amendment's reservation of unenumerated powers to the states, it "directly displaces the States' freedom to structure integral operations in areas of traditional governmental functions."[17]

Usery's revival of "states' rights" was both heralded and vilified as promising the return of judicial supervision of federal-state relations. The story of the legislation at issue in *Usery*, as well as *Usery*'s ultimate demise, however, reveals that federalism is principally about politics. The 1974 measure was the result of political compromise. Although Nixon had successfully vetoed analogous legislation in 1973 by characterizing the extension of minimum wage protection as "an unwarranted interference with State prerogatives,"[18] he relented in 1974 after Congress reenacted the measure *but* mandated that the increase take place over a longer period of time. Nixon, however, found other ways to pursue his commitment to a "New Federalism in which power, funds, and responsibility will flow from Washington to the states and to the people."[19] Most significant (for present purposes at least), Nixon appointed judges who believed that there were concrete limits to federal authority over the states. *Usery* is a vivid manifestation of this pursuit; four of the five justices who struck down the 1974 measure were Nixon appointees.

Usery's durability proved ephemeral. From the outset, the decision was in trouble. The Court, unable or unwilling to specify what constituted a "traditional governmental function," delegated to the executive the task of defining the ultimate meaning of *Usery*. This task fell on the Department of Labor, which published a "final rule" in December 1979 specifying both traditional and nontraditional functions.[20] To the chagrin of the Department of Transportation, mass transit systems were deemed nontraditional and therefore subject to fair labor laws. On 15 April 1980, the Transportation Department formally challenged the Labor Department's conclusion on both policy and constitutional grounds. In June 1980, however, the Justice Department's Office of Legal Counsel issued an opinion supporting Labor.

The stage was then set for challenges by the San Antonio Metropolitan Transit Authority (SAMTA) and others to the Labor Department ruling. When SAMTA's challenge reached the Supreme Court for oral argument (October 1984), the Court specifically asked the parties to discuss the appropriateness or inappropriateness of the Court's overturning of *Usery*. The election of Ronald Reagan provided another wrinkle in the Court's reconsideration of *Usery*. Reagan was a strong believer in states' rights, subscribing to the view that "the federal character of the Constitution was designed to ensure that the States continued to matter."[21] For the Reagan administration, *Usery* was a treasured precedent to be defended at any cost. Nonetheless, the administration did not disagree with the Carter Labor Department's conclusion that mass transit was not a traditional state function. The solution was to fiercely defend both *Usery* and congressional authority to regulate a broad array of nontraditional functions.

Thanks to Justice Harry Blackmun's switching sides, however, a bare five-member majority in *Garcia* v. *San Antonio Metro Transit Authority* overruled *Usery*, finding its "traditional function" standard unworkable and concluding that "the principal and basic limit on the federal commerce power is that inherent in all congressional action—the built-in restraints that our system provides through state participation in federal government action."[22] Congress and the Reagan administration, for quite different reasons, were troubled by *Garcia*. Attorney General Meese condemned the Court for disregarding "the framers' intention that state and local governments be a buffer against the centralizing tendencies of the national Leviathan."[23] President Reagan, too, got into the action, speaking of "the presumption of sovereignty [that] should rest with the individual states" and issuing an executive order directing departments and agencies to "refrain . . . from establishing uniform, national standards for programs."[24]

Congress was concerned less about the content of *Garcia* than about the decision's consequences. Recognizing that state and local employees would be entitled to billions of dollars in back-pay overtime claims, Congress approved legislation postponing the decision's effective date and authorizing the substitution of compensatory vacation time for overtime payments.[25] The bill, however, did not relieve states and municipalities of their post-*Garcia* obligation to satisfy the federal minimum wage law.

The question remains whether this legislation validates *Garcia*'s embrace of the political process. The bill's sponsors, such as Senator Howard Metzenbaum (D-Ohio), answered this question with an emphatic yes, claiming that the bill "vindicates the Supreme Court's faith . . . that the proper protection for the sovereign interests of States and their political subdivisions lies not in directives issued by the Federal Judiciary but rather the give-and-take of our federal system—especially the role of the States and cities in the political process."[26] Despite this claim of state influence over federal lawmaking, the fact remains that the states are now subject to greater regulation than *Usery* found constitutionally permissible. That Congress's response to *Garcia* did not lift minimum wage obligations for traditional state functions is proof positive that states are less well off under *Garcia* than under *Usery*.

Garcia's future, however, is far from clear. Changes in the Court's composition since 1985 cast grave doubt on *Garcia*'s bare five-member majority (with two members of the majority replaced by Republican appointees and no members of the dissent replaced by Democratic appointees). Indeed, in a 1992 decision, *New York* v. *United States,* the Court invalidated congressionally approved efforts to pressure states into enacting legislation on the grounds that these were outside Congress's commerce power.[27] More striking, in April 1995, the Court—again by a 5-to-4 margin—ruled that Congress had acted beyond its Commerce Clause authority when it made possession of a gun within one thousand feet of a school a federal crime. This decision, *United States* v. *Lopez,* further invigorated federalism-based limits on congressional regulation of matters "where States historically have been sovereign."[28]

Ironically, what may eventually save *Garcia* is the Court's reluctance to overturn past precedents. In *New York,* while raising doubts about *Garcia*'s durability, the Court nonetheless was careful not to formally overrule *Garcia.* As is true in the abortion context, the Court sees its institutional legitimacy as tied to its adherence to precedent. Yet, just as *Planned Parenthood* v. *Casey* gutted much of *Roe* (reaffirming abortion rights but overturning *Roe*'s trimester standard), *Garcia*'s survival may prove little more than a symbolic gesture. Whatever *Garcia*'s fate, it seems clear that federal-state relations will continue to be defined by the ebbs and flows of who sits on the Court, congressional preferences, and White House desires.

SEPARATION OF POWERS: THE LEGISLATIVE VETO

On 23 June 1983, the Supreme Court struck down more legislation with a single decision than it had previously done over the course of its nearly two-hundred-year existence. That decision, *Immigration and Naturalization Service* v. *Chadha,* declared unconstitutional the so-called legislative veto, a procedure by which departments or agencies would make proposals that would become law unless rejected by a majority vote of one or both houses of Congress. Noting that the Constitution demands that all legislation be approved by both houses of Congress and presented to the president for signature or veto, the Supreme Court concluded that the legislative veto procedure subverted the constitutionally prescribed lawmaking process.

The Court and elected government both perceived *Chadha* to be monumental. Writing in dissent, Justice Byron White thought "the Court's decision [to be] of surpassing importance," noting "the prominence of the legislative veto mechanism in our contemporary political system."[29] The executive shared this view. In petitioning the Supreme Court to hear *Chadha,* the Carter Justice Department spoke of the need to "secure a definitive ruling from [the] Court on an issue which, over the last decade, has created many occasions for confrontation between the executive and legislative branches."[30] When the Supreme Court resolved the dispute (after Ronald Reagan had assumed the presidency), Attorney General William French Smith perceived that "probably no other recent decision of the Supreme Court has had such an extensive and direct effect on existing statutes."[31]

Think again. From its 1932 inception, the legislative veto mechanism has been the province of Congress and the executive. It took the Supreme Court more than fifty years, despite a persistent and vigorous constitutional debate in the elected branches, to finally address the propriety of the legislative veto. Even more striking is the fact that since *Chadha*, Congress and the executive continue to make regular use of legislative vetoes. "In one form or another," as Louis Fisher observed in his definitive study of this device, "legislative vetoes will remain an important mechanism for reconciling legislative and executive interests. Neither Congress nor the executive branch wants the static model of government offered by the Court."[32]

Before *Chadha*, legislative vetoes had grown in popularity because they benefited both Congress and the White House. They allowed Congress to monitor executive-branch action without resorting to the cumbersome (and sometimes impossible) task of enacting legislation. The White House's grudging acceptance of the legislative veto mechanism is more complex but also understandable. While it heartily welcomes broad grants of delegated authority from Congress, it is less keen on conditions being set to limit the exercise of that authority. From Herbert Hoover through Gerald Ford, presidents were willing to swallow this bitter pill in order to expand their authority over executive-branch operations. By the late 1970s, however, this discomfort turned into outright hostility. With "Congress threaten[ing] to extend the legislative veto so that it covered every regulation issued by federal agencies,"[33] the legislative veto appeared more an offensive weapon of congressional micromanagement than a defensive check against broad delegation.

The executive decided to fight in court, supporting the challenge to the veto procedure in *Chadha*. After succeeding in the lower courts, a decision Carter praised as having "perhaps the most profound significance constitutionally" during his four years in office,[34] the Carter Justice Department successfully sought Supreme Court review to kill the legislative veto once and for all. By this time, however, Ronald Reagan had been elected president.

Reagan, although a strong believer in presidential prerogatives, supported the legislative veto mechanism in his 1980 campaign. Viewing this procedure as a check on excessive regulation, the Reagan administration seemed inclined to reverse course and defend the veto in *Chadha*. Attorney General William French Smith disagreed. "I pointed out," wrote Smith, "that the Republicans had controlled the presidency for one-half the time since 1952, but had controlled both houses of Congress only two years during that period. Why then sacrifice executive power for legislative power?"[35] This argument, thanks to a direct appeal to the president, ultimately prevailed. Before the Supreme Court, the Reagan Justice Department successfully challenged the legislative veto.

In the twelve years after *Chadha*, 1983–95, well over three hundred legislative veto provisions were enacted into law. Although when signing such legislation presidents sometimes cite *Chadha* and proclaim that the measures will be treated "as having no legal force or effect,"[36] it is quite clear that affected agencies comply with legislative veto provisions. "Agencies cannot risk . . . collisions with the committees that authorize their programs and provide funds."[37] Congress, moreover, can subvert *Chadha*, as then–appeals court judge Stephen Breyer noted, by requiring that agency regulations be introduced as legislation subject to "fast-track" approval by both houses of Congress.[38]

Not only has Congress continued to enact legislative veto provisions but an extraordinary number of informal and nonstatutory legislative vetoes have risen in *Chadha*'s wake. Two of these arrangements, one arising during the Reagan presidency and the other during the Bush presidency, make clear that legislative vetoes are an "irresistible force" that neither the White House nor the Congress wants to abandon.

In 1984, President Reagan proclaimed that Congress's continuing inclusion of legislative veto provisions "serves no constructive purpose" because they "will be implemented in a manner consistent with the *Chadha* decision."[39] The House Appropriations Committee responded in kind, threatening to repeal legislation that allowed the National Aeronautics and Space Administration (NASA) to exceed its spending caps subject to committee approval. From then on, NASA could only exceed its caps through the enactment of supplemental legislation, requiring approval from both houses of Congress and presentment to the president. NASA head James M. Beggs, not surprisingly, much preferred the limited legislative veto check to the onerous demand that NASA obtain formal, positive legislative approval before it exceeded its spending caps. Beggs successfully pleaded his case to Congress, seeking "an informal agreement" and promising "not to exceed amounts for Committee designated programs without the approval of the Committee of Appropriations."[40]

A more dramatic and highly visible arrangement, involving federal aid to the Nicaraguan Contras, was worked out between Bush's secretary of state, James Baker, and House Speaker Jim Wright (D-Tex.) in the spring of 1989. The agreement specified that Baker would not spend appropriated funds designated for the Contras *unless* he was authorized to do so by letter by the four relevant Senate and House authorization and appropriation committees.[41] Although recognizing that the granting of veto authority to the four committees was inconsistent with *Chadha* and understanding the "precedential aspects of this agreement,"[42] Baker embraced this arrangement as the best available compromise. Remarkably, Bush's counsel, C. Boyden Gray, much more concerned with presidential authority in general than with advancing only one part of the president's policy, attacked the Baker accord, warning that the four-committee veto was unconstitutional and set a dangerous precedent for congressional supervision of the president's foreign affairs power.[43] Gray's efforts accomplished little more than White House embarrassment and a public scolding, for the president's support of Contra funding outweighed separation-of-powers concerns.

The Baker accord and the NASA agreement reveal the obvious. The executive is more committed to its policy agenda and the acquisition of discretionary authority than it is to either the Supreme Court or abstract separation-of-powers concerns. Congress likewise is less committed to following the Court than to restricting executive-branch authority. "The predictable and inevitable result of *Chadha*," as Louis Fisher aptly observed, "is a system of lawmaking that is more convoluted, cumbersome, and covert than before. Finding the Court's doctrine incompatible with effective government, the elected branches have searched for techniques that revive the understanding in place before 1982."[44] For similar reasons, elected government has sought to sidestep disfavored rulings in a variety of areas. State lawmakers, for example, attempted to work around *Roe*'s recognition of a compelling state interest in fetal viability during the third trimester by requiring second-trimester viability testing.

RELIGION: FUNDAMENTALIST CHRISTIAN EDUCATORS VERSUS STATE REGULATORS

Controversies between state education officials and religious parents date back to the establishment of public schools and continue today. Early battles concerned states' authority to outlaw private schooling altogether; contemporary skirmishes center on the applicability of state regulations governing teacher certification, curriculum, and the like to religious parents and schools.

On one side, religious parents and educators claim that state-prescribed "minimum standards" and licensing procedures would violate their religious beliefs. This claim is rooted in the Free-Exercise Clause of the First Amendment and the implied Fourteenth Amendment right of parents to direct their children's upbringing. Over the past twenty years, this challenge to state authority has been championed principally by Christian educators and parents.

On the other side, state authorities assert their right to impose "reasonable" regulations on religious schools and religious home instruction. For the state, these regulations establish minimum criteria to protect children from the adverse consequences of an inadequate education. The state, moreover, asserts an independent interest in assisting the child in developing citizenship skills. Schools and parents that do not conform to these regulations violate compulsory school attendance laws and may be subject to criminal prosecution.

From 1975 to 1983, Christian educators and parents fought a holy war with state officials. Neither side seemed especially interested in accommodating the other, and lawsuits emerged in most states. Sometimes religious liberty claimants would succeed; most often the state would prevail. *But* state victories came at a substantial price. Unwilling to comply with court-approved regulations, religious parents and ministers were jailed, churches were padlocked, and the state threatened to terminate parental rights.

Since 1983 this struggle, while far from dormant, has become subdued. Both sides seem more accepting of the other. More significant, the battleground has shifted away from adversarial, winner-take-all litigation towards legislative reform. Thirty-two states have adopted home-schooling statutes or regulations since 1982, and twenty-three of these states have repealed teacher certification requirements. In the end, rather than jailing parents and ministers for noncompliance, state officials have backed down from *High Noon*-style showdowns with fundamentalist Christian educators and parents. This is the lesson of Nebraska and several other states.

The most controversial battle between the state and Christian educators centers around a January 1981 Nebraska Supreme Court decision, *State v. Faith Baptist Church*,[45] involving Pastor Evert Sileven's unaccredited Faith Christian School. After a three-year struggle with the state, Sileven—who publicly prayed for God to kill state education officials—proved the victor. That the state ultimately backed down suggests that enforcing state regulatory schemes may entail too great a cost to be practicable, despite court rulings upholding their constitutionality.

The events leading up to this widely publicized decision and its aftermath date back to 1977, when Faith Baptist Church of Louisville, Nebraska, opened a school without state approval. The leadership of the church maintained that "the operation of the school is simply an extension of the ministry of the church, over which the State of Nebraska has no authority to approve or accredit." Asserting that the state had no "right to inspect God's property," Pastor Sileven and the church officers refused to (1) provide a list of the students enrolled in the school; (2) seek approval for the educational program; (3) employ certified teachers; or (4) seek approval to operate the institution.[46]

The state sought to enjoin the operation of the school because of noncompliance with state regulations. The Nebraska Supreme Court supported these efforts, defending state authority to impose "reasonable regulations for the control and duration of basic education" and characterizing Sileven's actions as an "unreasonable attempt to thwart the legitimate, reasonable, and compelling interests of the State in carrying out its educational obligations, under a claim of religious freedom."[47]

The *Faith Baptist* decision, in Sileven's eyes, only meant that his school could no longer lawfully operate in Nebraska. Instead, it operated both in an Iowa church and "underground" in Nebraska until January 1982, when Sileven reopened the school at Faith Baptist Church. Refusing, because of his religious convictions, to close the institution, he was sentenced in February 1983 to four months in jail for contempt of court. When Faith Christian School reopened in August of that year without state approval, Sileven was arrested and returned to jail to complete the contempt-of-court sentence. To prevent continued operation of the school, the state, in October 1982, padlocked the church on weekdays. Efforts at compromise during the fall of 1983 again failed, and in November seven fathers of Faith Christian students were jailed (and remained jailed until February 1984) for refusing to answer a judge's questions concerning the school. Their wives and children then fled the state to avoid prosecution.

The succeeding events in the saga of Faith Christian School demonstrate the difficulty states have in enforcing their regulatory schemes against resistant Christian educators. This difficulty received national attention and ultimately was the subject of federal scrutiny. U.S. Secretary of Education T. H. Bell suggested that Nebraska's eligibility for federal education funds would be jeopardized if evangelicals could show that state education officials were practicing religious discrimination in their attempts to close the Faith Christian School. In addition to federal scrutiny, Nebraska became the subject of national publicity, frequently negative, for its jailing of individuals who acted on the basis of religious conscience. In January 1984, for example, the reverends Jerry Falwell and Jesse Jackson, on separate occasions, visited the Faith Christian School.

Possibly in response to this publicity and possibly just unwilling to keep on jailing Christian educators, Nebraska governor (and later U.S. senator) Robert Kerry established a four-member panel to examine and report on the public policy questions surrounding the Christian school issue. On 26 January 1984, the governor's panel issued its report, concluding, among other things, that existing procedures "violate[d]" the First Amendment religious liberty protections and that "some accommodation to the First Amendment freedom of religion claims of the Christian school supporters [had to] be recognized."[48] The panel thus recommended that standardized tests be offered to students in place of teacher certification and curriculum requirements. The governor's panel claimed that its recommendations struck "an appropriate balance between the legitimate interest of the State in the education of Nebraska youth and religious freedom."[49] In reaching this conclusion, the panel ignored its state supreme court decision in *State* v. *Faith Baptist Church,* as well as its own finding that the state "clearly has an obligation to establish reasonable and effective educational standards and to exercise an appropriate degree of control over all educational efforts."[50]

The state legislature acted on the panel's recommendations and enacted legislation in April 1984.[51] The 1984 law does not require schools to provide any information to state officials. Instead, parents who elect to send their children to a school that does not apply for state approval must provide the state with information about the education their children are receiving. Specifically, parents who find existing state regulations in conflict with their religious beliefs can satisfy state compulsory-education laws by submitting an "information statement" that declares that their children attend school for 175 days a year and are instructed on core curriculum subjects.

Nebraska's actions speak to the ability of fundamentalist educators to succeed in accomplishing before elected officials what they failed to achieve in court. This phenomenon is not limited to fundamentalist educators. Religious liberty interests generally have fared at least as well before elected officials as before appointed judges. Witness, as discussed in Chapter 3, Congress's enactment of legislation nullifying *Goldman* v. *Weinberger* and *Employment Division of Oregon* v. *Smith.* With the Supreme Court increasingly speaking of the need to defer to government on religious liberty questions, this trend will only continue. In areas other than religious liberty, elected government is also being increasingly called upon to provide individual rights protections where the Court will not. The Civil Rights Act of 1991 reversed several Supreme Court statutory rulings, thereby making it easier to challenge discrimination in contracts, employment, and elsewhere. Likewise, 1993 legislation on abortion clinic access filled a gap left open by the Court.

CONCLUSION

Constitutional decision-making is a fluid, ongoing enterprise involving all three federal branches and the states. The courts help to define but do not control constitutional interpretation. Even Supreme Court decision-making is but one part of a larger mosaic. Not only does elected-government action frame constitutional adjudication but the courts often revisit the same subject thanks to elected officials' interpretations of court rulings. That occurred with school desegregation, minimum wage laws, and the legislative veto. In other instances, elected government seeks to forestall subsequent judicial action by repudiating Court decision-making. Nonstatutory legislative veto regulations and the repeal of state laws regulating religious schools fit this category.

Decisions such as *Brown*, *Chadha*, and *Usery* certainly are an essential part of the stories of school desegregation, the legislative veto, and minimum wage laws. Nonetheless, these decisions have been overshadowed by elected-branch action. *Chadha* is a nullity; *Garcia* overturned *Usery* and then was itself statutorily modified; *Brown* was made meaningful principally by mid-1960s elected-branch action. The story of state regulation of religious schooling, while played out before state courts and officials, is much the same—with state court rulings trumped by elected-government action.

These tugs and pulls between elected government and the Court permeate constitutional decision-making. By considering several disparate subject areas, this chapter has demonstrated the dynamic nature of constitutional decision-making. These mini–case studies, however, provide only a glimpse of how pervasive and nuanced are the interchanges between the Court and elected government.

To better grasp this dynamic process, I will now consider elected-government participation in the abortion dispute. This examination will reaffirm what has come before: the last word on the Constitution's meaning is spoken neither by the Supreme Court nor by elected government. The last word, in fact, is never spoken. Through an ongoing dialectic that involves all of government, constitutional meaning is more a work-in-progress than a finished product.

5 / The Making and Unmaking of *Roe* v. *Wade*
The Rise, Fall, and Partial Resurrection of State Abortion Laws

ON 22 JANUARY 1973 THE SUPREME Court issued its decision in *Roe* v. *Wade*. Holding that a woman's substantive due process right to terminate her pregnancy in its early months outweighed state interests in maternal health and fetal protection, the Court struck down a Texas law permitting abortions only to save the life of the mother. The Court concluded both that the state's interest in potential human life is not compelling until the third trimester of pregnancy (once the fetus becomes viable) and that the state's interest in promulgating *reasonable* maternal health regulations is not compelling until after the first trimester of pregnancy. Consequently, during the first trimester the abortion decision is left to the woman (in consultation with her physician).

Prior to *Roe*, abortion had received some state attention and limited national attention. In the decade preceding *Roe*, after nearly a century of political dormancy, four states repealed and nineteen states—while still limiting abortion rights—liberalized their abortion laws. Congress and the White House, for the most part, were content to leave the abortion issue in the hands of state government: congressional action was limited and designed to preserve the antiabortion status quo ante, while executive-branch action was equally limited and typically reaffirmed state authority.

By placing a higher value on a woman's right to privacy than on potential human life and by imposing a trimester standard that reads like a legislative abortion code, *Roe* spurred elected government into action. It functioned as a political catalyst rather than the last word on abortion. While *Roe* became a lightning rod for all of government, state responses to *Roe* have proven more direct and more profound than federal responses. Between 1973 and 1989, states regularly challenged both the scope and the correctness of *Roe* by enacting abortion regulations that became the subject of the Court's post-*Roe* efforts to clarify the reach and the limits of abortion rights. In contrast, as will be shown in Chapters 6 and 7, below, federal abortion politics typically concerns matters peripheral to the central question of whether a woman possesses a constitutional right to terminate her pregnancy. Abortion funding, family-planning counseling, fetal tissue research, and the like, while undoubtedly of great practical and symbolic consequence, simply do not call into doubt the correctness of *Roe*. Indeed, the federal government eschewed absolutist solutions by rejecting constitutional amendment proposals as well as human life legislation. The only exception to this pattern was where federal and state abortion politics converged, namely, the filing of executive and congressional briefs in state abortion cases and the nomination and confirmation of the justices who were to decide those cases.

The state experience is illuminating for other reasons. State responses both to *Roe* and to the Supreme Court's loosening of *Roe* in its 1989 *Webster* v. *Reproductive Health Services* decision have played a prominent role in revealing public opinion and, with it, shaping the federal political agenda. Furthermore, in instances where the Supreme Court has validated state action, the abortion dispute highlights the power of state courts to provide broader protections under state constitutions than is required by the U.S. Constitution.

THE ROAD TO *ROE*

The story of *Roe* v. *Wade* begins in 1820, when Connecticut enacted the nation's first antiabortion statute. Prior to 1820, most states—following the common law—placed no restrictions on abortions performed before the first recognizable movement of the fetus in utero. This movement was known as the "quickening," and usually occurred between the sixteenth and eighteenth weeks of pregnancy. Under the "quickening" standard, which was very difficult to prove without the pregnant woman's admission, abortion prosecutions were rarely pursued. Instead, "abortion was advertised freely in newspapers, especially in the larger cities. Government was not particularly concerned about the practice."[1] Between 1820 and 1840, however, a movement led by physicians known as "regulars" prompted ten of the nation's twenty-six states to pass restrictive abortion legislation. This campaign against "irregular" medical practitioners such as pharmacists and midwives has been attributed to these physicians' desire "to upgrade themselves professionally and become the exclusive providers of health care services in the United States."[2] Beyond these pragmatic concerns, physicians saw themselves as "guardians of the rights of infants," and thus allegiance to the Hippocratic Oath contributed to their opposition to abortion.[3]

By campaigning for legislative restrictions on abortion, as the legal historian Reva Siegel observed, "the doctors were simultaneously entering the political arena on high moral grounds and seeking public power to close their ranks to professional competition."[4] In 1859 the American Medical Association (AMA) formalized these efforts through a resolution condemning abortion as an "unwarranted destruction of human life."[5] For the AMA, the woman seeking an abortion was "unmindful of the course marked out for her by Providence"; she "yield[ed] to the pleasures but [shrank] from the pains and responsibilities of maternity." Moreover, by claiming that life begins at conception, and thereby "asserting that women had abortions because they were ignorant of scientific knowledge, doctors shifted the focus of the debate from moral *values* to empirical *facts*."[6] Within two decades of the AMA resolution, more than forty states enacted antiabortion statutes, and by 1880 abortion was illegal everywhere. Most of these laws banned abortion in all circumstances, except when necessary to save the life of the mother.

In the decade preceding *Roe,* the abortion pendulum began to swing back. Seventeen states liberalized criminal statutes governing abortion. The triggering event for these reforms was the 1962 Model Penal Code, which authorized abortions when the health of the mother was endangered, when the infant might be born with incapacitating physical or mental deformities, and when the pregnancy was a result of rape or incest. Actions in the late 1960s by the AMA and religious organizations furthered these efforts. In 1967 the AMA endorsed the Model Penal Code's limited approval of abortion. In 1968 the American Baptist Convention, the Unitarian Universalist Association, and various Jewish groups favored liberalizing existing laws. By 1971 more far-reaching reform seemed likely. The National Conference of Commissioners on Uniform State Laws drafted a Uniform Abortion Act that would have placed no limitations on abortion during the first twenty weeks of pregnancy. Moreover, with American women undergoing close to 1 million illegal abortions per year, criminal sanctions against abortion were quickly unraveling. Matching these legislative reforms, several state courts invalidated abortion prohibitions as inconsistent with state constitutional demands.

Change was definitely afoot in the period immediately preceding *Roe*. By 1973 fourteen states had adopted some version of the Model Penal Code's abortion law, and four others had completely decriminalized abortion. Public opinion, too, had begun shifting—owing, in some measure, to two well-publicized episodes in which American women sought abortions to prevent the birth of severely deformed infants. One incident took place in 1962, involving Sherry Finkbine, an Arizona mother of four, who had taken thalidomide during her pregnancy. After learning that the drug often caused infants to be born with seal-like flippers or paralyzed faces, Finkbine unsuccessfully sought an abortion at home, and was ultimately forced to travel to Sweden to obtain an abortion. "Sherry Finkbine's very public ordeal, and the news coverage it received," observed the historian David Garrow, "altered the national consciousness concerning abortion far more profoundly than anything Alan Guttmacher (or other pro-choice activists) could say or do."[7] A Gallup poll taken at the time of the incident showed that 52 percent of Americans supported Finkbine's abortion and 32 percent opposed it. The second episode was a 1962–65 outbreak of rubella, which resulted in fifteen thousand babies being born with birth defects such as blindness, deafness, and mental retardation. In the midst of this outbreak, two California physicians were charged with unprofessional conduct for performing abortions.[8] These arrests prompted a public outcry, resulting in AMA efforts to loosen abortion restrictions and, ultimately, the California legislature's approval of the Therapeutic Abortion Act, reluctantly signed by then-governor Ronald Reagan. By 1972 a Gallup poll revealed that 64 percent of Americans, including 56 percent of Roman Catholics, agreed that "the decision to have an abortion should be made solely by a woman and her physician."[9]

Despite changes in state law, the medical profession, and public opinion, the reformers were fighting an uphill battle. Many states rejected the Model Penal Code reform, and some states that enacted reform legislation imposed so many restrictions that the number of legal abortions actually decreased. When *Roe* was decided, strict antiabortion laws remained on the books in nearly every state. The legislative battles leading up to *Roe* had led to the birth of the modern pro-life movement, which, in 1972, helped defeat Michigan and North Dakota referenda that would have repealed the laws that criminalized abortion in those states. In the months before the *Roe* decision, moreover, pro-life interests scored key legislative victories in Pennsylvania, where legislation allowing abortions only when the mother's life was threatened was approved by a 157-to-34 vote; and in Massachusetts, which approved by a 178-to-46 margin a bill that specified conception as the beginning of human life.[10] In New York, pro-life forces, headed by the Roman Catholic Church, were gaining momentum in an effort to repeal that state's permissive abortion legislation.

State legislative resistance to massive antiabortion reform convinced pro-choice leaders to pursue court-ordered abortion reform and, starting in the late 1960s, a "litigation avalanche" thrust the abortion dispute before lower federal courts throughout the country. In 1973, the Supreme Court suddenly intervened in the developing political struggle. *Roe* v. *Wade* made abortion a fundamental right and prohibited states from regulating it during the first three months of a pregnancy. Of the eighteen new state laws that the pro-choice reform movement had won between 1967 and 1973, only New York's even came close to *Roe* in force and breadth.

Single-Issue Politics and the Abortion Dispute

Roe v. *Wade* dramatically altered the ongoing battle between pro-choice and pro-life interests. By providing women an unqualified right to abortion in the first trimester of pregnancy, *Roe* turned abortion rights advocates' principal objective into a constitutional mandate. Consequently, reform efforts, rather than seeking to liberalize abortion, were now the province of groups seeking to chip away at, if not destroy, *Roe*.

Antiabortion interests had huge success. In the year following *Roe*, 260 bills aimed at restricting abortion rights were introduced in state legislatures, and thirty-one were enacted.[11] Many of these laws were struck down, while others were left unenforced. States nevertheless continued to pass legislation in the hope that a challenge might lead to a narrow interpretation of *Roe*. Between 1973 and 1978, as table 1 reveals, thirty-three states passed antiabortion measures. By 1989 forty-eight states had passed 306 abortion measures.

The principal weapons of *Roe* opponents were attempts to make abortion less attractive through so-called burden-creation strategies. These strategies included increasing the risks of undergoing an abortion (e.g., by passing statutes forbidding a safe abortion method—saline amniocentesis—while permitting more dangerous abortion techniques); reducing the accessibility of medical facilities that perform abortions (e.g., by passing statutes demanding that all abortions be performed in a hospital, or zoning laws restricting the number of abortion clinics); increasing the cost of abortions (e.g., by passing statutes requiring physician or pathologist involvement in abortion procedures); and establishing detailed preabortion procedures (e.g., by passing statutes requiring women to be informed of the "medical risks" of abortion

Table 1. Patterns of State Legislation on Abortion, 1973–1978

	LAW(S) ENACTED			
	No Restrictive Laws	Funding Restriction Only[a]	Consent Requirement Only[b]	Consent Requirement and Funding Limits
ALABAMA		✓		
ALASKA	✓			
ARIZONA [c]	✓			
ARKANSAS		✓		
CALIFORNIA	✓			
COLORADO [d]	✓			
CONNECTICUT		✓		
DELAWARE		✓		
FLORIDA		✓		
GEORGIA [e]		✓		
HAWAII [d,e]	✓			
IDAHO			✓	
ILLINOIS				✓
INDIANA				✓
IOWA [d]	✓			
KANSAS		✓		
KENTUCKY				✓
LOUISIANA				✓
MAINE		✓		
MARYLAND [d]	✓			
MASSACHUSSETTS [d]			✓	
MICHIGAN [e]		✓		
MINNESOTA				✓
MISSISSIPPI		✓		
MISSOURI				✓
MONTANA				✓
NEBRASKA				✓
NEVADA				✓
NEW HAMPSHIRE	✓			
NEW JERSEY		✓		
NEW MEXICO		✓		
NEW YORK [d,e]	✓			
NORTH CAROLINA [e]	✓			
NORTH DAKOTA				✓
OHIO				✓
OKLAHOMA		✓		
OREGON	✓			
PENNSYLVANIA				✓
RHODE ISLAND	✓			
SOUTH CAROLINA				✓
SOUTH DAKOTA				✓
TENNESSEE [e]		✓		
TEXAS	✓			
UTAH				✓
VERMONT [e]		✓		
VIRGINIA				✓
WASHINGTON	✓			
WEST VIRGINIA	✓			
WISCONSIN [d]	✓			
WYOMING	✓			

Source: Lee Epstein and Joseph F. Kobylka, *The Supreme Court and Legal Change: Abortion and the Death Penalty* (Chapel Hill: University of North Carolina Press, 1992), 212.

[a] All funding limits, except for those in Pennsylvania, Michigan and Ohio, were passed between 1976 and 1978.

[b] All consent requirements were enacted between 1973 and 1975.

[c] Arizona had no state Medicaid plan.

[d] Either legislation had been introduced in 1978 or a pro-life group had launched a lawsuit to prohibit funding.

[e] Enacted reporting requirement and/or prohibition against abortion advertising.

and to wait at least twenty-four hours after consenting to the abortion procedure).[12] During this period, however, the Supreme Court stymied most of these reform efforts. With few exceptions, these regulations were invalidated prior to *Webster.*

Throughout these years, the abortion debate in the state legislatures was singularly one-sided, because the pro-choice movement "essentially folded after abortion became legal."[13] Pro-choice groups, flush with satisfaction following their Supreme Court victory, diverted their energies away from the legislative arena and toward establishing abortion clinics and defending *Roe* and its progeny in court. So confident were pro-choice groups of succeeding in court that, as reported in a 1978 study, "under some circumstances these groups have advised their legislative allies not to struggle for minor concessions to bills. They prefer to leave state legislation strict and all the better to litigate."[14]

Meanwhile, the pro-life movement grew dramatically. The first efforts to develop a national network of pro-life activists originated in the Roman Catholic Church, whose leaders immediately called for opposition to the practice of abortion. Some of the church's tactics, such as the unprecedented appearance of four cardinals before Senate committee hearings in 1974, were highly publicized. In addition, however, the church also spent heavily ($4 million in 1973 alone) in support of pro-life groups. Indeed, there is now agreement "that the Catholic Church either supported or quietly ran most right-to-life organizations during the years immediately following *Roe.*"[15] These organizations included the National Right to Life Committee (NRLC), a Washington-based umbrella organization that received its first support from the United States Catholic Conference's Family Life Division and is now the largest of all the pro-life groups. "By its own count, the NRLC alone had almost 2000 chapters in all 50 states . . . with an estimated 11 million members in its affiliated state or pro-life groups."[16]

As the political parties' strength and cohesion declined during the 1970s and 1980s, the power of the "single-issue voter" increased; and among single-issue groups the pro-life activists were trailblazers. Within a few years the pro-life movement had grown to enjoy a wider base of support, particularly among fundamentalist Protestants of the "New Right." These activists adopted the pro-life cause "as one of a cluster of conservative issues" that attracted "voters frightened by the accelerating pace of social change." The other issues included opposition to gun control, to homosexuality, to atheism in the public schools, and to the Equal Rights Amendment.[17]

The methodology of the pro-life movement was simple: intensity of interest—particularly at early stages in the political process—is more powerful than majority sentiments. In the late 1970s and early 1980s, Gallup polls revealed that less than 5 percent of American voters considered abortion an issue of significance and only 20 percent of the population were in favor of banning all abortions.[18] Nonetheless, by contributing more money and participating more in grassroots letter-writing campaigns, pro-life interests proved to be a politically dominant force at that time. In Pennsylvania, for example, state legislators heard more from their constituents about abortion than about any issue other than taxes.[19] State legislators responded by approving a resolution that called for a constitutional convention on abortion. In describing this process, one legislator commented: "Judging from the visible support there was little to gain and much to lose by voting against the resolution. A no vote might mean a primary fight; a yes vote was unlikely to hurt."[20] More strikingly, Iowa's State Pro-Life Action Council capitalized on low voter turnout in defeating a front-running pro-choice state senator in a June 1978 primary. In a pamphlet sent out to antiabortion voters, the council contended: "Your vote . . . will have the impact of 10 votes or more since it is expected that less than 10 percent of the eligible voters will go to the polls. Don't pass up this unique chance you have to speak out loud and clear for pro-life."[21]

Because pro-life groups threatened the reelection chances of recalcitrant politicians while pro-choice groups did not, politicians stood to profit from openly declaring their opposition to abortion. From the mid-1970s until the end of the 1980s, pro-life politicians often controlled legislatures and governors' offices throughout America. Pro-life bills passed through some legislatures like hot knives through butter. This seemingly endless stream of pro-life legislation, coupled with a perception that pro-life sentiment among the American public was growing, led observers to predict that any weakening of *Roe* would lead to a flood of new abortion regulations.

From *Roe* to *Webster:* State Advocacy before the Supreme Court

Roe's approval of abortion rights set in motion a dialogue between the Supreme Court and state legislators which, sixteen years and fourteen decisions later, resulted in *Webster*'s recognition of broad state authority to regulate abortion. By enacting more than three hundred laws during this period, state legislators proved resilient and were ultimately successful in resisting *Roe*'s expansive definition of abortion rights. In each of these disputes, moreover, states' attorneys general played an instrumental role in chipping away at *Roe* through briefs filed and arguments made before the Supreme Court. Connecticut, Georgia, Missouri, Ohio, Pennsylvania, Texas, Utah, and Virginia all appeared as parties before the Court defending their abortion laws. During this period, amicus filings also were submitted by several states, including Arizona, Idaho, Kentucky, Louisiana, Nebraska, and Wisconsin (on the pro-life side) and California, Colorado, Massachusetts, New York, Texas, and Vermont (on the pro-choice side).[22]

Roe itself was a rather inauspicious start to state participation in Supreme Court abortion cases. Jay Floyd, who argued the case on behalf of Texas, began his argument with an off-color remark. Referring to Jane Roe's counsel, Sarah Weddington and Linda Coffee, Floyd commented, "It's an old joke, but when a man argues against two beautiful ladies like this, they are going to have the last word."[23] Following *Roe,* state advocacy improved quite a bit. The Supreme Court, however, remained steadfast in its commitment to both abortion rights and *Roe*'s stringent trimester standard. Between 1973 and 1986, the Court rejected efforts giving parents or spouses a right to veto a woman's abortion decision; obligating physicians to preserve fetal life; requiring physicians to report all abortions to the state and to dispose of fetal remains in a humane manner; requiring the presence of a second physician during the abortion procedure; prohibiting advertisements for abortion-related services; prohibiting saline amniocentesis abortions after the first trimester; requiring all post–first term abortions to be performed in a hospital; requiring "informed consent," which entailed telling a woman that life begins at conception, that medical assistance to carry the child to term is available, and that abortions have detrimental consequences, and describing to her the fetus's anatomical and physiological characteristics; and requiring a twenty-four-hour waiting period between the signing of a consent form and the performance of the abortion.

Not all state efforts failed. Abortion-funding prohibitions, parental notification for dependent minors, regulations requiring second-trimester abortions to be performed in licensed outpatient clinics, and restrictions on the performance of abortions at public hospitals were all upheld during this period. On balance, however, 1973–89 efforts to find cracks in *Roe*'s armor failed miserably. If anything, greater restrictions were placed on state authority. For example, while *Roe* recognized hospital-only abortions as an "example of permissible state regulation in this area," the Court struck down such a requirement in its 1983 *Akron* decision.[24]

Despite the failure of most state reform efforts, a vigorous dialogue nonetheless emerged between state legislatures and the courts. For example, following the Court's 1977 *Maher* v. *Roe* decision, upholding state denials of Medicaid funding for non-therapeutic abortions, most states approved funding restrictions. By 1992 thirty-one states had funding bans in place, and only twelve routinely provided Medicaid financing for abortions. That most states proved willing to enact this abortion restriction *but* only after the Court had ruled on its constitutionality is revealing in other ways. First, direct challenges to Supreme Court decision-making were rare because state legislators were not sufficiently ardent in their antiabortion convictions to engage in open conflict with the Court. Second, as table 2 demonstrates, a small group of states were responsible for a large proportion of these measures; just thirteen states accounted for more than half of all the pro-life legislation passed between 1973 and 1989.[25] Each of these states passed at least nine pro-life laws during this period, and seven passed a dozen or more measures. And third, the persistence of these "challenger" states kept the abortion issue before the Supreme Court and thereby ensured the Court a ready vehicle by which to examine *Roe*.

Changes in the Court's composition eventually paved the way for a loosening of *Roe*'s stranglehold on state regulatory authority. By the Court's 1987–88 term, three Reagan appointees—Sandra Day O'Connor, Antonin Scalia, and Anthony Kennedy—had joined *Roe*'s two dissenters—Byron White and William Rehnquist (who was now chief justice)—thereby setting the stage for the Court's reexamination of *Roe*. On 9 January 1989, the newly formed Rehnquist Court granted certiorari in its first abortion case, *Webster* v. *Reproductive Health Services.*

At issue on *Webster* was a 1986 Missouri statute that took aim at *Roe* v. *Wade* by mandating second-trimester fetal viability testing and, more dramatically, by decreeing in its preamble that "the life of each human being begins at conception." Authored by Missouri Citizens for Life and the Missouri Catholic Conference, the bill was designed to give the Court an opportunity to revisit *Roe*, "hopefully with some Reagan appointees sitting on the bench."[26]

On 26 April 1989 the Court, amidst much fanfare, heard oral arguments on a challenge to the Missouri law by Reproductive Health Services. In this case more than in any case before it, special interests—ranging from the Knights of Columbus to the Sierra Club—were determined to be heard and filed a record number of amicus briefs.[27] Adding fuel to this fire, Missouri, using language identical to that of a Reagan Justice Department brief, argued that *Roe* "is a source of such instability in the law that this Court should reconsider" and then abandon "the decision."[28] An amicus filing by several other state attorneys general was more moderate in tone, advocating "judicial deference to the political process at the State level . . . [as being] in conformity with the Framers' concept of the constitutional division of power between the federal and the state

Table 2. LEGISLATIVE REPONSES TO *ROE*, 1973–1989

CHALLENGERS	CODIFIERS OF PRO-LIFE DECISIONS	ACQUIESCERS	SUPPORTERS
IDAHO (10)	ARIZONA (8)	ALABAMA (2)	ALASKA (0)
ILLINOIS (15)	CALIFORNIA (5)	ARKANSAS (4)	COLORADO (1)
INDIANA (9)	FLORIDA (8)	DELAWARE (4)	CONNECTICUT (0)
KENTUCKY (13)	GEORGIA (8)	IOWA (4)	HAWAII (1)
LOUISIANA (12)	MAINE (6)	MARYLAND (4)	KANSAS (1)
MASSACHUSETTS (11)	MONTANA (7)	MICHIGAN (3)	NEW HAMPSHIRE (1)
MISSOURI (13)	OKLAHOMA (7)	MISSISSIPPI (3)	OREGON (1)
NEBRASKA (9)	SOUTH DAKOTA (8)	NEW MEXICO (3)	VERMONT (1)
NEVADA (9)	VIRGINIA (5)	NEW YORK (3)	WASHINGTON (1)
PENNSYLVANIA (14)	WISCONSIN (5)	NORTH CAROLINA (3)	
RHODE ISLAND (9)	WYOMING (7)	TEXAS (3)	
TENNESSEE (11)		WEST VIRGINIA (2)	
UTAH (14)			

Source: Glen Halva-Neubauer, "Abortion Policy in the Post-*Webster* Age," *Publius* 20 (summer 1990): 33; for 1973–80, *Family Planning / Population Reporter*; for 1981–89, "States Legislative Record–Fertility-Related Bills and Laws" (Washington, D.C.: Alan Guttmacher Institute).

Numbers in parentheses represent enactments. Hence the table does not reflect abortion battles that occurred before enactment, such as close defeats, tabled bills, and sustained vetoes.

governments."[29] For at least six attorneys general and 608 state legislators, however, this responsibility was too much. Arguing that "the judiciary, not the legislature, is the branch of government that interprets and applies the Constitution,"[30] these officials spoke of their "depend[ence] on the judiciary to define the constitutional boundaries within which to legislate."[31]

These legislators did not get their wish. Holding that "the goal of constitutional adjudication is surely not to remove inexorable 'politically divisive' issues from the ambit of the legislative process," a plurality of the Court approved the Missouri law and labeled "the rigid *Roe* framework" unworkable.[32] Not only did the Court prove willing to shake the doctrinal foundation of *Roe*, it encouraged state legislative responses to its decision. Without overruling *Roe*, the *Webster* plurality signaled a new era in abortion politics by recognizing that "there is no doubt that our holding today will allow some governmental regulation of abortion that would have been prohibited under the language of [earlier] cases."[33]

THE NEW POLITICS OF ABORTION

Webster touched off an explosion of discord, hostility, and political conflict that has fundamentally reshaped the abortion dispute. On the day the Supreme Court announced its decision, both pro-choice and pro-life leaders stood on the courthouse steps and proclaimed that *Roe* v. *Wade* was virtually done for, that the states were finally free to act, and that abortion legislation would meet with rapid approval in state legislatures around the country. Representative Chris Smith (R-N.J.), chair of the congressional Pro-Life Caucus, heralded *Webster* as "a truly significant victory for unborn children . . . [that] is likely to lead to the enactment of state laws."[34] Kate Michelman, executive director of the National Abortion Rights Action League (NARAL), went a step further, observing that "we are now careening down the slippery slope towards governmental control of our most fundamental right. Women's lives hang by a thread, and the Justices this morning handed state politicians a pair of scissors."[35]

The news media came to the same conclusion. *Time* calculated that nineteen states would likely restrict abortion. *Newsweek* predicted that the number would reach twenty, while *U.S. News and World Report*'s figure stood at twenty-seven. Politicians, too, believed that *Webster* had finally opened the floodgates. Governors called legislatures into special sessions for the sole purpose of enacting new abortion restrictions. Other states sought the lifting of injunctions that had banned the enforcement of pre-*Roe* criminal statutes. Indeed, in the year following *Webster*, more than 350 antiabortion bills were introduced in forty-three state legislatures. This flurry of activity was not a short-lived phenomenon; by May 1992 about 500 more bills had been introduced in forty-seven state legislatures. With National Opinion Research Center polls showing a slight decline in public support for abortion rights since *Roe*, there was good reason to think that a tidal wave of antiabortion restrictions was in the offing.

Webster, however, wound up producing a lot of smoke and little fire. Substantial restrictions on abortion were approved in only four jurisdictions—Pennsylvania, Utah, Louisiana, and the Pacific territory of Guam. Furthermore, three states—Connecticut, Nevada, and Washington—enacted abortion-rights legislation, and two states, Kansas and Maryland, enacted hybrid compromise laws. In many other states previously considered pro-life, such as Florida and Idaho, pro-life forces have suffered stinging defeats.

The Alan Guttmacher Institute, surveying this paucity of enacted bills, concluded that "the wholesale changes in abortion law that had been widely predicted by activists, political pundits and the media" were yet to occur.

Instead, "law makers stayed in the 'safe,' familiar, middle ground."[36] Indeed, only those states with a long history of enacting legislation challenging *Roe* gave serious consideration to new antiabortion measures.

Despite this legislative calm, it would be wrong to conclude that *Webster* turned out to be more lamb than lion. *Webster* set off a political firestorm throughout America, but the storm took a different shape than the one most pre-*Webster* observers had predicted. Within a few months it was clear that the decision had created a new class of single-issue voters who were generally opposed to abortion restrictions. New polls seemed to show a dramatic increase in support for abortion rights: 57 percent of Americans said they opposed *Webster*, 61 percent said they agreed with *Roe* v. *Wade,* and 70 percent said they opposed a constitutional amendment banning abortions.[37] But instead of accentuating the sharp ideological divisions that had characterized the abortion debate before *Webster,* the public's increased interest in abortion created a less polarized, more ambiguous political situation. Many restrictions on abortion continued to command broad public support: for example, 83 percent of Americans said that a girl younger than eighteen should be required to notify at least one parent before having an abortion, and 65 percent favored mandatory viability tests for fetuses more than twenty weeks old.[38] Moreover, a majority of Americans opposed public financing of abortions.

But the pro-choice "sleeping giant" was stirring. Acknowledging that it had been "lazy, complacent, and, because of that, caught off guard,"[39] the movement picked up steam. In the weeks just prior to the *Webster* decision, pro-choice groups experienced unprecedented growth in contributions and membership. NARAL increased its paid membership by 50 percent during the first six months of 1989 and saw its income surge from $3.3 million a year to $1 million a month. Federal Election Commission (FEC) records show that pro-choice political action committees (PACs) raised nearly $2.5 million during the 1989–90 election cycle, more than twice the amount they had raised in 1987–88.[40] Likewise, the number of pro-choice PACs registered at the FEC jumped from five in 1988 to fifteen in 1990. NARAL's budget grew from $3.4 million in 1986 to more than $9 million in 1989, while membership in the organization grew from about 150,000 in 1986 to more than 500,000 in 1992.[41] Pro-choice groups declared that public concern was the reason for the sudden swell in membership and funding. Pro-life groups such as the NRLC, the American Life League, and Americans United for Life experienced substantial yet less dramatic increases in contributions, a difference their leaders attributed to the widespread support their groups had enjoyed before the Supreme Court decided to hear *Webster.* Pro-life PAC revenues, however, actually declined after *Webster;* fundraising by pro-life PACs stood at about $2 million for the 1989–90 election cycle, down from $2.7 million in 1987–88.[42] Pro-life groups did their best to downplay these reverses, claiming that the fervor of their grass-roots supporters gave them an advantage despite their opponents' greater financial resources.

Irrespective of whether the pro-choice or pro-life side is stronger in absolute terms, one conclusion is inescapable: Improvements in pro-choice funding, membership figures, and organization after *Webster* created a new political force. The first manifestation of pro-choice forces' increasing muscle, occurring just four months after *Webster*, was seen in the 1989 off-year elections. The abortion issue seemed to have provided Democrats with an almost magical ability to defeat pro-life Republicans. Three pro-choice Democrats— L. Douglas Wilder in Virginia, James Florio in New Jersey, and David Dinkins in New York City—defeated opponents who either took pro-life positions or who flip-flopped on the abortion issue after *Webster* was decided. In Virginia, exit polls showed that a third of the voters considered abortion the most important issue in the election.[43] Furthermore, in addition to changing patterns of voter support for the candidates, the abortion issue affected many other aspects of the campaigns, such as the candidates' messages and their ability to recruit grass-roots support.[44] *Webster* shaped the campaign agenda by making the abortion issue newsworthy, thereby permitting candidates to use the media to communicate their positions to voters. Wilder took advantage of this attention by making the abortion issue a central aspect of his gubernatorial campaign strategy. This frontal attack forced Wilder's opponent, J. Marshall Coleman, to address the abortion issue directly, a particularly difficult task because Coleman had won his primary before *Webster* but had to run in a post-*Webster* general election. When Coleman tried to soften his position, his shift attracted media attention and eventually convinced some voters that he could not be trusted.

A similar pattern took shape in the New Jersey governor's race, in which 75 percent of the voters identified themselves as pro-choice, and of those, 70 percent voted for Florio. The Florio campaign did not emphasize the abortion issue as Wilder did, but abortion remained in the public eye anyway because activist groups and the media kept it there. Florio's opponent, Jim Courier, who had taken a very clear pro-life position prior to *Webster*, failed to take a firm stand in the weeks following the decision. He continued to issue contradictory statements throughout the campaign, and his waffling attracted so much media attention that it eventually developed into an issue of its own. In the New Jersey race, therefore, the abortion issue "became not only a substantive policy question but a character issue as well."[45] The New Jersey and Virginia campaigns thus seemed to show that while pro-choice candidates could choose either to ignore the abortion issue (like Florio) or to emphasize it (like Wilder), pro-life candidates would have no choice but to face endless media inquisitions.

Abortion's dominance in 1989 proved an aberration. Nonetheless, after *Webster*, "abortion [was] seen as a tool for attracting particular kinds of voters who could make a difference in close elections." In 1990, *Congressional Quarterly* dubbed abortion "the most critical non-money issue" in gubernatorial races.[46] When the dust settled, the raw numbers seemed to indicate that the abortion lobbies had fought each other to a draw. The governorships of seven states—California, Florida, Georgia, Minnesota, New Mexico, Rhode Island, and Texas—had passed from pro-life to pro-choice candidates, while in four other states—Alaska, Kansas, Michigan, and Ohio—the reverse was true. Oregon voters had rejected two pro-life referenda, while in Nevada voters had approved a pro-choice ballot initiative. Pro-choicers had also gained eight seats in the House of Representatives and two seats in the U.S. Senate, but polls nevertheless appeared to indicate that the abortion issue had helped Republican congressional candidates more than it had helped Democrats. Although these mixed results showed that the abortion issue was not the "magic bullet" for which the Democrats had hoped, a closer analysis shows that abortion was nevertheless extremely important in the campaign. For although the abortion issue decided few races, the pro-choice groups' new-found strength had forced every politician to define a stance on the issue, had convinced some that they should change their position, and had even caused a few candidates to launch campaigns that focused on abortion alone.

FROM *WEBSTER* TO *CASEY:* THE STATES AND ABORTION

State legislators did not welcome *Webster*. Although the decision had dramatically expanded their authority, many state lawmakers—when it came to abortion—preferred to pass the buck back to the courts. Grace Duke, a Republican state legislator in Ohio, spoke of "everyone hoping the courts would decide and it wouldn't go through the legislatures."[47] William Black, a Republican legislator in Illinois, began to support abortion rights in the aftermath of *Webster*, "which he said had given new weight and effect to his votes on abortion."[48] Even in Missouri, *Webster* came as a not-entirely-welcome surprise to state legislators. "Ninety-five percent who voted for this bill [upheld in *Webster*] believed it didn't have a chance," argued Missouri pro-choice activist Mary Bryant. "They looked at that preamble [specifying that life begins at conception] and laughed. 'This is stupid. The court will never go for it.'"[49]

The *Webster* Court, of course, did go for it, and state legislators were forced to confront a burgeoning pro-choice movement that recognized that "in the short term at least, some of our greater victories will have to come on the legislative level."[50] In the initial round, the first priority of the abortion rights movement was to prevent the enactment of antiabortion legislation. Pro-choice leaders were reluctant to try to pass laws that would guarantee abortion rights at the state level. "Unless we have a strong majority in both houses, we run the risk of damaging our own cause," said NARAL's Kate Michelman. "So a better strategy for a while is to hold the line, because we still have *Roe*—or at least what's left of it."[51] The real measure of *Webster*'s impact then would be revealed in states that had previously opposed *Roe*. If these states altered their practices, *Webster* would have fundamentally changed the face of abortion politics. On this score, post-*Webster* disputes in Florida and Idaho are especially relevant.

Florida was the first battleground in the new abortion wars. Just two days after *Webster*, Republican governor Bob Martinez announced that he would call a special session of his state's legislature to enact new abortion restrictions. For the next three months, pro-choice and pro-life groups blitzed the state with television advertisements and rhetoric. Polls showing that a majority of Floridians supported abortion rights convinced Martinez that the legislature would not accept a broad antiabortion package, so he put forward a menu of proposals, including a seven-day wait before clinics could perform abortions, a ban on public funding of abortions, and fetal viability tests. At the two-day special session, where Martinez himself led a rally of eight thousand antiabortion demonstrators outside the state capitol, the legislature killed all his bills in committee and adjourned without passing a single abortion restriction. "Once a right is established, it's not easily removed," said Democrat Tom Gustafson, speaker of the Florida House of Representatives. "There has been a very clear response from people that felt a right was being taken away."[52]

Because the abortion question reentered the political arena with such force, politicians who attacked the constitutional deficiencies of antiabortion bills often concealed their real reasons. This may have been the case in Idaho, where the legislature passed a restrictive abortion bill on 23 March 1990. Based upon the National Right to Life Committee's model legislation, the bill sought to ban abortions except in cases involving rape, incest, or danger to the mother's life, and probably would have outlawed between 93 and 98 percent of all abortions in the state. While the bill awaited the signature of Idaho's antiabortion governor, Democrat Cecil Andrus, the Idaho pro-choice movement suddenly came alive. "It's a tragedy, but sometimes it takes a tragedy to shake people up and shake them out of apathy to protect their rights," said an official from the National Organization for Women.[53]

The pro-choice groups' most well-publicized tactic was their announcement of a national boycott of Idaho's chief cash crop, potatoes. The boycott attracted national media attention, and in a final dramatic gesture staged the day before Andrus announced his decision, pro-choice college students dumped ten thousand Idaho potatoes on the steps of the capitol. Some of their signs read, "Veto House Bill 625. No dic-tater-ship." When Andrus finally announced that he had decided to veto the bill, he cited its inadequate rape and incest provisions as his primary justification. But he also objected to the bill's constitutional deficiencies: "I am advised by legal scholars of both political parties that, in their opinion, there is not the remotest chance of this legislation's being found constitutional by the Supreme Court."[54] Andrus pointed out that the bill "was conceived outside our state for the sole purpose of getting this issue back before the Supreme Court" and that "the financial burden to Idaho will be excessive if we litigate this issue." He denied that boycotts and political pressure had influenced his decision. Pro-lifers disagreed. One of Andrus's opponents in his race for reelection said he had "erred grievously in judgment. . . . When he was under awesome pressure, he didn't stick to his" principles.[55] Antiabortion groups also attacked Andrus's rationale for vetoing the bill. "Let's face it," said one newspaper advertisement, "this whole business about [House Bill] 625 being unconstitutional is just a smokescreen for anyone who doesn't want to support the bill but needs a fine-sounding excuse."[56] The National Right to Life Committee targeted Andrus for defeat in November 1990, but he easily won reelection, and abortion rights supporters gained a commanding majority in the Idaho Senate.

Andrus's resolve reveals that governors, armed with their veto power, wield enormous influence on the lawmaking process.[57] In Louisiana, however, Governor Buddy Roemer was unable to fend off state legislature opposition to abortion through his veto power. On 14 June 1991, Roemer—for the third time in less than a year—vetoed restrictive antiabortion legislation. In each instance he proclaimed that he was willing to sign an abortion bill but that the state legislature had approved measures without "meaningful exceptions . . . [and] I cannot close my eyes to that."[58] Roemer's actions did not sit well with the Louisiana legislature. Ridiculing Roemer for statements such as "I still consider myself pro-life, but I'm more pro-choice now,"[59] Allen Bares, a co-sponsor of the bill, declared it time to "send a loud and clear message to the people of this state and this nation that this [legislature] is pro-life."[60] On 18 June 1991,

the Louisiana legislature reinstated its antiabortion measure, overriding a gubernatorial veto for the first time in its history.

The Louisiana legislature's willingness to stare down Roemer's third veto
is attributable to the political potency of the religious interests opposed to abortion, most notably fundamentalist religious groups from northern Louisiana,
and Roman Catholics from southern Louisiana. Religious convictions and a
desire to overturn *Roe* v. *Wade* also played an important role in Pennsylvania.
On 17 November 1989, Pennsylvania passed a law banning most abortions at
public hospitals, prohibiting abortions after the twenty-fourth week of pregnancy, requiring spousal notification and waiting periods, and outlawing abortion for sex selection. The Pennsylvania House passed the measure by a vote of
143 to 58, and the Senate approved it 33 to 17. Political analysts, however, said
that Pennsylvania was unrepresentative of national opinion on abortion, and
pointed out that the state had a history of social conservatism owing to its relatively large rural population and its many Roman Catholics and fundamentalist Christians. Even with such firm support for abortion restrictions, Pennsylvania's legislators faced a tough choice. "In the past, these lawmakers could pass
restrictive bills while knowing that the courts would enjoin most of their handiwork," wrote one observer. "Now, they are sobered by the realization that what
they adopt could well become law."[61]

Pro-choice groups held a vigil outside the Harrisburg mansion of Governor Robert P. Casey, but Casey signed the bill into law two days later,
proudly proclaiming, "We are the first state in the country after the *Webster*
case to move and speak forcefully on the subject of protection of unborn life.
I have seen politicians cutting and running, and states waffling on that issue.
Pennsylvania did not."[62] Pro-choice groups then obtained a preliminary in-
junction in federal district court, and in August 1990 the court struck down
most of the law's provisions. Abortion foes expressed their hope that the law
would serve as a vehicle to challenge *Roe*.

CASEY AND BEYOND

The Rehnquist Court granted abortion foes their wish, but *Planned Parenthood*
v. *Casey* proved an unsatisfying culmination to a two-decade campaign to overturn *Roe*. On the one hand, by reaffirming the "central holding of *Roe*,"[63]
Casey made clear that five Reagan-Bush Supreme Court appointments were not
enough to undo abortion rights. On the other hand, *Casey* utilized a deferential

"undue burden" standard to uphold all but the spousal notification provision of the state's law. In so doing, *Casey* "reject[ed] the trimester framework" and overruled prior decisions "incompatible with the recognition that there is a substantial state interest in potential life throughout pregnancy."[64] Despite this mixed result, *Casey* was a major blow to pro-life forces. Symbolically, *Casey* stood more for the Rehnquist Court's approval of abortion rights and not for its gutting of *Roe*'s stringent trimester standard. Under *Casey*, for example, the highly restrictive post-*Webster* abortion laws of Guam, Louisiana, and Utah have all been invalidated by federal courts.

Casey's middle-ground approach to both abortion rights and broad state regulatory authority matched public opinion. Sixty percent of voters supported the Pennsylvania law, although, by a margin of 59 percent to 21 percent, voters also said that they were more likely to support candidates who supported abortion rights in the 1992 elections.[65] More specifically, "many Americans . . . support such restrictions on access to abortion services as requiring women younger than 18 years to get a parent's permission (70% to 73% approve), a 24-hour waiting period (69% to 81%), and requiring married women to inform their husbands before receiving an abortion (62% to 69%)."[66]

Casey's matching of public opinion prompted the ire of some conservative commentators who claimed that "the current Court is driven more by public opinion than by constitutional principle."[67] Nonetheless, the Court's decision seems to have stabilized state abortion politics. Most state attorneys general, for example, have resisted enforcing existing state laws with Pennsylvania-type restrictions. Instead, attorneys general have returned the issue to the state legislatures, claiming that lawmakers need to reaffirm their support for abortion restrictions by writing new laws. State legislators, however, seem reluctant to enact antiabortion measures. Although *Casey* has hardly slowed down the pace of abortion-related proposals (roughly three hundred measures were introduced in each of the two years following the decision), state responses to *Casey* reinforce the post-*Webster* trend of diminishing state intervention in abortion. Most strikingly, according to Alan Guttmacher Institute studies, "antiabortion legislators [have] heeded . . . [*Casey*] and curtailed their attempts to make abortion illegal."[68] In 1994, for example, no legislation was introduced to outlaw abortion.[69] Furthermore, in the two years following *Casey*, one-third of abortion-related legislative initiatives would have guaranteed the right to abortion. Finally, of the handful of abortion regulation measures adopted since *Casey*, all involve restrictions approved by the Court: waiting periods, informed consent, and parental notification.

STATE COURTS STEP IN

The federal Constitution is not the only source of fundamental rights. Each state has the right to adopt more expansive individual liberties in its own constitution than are provided by the U.S. Constitution.[70] Not surprisingly, in states whose judges are subject to popular election or removal, expansive state court interpretations may trigger an electoral firestorm. California and Florida, states whose judges are subject to popular election and removal, exemplify the perils that may arise when state courts provide more sweeping abortion rights than the U.S. Supreme Court.

Following *Webster,* pro-choice groups scored impressive victories in California and Florida. In 1989, the California Court of Appeals struck down a law requiring unwed minors to obtain parental consent or a court order before having an abortion. The court cited the California Constitution's explicit right to privacy, which declares that "all people are by nature free and independent and have inalienable rights," and that "among these are . . . pursuing and obtaining safety, happiness, and privacy."[71] "Indeed," said the court, "the right to privacy was added to California's Constitution in order to prevent government intrusion[s] . . . permitted under the federal Constitution."[72]

Also in 1989, the Florida Supreme Court achieved a similar result by interpreting its state's express privacy right, which declares that "every natural person has the right to be let alone and free from governmental intrusion."[73] The court, in *In Re T. W.,* voted 6 to 1 to strike down a statute that required a minor to obtain parental consent before undergoing an abortion, reasoning that the people of Florida would not have included this explicit provision in the state constitution if they had been satisfied with the federal right to privacy.[74]

Victories in court do not end the political struggle. Although in 1981 the California Supreme Court declared that the legislature cannot restrict state funding for abortions for indigent women, the legislature persistently passed laws restricting such funding. Pro-life ire eventually turned into an attack against the courts. Conservatives attempted to make use of the ballot box to remove liberal judges, but this approach has not had the desired effect. California chief justice Rose Elizabeth Bird and two other justices were ousted in 1986 when conservatives targeted them for electoral defeat. While the 1986 election resulted in a conservative majority on the court, the California Supreme Court nonetheless continued to issue expansive interpretations of California's privacy right.

Antiabortion activists in Florida also devoted energy to unseating justices who supported abortion rights. Florida's justices must undergo a "merit retention" vote every six years, and Justice Leander Shaw, author of the court's opinion *In Re T. W.*, faced his vote in November 1990. Shaw was the right-to-life groups' primary target. "This thing is cut clearly," said the Rev. Bobby Welch, a religious broadcaster who led the fight against Shaw. "You watch. You watch and see what happens. Whether we win or lose, I'll guarantee you there's going to be a cold chill sent down every politician's back."[75] Justice Shaw agreed. "It's scary," he said, noting that if the pro-life groups defeated him "they can hold my scalp up all over the country and go around saying, 'you see what we did in Florida?'"[76] Despite the efforts of pro-life leaders, however, Shaw won 60 percent of the vote in his re-election bid that November.

CONCLUSION

The states are as prominent as the federal government in shaping the abortion dispute. Prior to *Roe* v. *Wade,* abortion battles were the near-exclusive province of the states. Since *Roe,* the states have been afforded and have taken advantage of "multiple opportunities for thwarting compliance with, or implementation of *[Roe]*."[77] With decisions such as *Webster* v. *Reproductive Health Services* and *Planned Parenthood* v. *Casey* acknowledging broad state authority to regulate (although not prohibit) abortion, the scope of abortion rights seems to hinge on state politics.

Webster and *Casey,* while promising a revolution, have had a modest impact on abortion rights. State legislatures have enacted few measures in response to these decisions. State courts, in the years following the decisions, continued to serve as a limited countermajoritarian check. This outcome is hardly surprising. "In a manner consistent with the expectations of federalism, diverse policies were developed after *Roe,* that reflected local political and cultural factors. Once these policy approaches were institutionalized, they became rather resistant to change."[78]

Without doubt, as former Reagan policy adviser Gary Bauer put it, "it's going to be . . . a long, ground-out struggle by both sides."[79] At the same time, the struggle may be far less intense than interest group leaders would have us believe. While hundreds of abortion-related bills continue to be introduced each legislative session, state lawmakers now seem extraordinarily disinclined to reenter the abortion fray. That no significant abortion measures have been passed in the two years since *Casey* is a testament to the growing state inclination to steer clear of the abortion dispute. State attorneys general, likewise, saw little political gain here. Their reluctance to enforce preexisting abortion regulations that, after *Webster* and *Casey*, might now pass constitutional muster is a significant departure from past practices. Finally, since *Casey*, abortion appears to be losing the political edge in gubernatorial and other state races.

That abortion appears less salient, however, does not mean that the abortion wars will not rage again. Utah, Louisiana, and Guam, for example, may continue to serve up new abortion restrictions. Interest group politics also may bring abortion to the fore in other states.

Too much should not be read into the relative quiet of post-*Casey* state abortion politics. The notion that *Roe* and its progeny accomplished little other than preventing state legislatures from devising pro-choice regulatory schemes similar to the ones now in place, for example, finds little support in the historical record. Instead, *Roe* was instrumental in establishing abortion rights. Likewise, the persistent volleys between the states and the Court, after *Roe*, have proven equally instrumental in defining the reach of state regulatory authority. Whether the return of most of the abortion issue to the states by *Webster* and *Casey* is heralded or condemned, it is undeniable that *Roe* transformed the states and that the states transformed *Roe*.

6 / Congress and Abortion

ROE V. *WADE* TRANSFORMED Congress as well as the states. In the decade before the decision, only ten abortion-related bills were introduced in Congress. Congressional action, for the most part, was limited and was designed to preserve the antiabortion status quo ante. During the decade after the Court's decision, five hundred abortion bills were introduced. Congress's record here is mixed. It has done much to limit *Roe*, accepting numerous restrictions on federal abortion funding, prohibiting the performance of abortions at military hospitals and federal penitentiaries, and funding pro-life counseling programs. Nonetheless, Congress has been unwilling to overturn *Roe* by means of a constitutional amendment or through legislation either defining life at conception or curtailing federal court jurisdiction in this area. Congress even has approved some pro-choice initiatives, most notably legislation prohibiting abortion clinic blockades and funding fetal tissue research. However, Congress has been unwilling to codify *Roe* and thus far has rejected various proposals for legislation to ensure freedom of choice.

Congress's ambivalence here extends beyond its mixed lawmaking record. It has confirmed both pro-life and pro-choice officials, including attorneys general, secretaries of health and human services, and surgeons general. It has grilled Supreme Court nominees about *Roe* but is unwilling to demand that nominees state their views about the correctness of *Roe*. It has attacked the executive branch in oversight hearings, sometimes for its pro-choice interpretations and other times for its pro-life interpretations of federal statutes. Individual members, finally, have filed briefs before the Supreme Court both defending and condemning *Roe*.

Congress's conflicting abortion record seems a microcosm of the sharp divide that separates pro-choice and pro-life interests. Congress operates within this divide and, absent a national consensus on abortion, is unwilling to fully embrace either pro-choice or pro-life positions. Furthermore, because of an unwillingness to alienate pro-choice or pro-life interests by taking a firm position on abortion, congressional action has focused on critical but peripheral issues such as clinic access and abortion funding. Albeit muddled, congressional decision-making nevertheless has played a profound role in the abortion dispute. In shaping the national debate on abortion, Congress, in the twenty-plus years since *Roe,* has actively considered making use of all of its powers.

This congressional role likely will continue. Even if the Supreme Court could devise a solution to the abortion dispute that would satisfy both pro-choice and pro-life interests, abortion funding, health care, and other perennial issues will force Congress to confront abortion. This has been the lesson of the past few years. While the Court's reaffirmation of abortion rights in *Casey* has reduced the decibel level of Supreme Court confirmation hearings, and while absolutist efforts to codify or repeal *Roe* are not being seriously pursued, abortion has hardly dropped off the legislative radar screen.

ABORTION FUNDING

Roe promoted an immediate and intense response by several members of Congress. Within months of the decision, numerous antiabortion measures had been introduced in Congress. One statute would have defined a "person," for Fourteenth Amendment purposes, as including "any animate combination of viable human cells"; another statute would have limited abortion protection to instances in which the life of a pregnant woman was at stake; a constitutional amendment would have returned abortion policy to the states; and another amendment proposal would have extended Fourteenth Amendment protection to "unborn offspring."[1] However, these proposals failed—in part, because the congressional committees with jurisdiction to consider them refused to act. Frustrated by these tactics, antiabortion forces turned their attention to the subterranean world of appropriations-based policy-making. Riders were attached to appropriations bills to prohibit the use of appropriated funds to finance abortions.

Policy-making through appropriations has multiple problems. First, the process is conducted without the benefit of review by the authorizing committee with appropriate subject-matter expertise. Second, the often hurried and high-pressured appropriations process does not allow for reflective examination, especially on emotionally divisive issues. Indeed, since appropriation riders often are introduced on the floor of Congress, members have little opportunity to study a proposed restriction before they cast their votes. Third, House and Senate rules prohibit attaching substantive legislation to appropriations bills, so the content of riders is limited. Fourth, since most appropriations are reenacted every year, appropriations-based policy-making is extraordinarily contentious. Battles are neither won nor lost: this year's victory may be next year's defeat. Since appropriations-based policy-making is in a constant state of flux, agency rule-making and administration is likewise uncertain. Nonetheless, because appropriation riders cannot be killed in committee and only bind Congress for a year at a time, appropriations-based policy-making is common.

In 1974 Congress considered and *rejected* limitations on federal funding of abortions. At that time, the prevailing view in Congress was that "an annual appropriation bill is an improper vehicle for such a controversial and far-reaching legislative provision whose implications and ramifications are not clear, whose constitutionality has been challenged, and on which no hearings have been held."[2] After this action, antiabortion forces scored a stunning victory in 1976. During debates on the appropriations bill for the Department of Health, Education, and Welfare (now the Department of Health and Human Services), Representative Henry Hyde (R-Ill.) decided that it would be "a nice idea if we could just sneak an amendment in there that would halt this nefarious practice" (government-supported abortion) and "scribbled . . . out" a funding prohibition "in longhand right on the spot."[3] At that time, Health, Education, and Welfare, through its Medicaid program, was paying for 250,000 to 300,000 of an estimated 1 million abortions a year at an estimated cost of $45 million. The Hyde Amendment specified that "none of the funds appropriated under this Act shall be used to pay for abortions or to promote or encourage abortions."[4]

Debate over this proposal was dramatic and emotional. Hyde spoke of the "unborn child . . . as a member of the innocently inconvenient . . . [who] in a caring and humane society deserves better than to be flushed down a toilet or burned in an incinerator."[5] Opposing the amendment, Daniel Flood (D-Pa.) characterized the measure as "blatantly discriminatory" because the denial of Medicaid funds effectively "prohibits abortion for poor people."[6] Amendment supporters answered this charge, pointing to their failed efforts to outlaw all abortions through a constitutional amendment and noting that "if we could protect the right to life for all children" regardless of poverty or wealth, "we would do it."[7]

The 1977 battle over abortion funding proved more divisive than its predecessor. House forces (who had approved the Hyde Amendment without compromising exceptions) were deadlocked with their Senate counterparts (who endorsed exceptions in cases in which the life of the mother was threatened or a physician judged the abortion to be "medically necessary," and in cases of rape or incest). For five months (from 17 June to 7 December), this imbroglio consumed Congress. Before the matter was decided, twenty-eight roll call votes were taken (seventeen in the Senate and eleven in the House), two continuing resolutions expired, and thousands of federal employees were threatened with delays in their paychecks. When the dust finally settled, Senate forces had largely succeeded in securing a Hyde amendment with both maternal health and rape exceptions.[8]

This hard-fought compromise did not survive. In 1979 the exemption for medically necessary abortions was dropped. In 1980, a caveat added to the rape exemption demanded that rape victims report the crime within seventy-two hours. Finally, in 1981, Congress dropped the rape and incest exemption. The 1981 language remained intact until 1993, when Congress restored the rape and incest exception.[9]

Nineteen eighty-nine, however, witnessed another fierce battle over the Hyde Amendment. In the wake of the Supreme Court's July 1989 decision in *Webster* v. *Reproductive Health Services,* Congress sought to liberalize its law on abortion. Pro-choice member Les Au Coin (D-Ore.), in leading the effort to change abortion-funding restrictions, sounded a message that resonated with many of his colleagues: "A new political era begins right now, friends. . . . Those of us who defend a woman's freedom of choice are drawing a line in the sand today, a line of decency, a line of fair play—and a line of serious politics."[10] Twenty-seven members of Congress (twenty-one Democrats and six Republicans), perhaps fearing the consequences of a pro-life vote in their re-election bids, moved from the pro-life camp to the pro-choice camp. In the House, after efforts to provide rape and incest exceptions to the 1988 Hyde Amendment were defeated by a vote of 216 to 166, such exceptions were agreed to by a vote of 212 to 207.[11]

Congress's 1989 loosening of the Hyde Amendment ran into a stone wall when George Bush successfully vetoed the measure. With the 1992 election of Bill Clinton, that wall had crumbled, paving the way for congressional reform efforts, including the restoration of the rape and incest exception.

The 1993 liberalization of the Hyde Amendment is revealing both for what it did accomplish and for what it did not accomplish. On the one hand, there is clearly a chink in the amendment's armor. In addition to the rape and incest exceptions, Congress eliminated restrictions on District of Columbia abortion funding and on the use of Federal Employee Health Benefit program funds for abortion-related services. On the other hand, the Hyde Amendment remains. Despite Clinton administration opposition to funding prohibitions, and despite increasing public support of pro-choice policies, Congress reenacted and the president signed *a* Hyde Amendment.

The fate of the Hyde Amendment will have broad ramifications elsewhere. The amendment typifies Congress's use of appropriations as the principal weapon in its anti-*Roe* arsenal. Specifically, since funding prohibitions do not directly challenge the correctness of *Roe*, Congress can express its displeasure with the Court without either taking a firm position on abortion rights or challenging the Court's institutional legitimacy. Moreover, since appropriations must be enacted each year, appropriations-based policy-making allows Congress to react to judicial or executive-branch action. Efforts to moderate the Hyde Amendment in 1989 (in response to *Webster*) and in 1993 (in response to Clinton's 1992 election) exemplify such reactive fine tuning.

Another example of such reactive fine tuning occurred in 1995, when the Republican takeover of both houses of Congress prompted yet another wave of proposed abortion-funding restrictions. The House Appropriations Committee, for example, voted to prohibit federal research on human embryos created outside the womb; to allow states to decide for themselves whether or not to provide matching state Medicaid funding for the abortions of low-income women; and to replace the government's principal family-planning program with a block grant program that would allow states to shift federal funds away from family planning and to other child and maternal health programs.[12] For both abortion rights supporters and opponents, this shift reveals Congress's desire to respond to changing conditions, especially the demands of the Christian Coalition that the new Republican majority gut federal abortion funding.[13]

Congress's reliance on its power of the purse is to be expected. Other funding restrictions apply to appropriations for the Department of Defense (prohibiting the use of funds to perform abortions unless the life of the woman would be endangered); the Peace Corps (stipulating that no funds may be used to pay for abortions); the Legal Services Corporation (prohibiting legal assistance for the procurement of abortions in federally funded legal assistance programs); the Bureau of Prisons (prohibiting the use of funds to perform abortions); federal family planning programs (prohibiting the use of funds for programs in which abortion is a method of family planning); and the Small Business Administration (prohibiting the awarding of funds to any organization involved in activities relating to abortion). Congress also has approved conscience clauses guaranteeing that receipt of federal funds would create no obligations to perform abortions on the part of hospitals and physicians as well as medical and nursing schools.

CONGRESS IN COURT: FROM *HARRIS* TO *CASEY*

The controversy over the Hyde Amendment was not limited to the halls of Congress. In the courts, the amendment came under sharp constitutional attack. A brief filed by the Center for Constitutional Rights emphasized privacy concerns, arguing that the Hyde Amendment was premised on the belief that "abortion is . . . murder" and therefore served an unconstitutional purpose.[14] Equality concerns were highlighted by the National Organization for Women, which argued that "the purpose and effect of this exclusionary funding scheme is to induce indigent women to carry unwanted pregnancies to term."[15] Finally, the American Civil Liberties Union characterized the Hyde Amendment as "'religious gerrymandering' which cannot survive the neutrality demanded by the Establishment Clause." A federal district judge, John Dooley, agreed with these claims, holding that "to deny necessary medical assistance for the lawful and medically necessary procedure of abortion is to violate the pregnant women's . . . rights" to personal privacy and equal protection.[16]

On appeal to the Supreme Court, briefs filed by the Carter Department of Justice and a coalition of more than two hundred members of Congress answered these charges. The congressional brief was truly extraordinary, involving both pro-life and pro-choice legislators and speaking exclusively to Congress's lawmaking power, especially its appropriations powers, with no mention of the reasonableness of the Hyde Amendment as a matter of public policy. Perceiving that "any judicial order to expend money for abortion puts the federal judiciary squarely in the legislative area," Hyde supporters and opponents joined forces in an effort to defend Congress's Article I section 9 authority, which commands that "no money shall be drawn from the Treasury but in Consequence of Appropriations made by Law."[17] According to these congressional amici, "the inviolable and exclusive power of the purse is one that touches on all of what Congress does. To tamper with that exclusive power is to tamper with the very essence of constitutional, representative government."[18]

The Supreme Court agreed and upheld the Hyde Amendment in *Harris* v. *McRae*. The Court ruled that "whether freedom of choice that is constitutionally protected warrants federal subsidization is a question for Congress to answer, not a matter of constitutional entitlement."[19] Noting that Congress has a "legitimate . . . interest in protecting potential life," it deemed the refusal to subsidize abortions permissible.[20] The establishment claim was likewise rejected, because the fact that a statute happens to coincide with the tenets of some religions is not dispositive in cases involving church-state separation.

Congress's coalition defense of the Hyde Amendment stands in sharp contrast to other legislative filings in abortion cases. After *Harris*, pro-choice and pro-life legislators lined up on opposite sides of state regulation cases. Since what is at issue here is the correctness of *Roe* and not the powers of Congress, state regulation cases highlight ideological differences between pro-choice and pro-life legislators. In *Thornburgh* v. *American College of Obstetricians and Gynecologists* (1986), eighty-one pro-choice legislators publicly scolded Solicitor General Charles Fried for having "taken an extraordinary and unprecedented step" in calling for *Roe*'s reversal.[21] More typically, pro-choice and pro-life legislators share with the Court their competing conceptions of the correctness of *Roe*.

Pro-life legislators argue that "*Roe v. Wade* has expanded federal judicial powers into areas that are within the rightful legislative domain of Congress and the states" and that this expansion has harmed "the constitutional allocation of powers between the judicial and legislative branches and between the states and the federal government."[22] Pro-life legislators also attack *Roe* as internally incoherent, characterizing the "flow of *Roe v. Wade*'s reasoning" as both "cryptic" and likely to foster "arbitrary judicial decisions."[23] Pro-choice interests, in contrast, speak of "the soundness of *Roe*" and claim that "abortion is particularly unsuited to a multiplicity of inconsistent state and local laws."[24] Rejecting calls to overrule *Roe* on balance-of-powers grounds, pro-choice legislators note their "concern for the stability and integrity of our system of government" and assert "that if the system is to work, certain fundamental rights of individuals must be insulated from the shifting winds of politics."[25]

It comes as no surprise that pro-choice and pro-life legislators would seek to shape constitutional doctrine through their participation in litigation. As one congressional brief noted, the Court's "articulating a clear standard of review would resolve lingering doubts of constitutional infirmity that plague much abortion-related legislation and, therefore, would directly affect Congress' continued attempts to act in this area."[26] Of equal significance, House and Senate members are aware of the political culture surrounding a decision, and recognize that signing onto an abortion brief is an act of partisan symbolism.

SUPPORTING ALTERNATIVE VALUES: CONGRESS ENCOURAGES WOMEN TO CHOOSE BIRTH

Congressional efforts to discourage abortion and encourage women to choose birth are not limited to increasing the cost of an abortion by imposing funding restrictions. Congress also has acted affirmatively, both in creating workplace incentives to choose birth and in facilitating access to pro-life information. Like prohibitions on funding, these measures do not directly challenge the correctness of *Roe* or the authority of the Supreme Court. The 1978 Pregnancy Discrimination Act (PDA) and the 1982 Adolescent Family Life Act (AFLA) are prime examples of congressional attempts to encourage birth.

The impetus for the PDA was the Supreme Court's 1976 finding that an employer did not violate Title VII gender discrimination protections by excluding pregnancy disability from its sickness and accident benefit policy. In prohibiting discrimination based on "pregnancy, childbirth, and related medical conditions,"[27] and by allowing employers to exempt abortion from health insurance benefits, the PDA creates economic incentives for a woman to carry her pregnancy to term.

The Adolescent Family Life Act is a pro-life elaboration of Congress's prior efforts to tackle the teenage pregnancy problem. Specifically, in response to a perceived emphasis on abortion in federal family-planning efforts, Senator Jeremiah Denton (R-Ala.) reworked the Adolescent Health Services and Pregnancy Prevention and Care Act of 1978, rechristening it the Adolescent Family Life Act. The revised legislation contained four new provisions: it required the active involvement of religious groups; it prohibited provision of funds to any organization involved in abortion; it instructed groups to advise teens to choose adoption; and it required emphasis on premarital abstinence. AFLA survived congressional scrutiny because of a deal struck in a 1981 House-Senate conference committee: if pro-choice members supported AFLA, pro-life members would continue to support other, broader family-planning projects.

After 1981, AFLA became highly controversial. Referred to in the media as the "Chastity Act," it was at times touted as a heroic bipartisan effort to address the epidemic of teen pregnancy and was at times denounced as "an $11 million concession to the right."[28] Although the moral overtones of the legislation made some interest groups uneasy, the bulk of the criticism was aimed at the mandated involvement of religious organizations in the program's administration. The act also drew approval from a wide range of interest group leaders. Its supporters steadfastly argued that federal money had been provided to church-operated social service organizations for years.

In 1983 a coalition of civil rights and women's groups, including the American Civil Liberties Union and the American Jewish Congress, launched a constitutional challenge to the program. The plaintiffs argued that the act represented an unconstitutional establishment of religion, first, by discriminating against religious organizations that favored abortion rights; and second, by subsidizing religious pro-life family-planning programs. The Supreme Court disagreed. Its 1988 decision in *Bowen* v. *Kendrick* upheld the constitutionality of the act.[29] The Court found that the statute had a legitimate secular purpose of addressing teenage sexuality and pregnancy; and that the primary effect of the act was not to promote religion, because the act did fund nonreligious institutions as well as religious institutions.

Like *Harris* v. *McRae*'s approval of the Hyde Amendment, *Bowen* recognized Congress's ability to participate in the abortion dispute through indirect attacks on *Roe*. Through these decisions—as well as legislation, such as the PDA, overturning Court interpretations of federal statutes—Congress is empowered to express its disapproval of the Court's constitutional decision-making without engaging in open conflict with the judiciary. Being able to indirectly challenge the Court, among other things, reduces pressure on Congress to directly challenge judicial authority through court stripping or constitutional amendment.

Overruling *Roe* on the Floor of Congress: Human Life Legislation and Proposed Constitutional Amendments

Soon after the Supreme Court handed down *Roe* v. *Wade*, antiabortion factions began persistently lobbying Congress to ban abortion. Over the years, they have advocated a variety of legislative strategies for decreasing or eliminating the practice of abortion. The most radical of these strategies have been proposed constitutional amendments and legislation designed to nullify *Roe* entirely.

Despite extensive hearings on abortion held by the Senate in 1974 and 1975 and by the House in 1976, none of these drastic antiabortion measures survived even subcommittee review until 1981. The ninety-seventh Congress convened in 1981 with a newly won Republican majority in the Senate. Strom Thurmond (R-S.C.) replaced Edward Kennedy (D-Mass.) as chairman of the Senate Judiciary Committee and filled vacancies on the committee with fellow conservatives. Soon after, two Judiciary subcommittees reported separate antiabortion measures.

The Separation of Powers Subcommittee, led by freshman senator John East (R-N.C.), held hearings on the "Human Life Bill." Sponsored by Jesse Helms (R-N.C.), this measure was in part a court-stripping bill—like many that had come (and gone) before in the areas of abortion, school prayer, and busing—in that it sought to remove jurisdiction over the subject matter from the lower federal courts. The Human Life Bill, however, was more than just another court-stripping bill. The legislation also stated that "for the purpose of enforcing the obligation of the States under the fourteenth amendment not to deprive persons of life without due process of law, each human life exists from conception . . . and for this purpose 'person' includes all human beings."[30] The effect of this would have been to overturn *Roe* v. *Wade* by statute. The bill was reported to the Senate Judiciary Committee by a vote of 3 to 2.

Before the bill made it out of the subcommittee, however, its supporters and opponents engaged in a fierce battle. Subcommittee hearings got off to a less than auspicious start thanks to East's refusal to schedule witnesses selected by Democratic members or to allow Democratic members' counsel to ask questions of the witnesses. The bill's opponents, moreover, "simply dismissed representatives supporting fetal rights as tyrannic, religious fanatics."[31] For Robert Packwood (R-Ore.): "Every generation witnesses a new group of citizens who believe themselves the keepers of the faith, . . . moralists who are so convinced they are right that they choose to impose their morality on us" and thereby threaten "the liberties of all Americans."[32] The bill also came under sharp criticism by six former attorneys general who, despite coming from different parties and having varying views on abortion, wrote that "to overturn [the *Roe*] decision by enacting a statute . . . [is] an attempt to exercise unconstitutional power and a dangerous circumvention of the avenues that the Constitution itself provides for reversing Supreme Court interpretations of the Constitution."[33]

Human life legislation also had its supporters. Pointing to *Roe*'s refusal "to determine whether unborn children are human life," Charles Dougherty (R-Pa.) argued on the House floor that "it is unreasonable to assume that the Supreme Court's definition of 'person' in *Roe v. Wade* is so inflexible that it cannot change in response to a legislative determination that unborn children are human beings."[34] John East echoed these concerns in his opening statement at the subcommittee hearings. Describing the proposal as an "exercise [of] the authority of Congress . . . based on an investigation of facts and on a decision concerning values that the Supreme Court has declined to address,"[35] East contended that the human life bill did little more than "invite the Court to reconsider what it had done" in *Roe*.[36]

Interestingly, the schism in this debate was not simply along pro-choice/pro-life lines. While consideration of abortion-related measures tends to focus on the substantive ends of the proposed legislation, debate on the Human Life Bill seems to reflect a genuine concern over means. Witness the criticism of Senator Orrin Hatch (R-Utah), a staunch member of the antiabortion camp: "Congress is doing far more in this bill than simply stating Congressional findings of fact and attempting to call these to the attention of the Court. . . . It is attempting to enact a law in the face of an absolutely contrary Supreme Court decision."[37] Hatch, like many senators and constitutional law scholars, believed that the only way to overturn *Roe* v. *Wade* and its progeny would be by constitutional amendment.

Constitutional amendments, however, are far more difficult to enact than laws. For a constitutional amendment to succeed it would require a two-thirds majority of both houses of Congress and ratification by three-fourths of the states. As a result, the Senate Judiciary Committee divided into three groups: pro-choice senators who opposed any antiabortion measures; pro-life senators who felt constitutionally bound to achieve their ends through amendment of the Constitution itself; and pro-life senators who, while perhaps preferring the permanency of a constitutional amendment, viewed an amendment as an unrealistic goal and thus supported the Human Life Bill. In the end, a deal was struck to set the bill aside until the Subcommittee on the Constitution had a chance to act on the pro-life constitutional amendment proposals before it.

Proposals for constitutional amendments on abortion have been made in nearly every Congress since *Roe* v. *Wade* was decided in 1973. The proposals generally are of two sorts: "human life" amendments and "federalism" amendments. A federalism amendment allows each state to decide whether and how abortion is to be prohibited or regulated. By leaving abortion regulation to the states, federalism amendments seek a return to the pre-*Roe* status quo and no more. In contrast, a human life amendment typically states that life begins at conception or fertilization. Thus, state lawmakers could not choose—as New York and other states had done before *Roe*—to legalize abortion. One of the proposed amendments before the Constitution Subcommittee in 1981 was the "Human Life Federalism Amendment" (HLFA). Proposed by subcommittee chairman Orrin Hatch, it was a federalism amendment with a definite human life slant in the form of a preference for more restrictive antiabortion laws. As finally reported by the Senate Judiciary Committee the HLFA stated: "A right to abortion is not secured by this Constitution. The Congress and the several States shall have concurrent power to restrict and prohibit abortion: Provided, That a provision of a law or a State which is more restrictive than a conflicting provision of a law of Congress shall govern."[38]

Remarkably, despite significant congressional disagreement with *Roe*, the HLFA was the only instance of a measure directly attacking *Roe* which survived the entire committee process in any session of Congress. When the amendment finally came to a vote, 50 senators—a surprising total of 19 Republicans as well as 31 Democrats—voted no. The yeas were 49, with Jesse Helms voting "present" in an attempt to manifest disagreement with both sides. It would have required 67 yeas to pass the Senate.

After this defeat, the Senate antiabortion forces did not regain their momentum. Although antiabortion legislation and constitutional amendments continue to be introduced in Congress after Congress, none has met with even the limited success of the measures considered by the Senate in the early 1980s. The failure of and general disinterest in repeal measures comes as no surprise. Unlike funding prohibitions or congressional efforts to encourage women to choose birth, repeal measures come at a much higher price, challenging the correctness of *Roe* and the legitimacy of the Supreme Court. This is especially true with human life legislation that attempts to make an end run around the constitutionally prescribed amendment process. Congress, unwilling to absorb these decisional costs, has limited its attacks on *Roe* to indirect techniques.

PRO-CHOICE INITIATIVES: FREEDOM-OF-CHOICE AND CLINIC ACCESS LEGISLATION

From 1973 until 1989, *Roe*'s protection of a woman's right to choose abortion remained largely unaltered. In 1989, *Webster* v. *Reproductive Health Services* narrowed the right to choose abortion by permitting some state regulation.[39] Pro-choice legislators sought to statutorily nullify *Webster* through the Freedom of Choice Act (FOCA). Introduced on 17 November 1991, FOCA prohibited states from restricting abortion before viability and at any time when the abortion was necessary to save the life or health of the mother. Supporters of FOCA argued that Congress had to protect the right established in *Roe* as the Court began to retreat from recognition of that right.

FOCA, as amended in 1992, outlined Congress's authority under section 5 of the Fourteenth Amendment, which had been the original basis for the legislation, and Congress's commerce power, which was utilized for the first time in 1992 to help shore up FOCA's constitutional foundations.[40] Specifically, FOCA 1992 found that recent Supreme Court decisions on abortion had (1) resulted in physical harm and death to women; (2) burdened interstate travel by forcing women to travel from states where abortion is illegal and unsafe to states where it is safe; and (3) discriminated among people on the basis of their ability to travel, causing disproportionate harm to poor minorities who can not afford to travel.[41] FOCA supporters therefore contended that the bill did not extend the rights granted in *Roe* and thus added nothing new to the constitutional law that existed before *Webster*.

FOCA supporters, in distinguishing their proposal from human life legislation that they had savaged a decade earlier, emphasized that FOCA both codified rights previously recognized by the Court and, like the 1964 Civil Rights Act's public accommodations provision, made use of Congress's commerce power.[42] FOCA's congressional opponents, surprisingly, did not launch a constitutional counterattack. Complaining that "this bill is a classic example of overzealous federal meddling in matters Congress should trust the American people in their respective States to address,"[43] FOCA opponents Orrin Hatch, Strom Thurmond, and others invoked federalism as a public policy rationale for voting against the bill.

The Bush administration was unequivocally opposed to FOCA. On 3 March 1991, the day before House subcommittee hearings began on FOCA, Bush addressed the National Association of Evangelicals and promised that FOCA would not become law as long as he was president. Furthermore, the Bush Justice Department issued an opinion letter declaring FOCA unconstitutional and testified before Congress about the bill's constitutional failings.[44]

The Bush administration's opposition was nullified by the election of Bill Clinton, who during his presidential campaign had come "out strongly for . . . the Freedom of Choice Act."[45] What Clinton and pro-FOCA lawmakers did not take into account was the Supreme Court's June 1992 decision in *Planned Parenthood* v. *Casey*. *Casey* stopped FOCA in its tracks. The Supreme Court had adopted a moderate stance that better reflected the beliefs of Americans than did the absolutist Freedom of Choice Act. By making FOCA look extremist by comparison, the *Casey* decision caused a great many pro-choice lawmakers to abandon FOCA. Furthermore, after his election Bill Clinton's support of FOCA diminished. He has said little about FOCA, and although he has taken several pro-choice positions, he has taken no action in support of the bill. Not surprisingly, by 1995 pro-FOCA lawmakers had abandoned their campaign to statutorily codify abortion rights.

The counterpart to the *Casey*-inspired failure of FOCA is the Freedom of Access to Clinic Entrances Act of 1994 (FACE). Whereas a Supreme Court decision proved the undoing of FOCA, FACE was largely a by-product of Congress's disapproval of the Supreme Court's 1993 decision, in *Bray* v. *Alexandria Women's Health Clinic*,[46] that then-existing federal civil rights legislation was not applicable to blockades of abortion clinics by Operation Rescue and other pro-life groups. In addition to *Bray*, clinic access reform was spurred on by the fatal shooting of Dr. David Gunn, an abortion provider, by a pro-life activist two months after the Supreme Court's ruling. Specifically, FACE prohibits threats of force against women seeking abortions or individuals assisting such women.

Congressional sponsors emphasized that, with more than 6,000 clinic blockades and other disruptions since 1977 (including 28 bombings, 266 bomb threats, 62 arsons, and 394 incidents of vandalism), federal remedies were necessary to guarantee "the constitutionally protected right to choose."[47] Pro-life congressional interests, while "deplor[ing] the violence . . . connected with this emotional debate,"[48] nevertheless rallied against the bill. Characterizing the measure as "a piece of legislation seeking to silence an unpopular minority and doing so in the best traditions of political correctness,"[49] clinic access opponents launched a First Amendment counterattack.

The bone of contention here was that the act contained language that criminalized "physical obstruction [that] . . . intimidates, or interferes with . . . providing reproductive health services." Finding this language overly vague and arguing that this risk of criminal sanction would "chill" pro-life individuals peacefully approaching someone walking into a clinic for an abortion, opponents of FACE contended that "Congress has selected a single point of view—opposition to abortion—and subjected it to penalties not applied to other points of view."[50] Supporters of the bill, while tightening the act's language in response to these charges, argued that the bill did not target expression but sanctioned *conduct* (use of force, threat of force, physical obstruction, and destruction of property).[51]

While these claims did not fully satisfy opponents, supporters of the bill persevered, and on 26 May 1994 Bill Clinton signed the clinic access bill. In an emotional ceremony, prominently featuring the children of Dr. David Gunn, the president hailed FACE as reinforcing our nation's "commit[ment] to the rule of law" by "ensur[ing] that all citizens have the opportunity to exercise all their constitutional rights, including their privacy rights."[52] Predictably, the law was immediately challenged by antiabortion groups, and the cycle of the dialogue again returned the issue to the courts.

CONGRESS VERSUS THE EXECUTIVE

In addition to legislation and litigation, Congress participates in the abortion dispute through its oversight of governmental programs and through its power to confirm presidential appointees. Just as the White House checks Congress through its veto power, congressional oversight and confirmation powers ensure that the executive does not stray too far from legislative preferences.

Indeed, starting with the Ford administration, Congress and the White House have warred over a broad array of abortion-related issues.

The most visible (and perhaps most important) of these battles centers on judicial appointments, especially to the Supreme Court. The classic example, which will be considered at length in Chapter 7, is Ronald Reagan's failed nomination of Robert Bork, a nominee who attacked as "unprincipled" the doctrinal foundation of *Roe*, specifically, the Warren Court's recognition of privacy and other substantive due process rights. In the post-Bork era, members of the Senate Judiciary Committee have come to view the confirmation process as a mechanism to influence Court decision-making through their questioning of and pontificating before judicial nominees. After Bork, every Supreme Court nominee has sworn allegiance before the altar of unenumerated rights, especially the right of privacy. Anthony Kennedy noted that "the concept of liberty in the due process clause is quite expansive, quite sufficient, to protect the values of privacy that Americans *legitimately* think are part of their constitutional heritage."[53] The first question asked of David Souter concerned privacy; and he unhesitatingly replied, "I believe that the Due Process Clause of the 14th Amendment does recognize and does protect an unenumerated right of privacy."[54] Even Clarence Thomas told Senator Biden on the first day of his hearings that "my view is that there is a right to privacy in the Fourteenth Amendment."[55] Needless to say, Clinton nominees Ruth Bader Ginsburg and Stephen Breyer embraced privacy rights at their confirmation hearings. For Ginsburg, privacy, and with it, abortion, "is something central to a woman's life, to her dignity. It's a decision that she must make for herself."[56]

That Supreme Court nominees now view the privacy mantra as simply part of the confirmation routine, however, has not prevented candidates from refusing to answer questions about abortion. David Souter, who described *Roe* as "the one case which has been on everyone's mind and on everyone's lips since the moment of my nomination," nonetheless refused to discuss "the concept of *Roe v. Wade*."[57] Clarence Thomas went a step further, proclaiming to an incredulous Patrick Leahy (D-Vt.) that he had "never debated the contents of *[Roe]*" and could not "remember personally engaging in" discussions of *Roe*,[58] which was decided when Thomas was a law student. For Leahy, who found it "hard to believe that there is a thoughtful lawyer in this country . . . who has not discussed or expressed his view on *Roe v. Wade*,"[59] this exchange was decisive. Nevertheless, despite being further weighed down by the Anita Hill sexual harassment scandal, Thomas survived his Senate confirmation hearings by a vote of 52 to 48.[60]

The confirmation process, of course, extends to executive-branch officials as well as federal court judges. Starting with the Carter administration, presidential appointees for such positions as secretary of health and human services, surgeon general, attorney general, solicitor general, and director of the Office of Personnel Management have come to the Senate with a track record on the abortion issue. The Senate grants the president great leeway in executive-branch appointments. Although the Senate will explore a nominee's personal views on abortion and how those views will affect his or her management of governmental resources, the abortion issue is not a litmus test. Charles Fried, who had filed a brief calling for *Roe*'s reversal prior to Reagan's nominating him as solicitor general, spoke of being "surprised by how pleasant and interesting the [courtesy call] meetings with the most liberal Democratic Senators—Kennedy, Metzenbaum, Simon—turned out to be."[61] Nonetheless, the Senate uses hearings to make nominees well aware of the high-stakes nature of abortion politics. Joseph Califano, secretary of health, education, and welfare under Carter, put it this way when describing his own confirmation hearings: following a round of questioning about abortion, "the tension in the room eased a little as other senators asked questions on Social Security, balancing the budget, eliminating paperwork, busing, race discrimination, [etc.]."[62]

Congress's bark here is worse than its bite, for abortion never has been the downfall of any executive-branch nominee. The Senate's June 1995 refusal to vote on Clinton surgeon general nominee Henry Foster, for example, was as much a by-product of the White House's initial misrepresentations of the number of abortions Foster had performed as it was of Foster's pro-choice stance.[63] Specifically, by initially misstating his abortion record, Foster opened the door to attacks on his credibility. Indeed, by winning approval from the Senate's Labor and Human Resources Committee and receiving 57 of the 60 votes needed to force a vote (which he almost certainly would have won) on his nomination,[64] the Foster nomination revealed that the Republican Senate was willing to confirm a pro-choice surgeon general. Along these lines, after the initial uproar about Foster's abortion record, the White House sought to transform the Foster nomination into a referendum on abortion rights.

Congress's willingness to let the president people the executive branch as he sees fit is vividly illustrated in the Senate's approval of two surgeons general who were polar opposites—Ronald Reagan's pro-life nominee C. Everett Koop, and Bill Clinton's pro-choice nominee Joycelyn Elders. Koop, whose nomination the *Los Angeles Times* described as a "political sop to antiabortion forces,"[65] garnered opposition from pro-choice interests, women's groups, and such newspapers as the *Boston Globe*, the *Los Angeles Times*, and the *New York Times*. Of particular concern to Koop's opponents were his writings on the sanctity of life—writings that accused pro-choice religious groups of "superficial theology, lack of morality, and an insensitivity to the eventual reward for their depravity."[66] Koop nonetheless prevailed by a lopsided 68-to-24 vote because, as Senator Slade Gordon (R-Wash.)—in a statement otherwise critical of the nominee—put it, "the President is, absent extraordinary circumstances, entitled to the appointment of his choice to offices in which the appointees serve at his pleasure."[67] The nomination of Joycelyn Elders followed a similar script. Elders outraged pro-life interests both by characterizing abortion foes as "non-Christians with slavemaster mentalities" who need to get over their "love affair with the fetus" and by defending abortion as "the single most important factor" in decreasing infant mortality and having other "important public health effect[s]."[68] Despite arousing ardent opposition, Elders prevailed by a vote of 65 to 34. In the end, most senators concurred with Edward Kennedy's assertion that "Dr. Elders' pro-choice views are the same as those of the President who appointed her . . . and who deserves to have the pro-choice nominee of his choice confirmed."[69]

That Congress allows the president great leeway in executive-branch appointments does not translate into legislative acquiescence to the administration of governmental programs. Congress actively participates in the abortion dispute through its oversight of governmental programs. When the U.S. Commission on Civil Rights published a report advocating abortion rights in 1975, Congress expressed its displeasure with the agency by forbidding future studies on this issue. Congress likewise used its oversight powers to express its dissatisfaction with the Office of Personnel Management's (OPM's) treatment of Combined Federal Campaign contributions to Planned Parenthood. OPM, then headed by pro-life activist Donald Devine, excluded Planned Parenthood from the list of approved charities to which federal employees could donate by means of payroll deductions. Following a series of court decisions, including a Supreme Court decision suggesting that the Planned Parenthood exclusion might be an impermissible attempt to snuff out a particular point of view, Congress enacted legislation in 1985 blocking the exclusion of advocacy groups from the list of approved charities.

In addition to the enactment of punitive legislation, congressional oversight also, and more typically, takes the form of legislative jawboning. For example, implementation of the Hyde Amendment by the Carter administration prompted sharp criticism but nothing more. When the Reagan administration suspended fetal tissue research, Ted Weiss (D-N.Y.), chair of the House Committee on Human Resources, made an extraordinary request that the administration turn over all "research evidence" and "all documents, including letters, memoranda, minutes of meetings, and internal or draft documents."[70]

CONCLUSION

Congressional participation in the abortion dispute does not lend itself to easy generalization. Unwilling to squarely support pro-choice or pro-life policies, Congress vacillates between sometimes-contradictory policy objectives. Nevertheless, some tentative conclusions can be inferred. First, congressional action must be placed in context, especially as it relates to Supreme Court decision-making. When the Court ardently supports abortion rights, pro-choice interests are less vocal and pro-life interests in Congress are more likely to get their way. This is the story of the Hyde Amendment and other funding restrictions. In contrast, when *Roe* appeared ready to be overruled, it seemed likely that Congress would enact some form of freedom-of-choice legislation. Moreover, Congress's weakening of the Hyde Amendment and other funding restrictions is very much linked to the Court's chipping away at *Roe*. Second, Congress prefers to avoid confrontational or absolutist responses to Court action. The failure of human life legislation, constitutional amendments, and freedom-of-choice legislation (once *Roe* was reaffirmed) indicates Congress's desire to minimize the costs of its action. Third, and relatedly, Congress seems quite willing to delegate decision-making authority rather than bear the costs of choosing between pro-choice and pro-life interests. The Pregnancy Discrimination Act and health care reform proposals, for example, leave the abortion coverage decision to private sector employers and insurers. Fourth, in rare instances, institutional customs transcend policy objectives. The joining of pro-choice and pro-life forces in defending Congress's appropriations powers before the Supreme Court, and the deference typically accorded the White House in executive-branch appointments, are relevant here. Fifth, Congress is willing to modify legislation to meet constitutional objections. The invocation of Congress's commerce power in freedom-of-choice legislation, as well as modifications made in clinic access legislation, were responses to perceived constitutional defects. Sixth, congressional action often requires executive-branch approval. Through his veto power, Bush successfully fought off 1989 efforts to moderate the Hyde Amendment and other funding restrictions.[71]

The abortion dispute also highlights the numerous devices available to Congress both to shape constitutional values and to interface with the execu-

tive and judicial branches. On constitutional matters, Congress may check judicial action through funding restrictions, constitutional amendments, and
statutory repeal proposals. On statutory matters, Congress reigns in the courts
as well as the executive through legislation such as that governing the Combined Federal Campaign, clinic access, and pregnancy discrimination. Through
its participation in litigation as well as its oversight and confirmation powers,
Congress also is involved in judicial and executive-branch decision-making.
Congress, finally, engages in constitutional interpretation through its independent assessment of the constitutionality of family-planning and clinic access
legislation.

Congressional involvement in the abortion dispute will continue. Whether
the issue is health care reform, Medicaid funding, or foreign aid, abortion is likely
to play a pivotal role in legislative deliberations. However, because of *Casey*'s
reaffirmation of both abortion rights and state regulatory authority, Congress
has little incentive to pursue absolutist pro-choice or pro-life measures. Moreover, with Clinton's shoring up of *Casey*'s pro-choice foundations through his
appointments of Ruth Bader Ginsburg and Stephen Breyer to the Supreme
Court, the future of *Roe* v. *Wade* is no longer at stake; consequently, Senate confirmation hearings likely will pay far less attention to the abortion issue. Indeed,
the abortion issue never was seriously explored at Stephen Breyer's confirmation hearing. Only Strom Thurmond asked Breyer about the constitutional status of abortion rights, to which Breyer responded, "That's the law."[72]

Congress, however, cannot extricate itself from abortion. It is a reactive
body, and the abortion dispute will create circumstances that prompt legislative
decision-making. Clinic access legislation and health care reform are two recent examples of this phenomenon. Congress simply has too many tools available to it and too many roles to play to refuse to be actively engaged in the abortion dispute.

7 / The Executive and Abortion

CONGRESSIONAL AMBIVALENCE ABOUT abortion stands in sharp contrast to executive-branch decisiveness on this question. Starting with the 1980 election of Ronald Reagan, presidential candidates (as well as the party platforms on which they run) have taken sharply opposing views on the correctness of *Roe* v. *Wade*. For the Republican party and its candidates (from 1976 to 1992 at least), "the unborn child has a fundamental individual right to life which cannot be infringed";[1] for the Democrats, "reproductive freedom" is recognized "as a fundamental human right."[2] That the Democrats are more sensitive to pro-choice interests and the Republicans to pro-life interests, while critically important to single-issue voters, tells precious little about how the abortion dispute has affected the executive and, more importantly for our purposes, how the executive has transformed the abortion dispute.

There is no doubt, as was the case with Congress, that the executive makes use of all its powers in this area. Presidents have advanced their pro-choice or pro-life agendas through spiritual leadership, legislative and constitutional amendment proposals, judicial and executive appointments, judicial filings, and regulatory reform. Of equal significance, an extraordinary number of executive-branch entities have found themselves immersed in the abortion controversy, including such unlikely participants as the Veterans Administration, the Community Service Administration, the Civil Service Commission, the Office of Personnel Management, the Legal Services Corporation, the Agency for International Development, and the Departments of State and Defense. There also have been controversies involving the usual suspects—the Civil Rights Commission, the Equal Employment Opportunity Commission, the Office of the Surgeon General, the Food and Drug Administration, the Department of Justice, and the Department of Health and Human Services. With so many actors and presidential powers involved, there is little doubt that the abortion dispute permeates executive-branch operations.

Although it is true that activist presidential involvement in the abortion issue began with the Reagan administration, the origins of direct White House involvement in the dispute date back to Richard Nixon. Starting during the Nixon administration, the president and his staff have been attentive to the abortion issue in personnel decisions, legislative initiatives, presidential vetoes, White House oversight of administrative enforcement, presidential bully-pulpit statements, and campaign decision-making. Nevertheless, the decisiveness and authority of the executive branch should not be overstated. Presidents serve no more than eight years and often serve only for four years. Consequently, while one executive may be somewhat single-minded about abortion, a different administration may have diametrically opposed policies. As a result, executive-branch initiatives are inevitably subject to reversal or modification "at the stroke of a pen." Furthermore, not only are some executive-branch policies short-lived but it would be wrong to assume that all future administrations will continue to take a hard-line position on abortion. Before the election of Ronald Reagan, for example, abortion was an important but not a front-burner issue for the executive.

ABORTION AND THE SOUL OF THE WHITE HOUSE: PRESIDENTIAL CAMPAIGNS AND BULLY-PULPIT STATEMENTS

Abortion politics often is symbolic politics. Rather than seeking to affect the enactment of a law, the resolution of a judicial dispute, or the administration of a governmental program, the president and presidential candidates communicate a moral vision and signal the ways in which they will use the presidency to advance that vision. Presidential campaigns and bully-pulpit statements provide the most vivid examples.

Prior to *Roe*, the White House saw abortion as fundamentally a states' rights issue and, for the most part, left it alone. In the 1972 election, for example, Richard Nixon spoke of "abortion [as] an unacceptable form of population control" but proposed no federal action, while George McGovern made clear that he had "never advocated federal action to repeal [abortion] laws" and that, if elected, he "would take no such action."[3] The Nixon White House, however, did recognize the political significance of abortion, and Nixon himself participated in the abortion dispute in several ways. Most strikingly, to the chagrin of New York's Republican governor (and later Gerald Ford's vice-president) Nelson Rockefeller, Nixon commended Cardinal Cooke for spearheading pre-*Roe* efforts to repeal New York's "liberalized abortion laws." After the Supreme

Court's 1973 abortion decision, the Nixon White House seriously considered entering the abortion fray. In a memo to the president from White House aide Patrick Buchanan, Nixon was encouraged to support a constitutional amendment proposal seeking to overturn *Roe*. For Buchanan, "the issue is a 'moral' one; it will engage us on the 'moral' side of an issue—and place us into a controversy which would be both politically advantageous" (since "the women's libbers . . . [are a] group we never had, and never will have") "and advantageous from the standpoint of legitimate controversy, other than Watergate."[4]

Buchanan was certainly correct in concluding that abortion was too much on the national political agenda to be dismissed by the White House. The Ford administration, for example, could not help but confront questions regarding the eligibility of abortion under federal health care programs. Ford sought to walk a tightrope, claiming that "abortion is a matter better decided at the State level" but also that "as President I am bound by my oath of office to uphold the law of the land as interpreted by the Supreme Court."[5] In the 1976 election, however, Ford sought out the Catholic electorate by opposing public funding of abortion; he wrote the National Conference of Catholic Bishops that "the Government has a responsibility to protect life—and indeed to provide legal guarantees for the weak and unprotected."[6]

Abortion proved to be only of secondary importance in the 1976 elections. Carter and Ford bested, in their party primaries, candidates with stronger views on abortion—with Ford defeating Ronald Reagan and Carter triumphing over Birch Bayh and Frank Church. The principal difference between Ford and Carter was that Ford supported efforts to return control over abortion to the states through a constitutional amendment. In June 1976, Carter declared his opposition to these efforts. Three months later—in an appeal to Catholic voters—Carter modified his position, stating that he would neither support nor oppose an abortion amendment. This policy shift, however, raised questions in the minds of pro-choice and pro-life voters. More tellingly, Carter's flip-flop proved emblematic of his administration's handling of the abortion issue. Recognizing the legal and moral difficulties involved, Carter sought out a non-confrontational, middle-ground approach to abortion only to find himself alienating both pro-choice and pro-life interests. For the most part, and like his predecessors, Carter eschewed an activist role in the abortion dispute. Abortion did not figure prominently in his judicial appointments; his solicitor general did not ask the courts to affirm or to disavow *Roe;* he did not propose legislation or constitutional amendments; and his regulatory initiatives were modest in scope and sweep.

When Carter acted, he sent out an inconsistent message, and this cost him dearly. Opposed to public funding of abortion, he justified the disproportionate burden that poor women suffer under the Hyde Amendment by observing, "There are many things in life that are not fair, that wealthy people can afford and poor people can't."[7] These remarks, combined with his inclusion of the Hyde Amendment in budget proposals submitted to Congress, prompted the *New York Times* to characterize Carter's abortion policies as "deplorable social policy" and "cruel[,] . . . curious and misguided."[8] Carter fared no better with pro-life interests. Pointing to his pro-choice nominees and his refusal to actively support pro-life legislation, March for Life prepared a "Declaration of Grievances" accusing Carter of paying "lip service to the principle of the right to life" and describing "the record of this administration [as] an unrelieved series of betrayals and hypocrisy."[9] Carter's inability to successfully carve out a middle ground in this area highlights the perils of a cautious approach to the abortion dispute. The 1980 election of Ronald Reagan proved that. Reagan campaigned on a platform that "support[ed] a constitutional amendment to restore protection of the right to life for unborn children" and "support[ed] . . . the Congressional efforts to restrict the use of taxpayers' dollars for abortion."[10]

Reagan honored his campaign commitment to "unborn children" through, among other actions, presidential proclamations and speeches to the right-to-life community. He wrote in the *Human Life Review* that *Roe* v. *Wade*, by denying "the value of certain human lives," was as divisive and as wrong as the decision in *Dred Scott*.[11] Reagan also lamented that "the consequences of this judicial decision *[Roe]* are now obvious: [from 1973 to 1983] more than 15 million unborn children have had their lives snuffed out by legalized abortion. That is over ten times the number of Americans lost in all our nation's wars."[12] In a briefing to right-to-life leaders, Reagan referred to Terrence Cardinal Cooke's message that "it is through the weakest of human vessels that the Lord continues to reveal the power of his love."[13]

Reagan's willingness to confront the morality of abortion head-on dramatically affected public discourse on abortion rights. Reagan won not only this battle but a much larger war. His moral campaign against *Roe* served as the foundation for a host of White House legislative and regulatory initiatives. Correspondingly, Congress's abortion-related activity (as discussed in Chapter 6) grew exponentially. Reagan therefore succeeded, as Alexander Hamilton put it, in undertaking extensive and arduous enterprises for the public benefit because he understood that, without his aggressive use of the bully pulpit, "the very notion of presidential leadership in a legislative context would be compromised."[14]

The most visible manifestation of Reagan's campaign against abortion was the transformation of George Bush. When running against Reagan in the 1980 primaries, Bush said bluntly, "I happen to think *[Roe]* was right."[15] Once ensconced in the White House, Bush echoed the Reagan administration's anti-abortion refrain in speeches to right-to-life groups. Before the annual March for Life rally, Bush referred to abortion on demand as "our American tragedy" and called for the overturning of *Roe*.[16] On National Sanctity of Human Life Day, moreover, Bush issued an annual proclamation seeking to prevent "another unborn child" from becoming "the innocent victim of abortion."[17]

When Bush sought reelection in 1992, dramatic changes had occurred in the abortion landscape. In June of that year, the Supreme Court had handed down *Planned Parenthood* v. *Casey*, a decision that was in keeping with prevailing public opinion because it upheld abortion rights *but* recognized broad state authority to regulate access to abortion. Public attention, moreover, focused on the economy and other issues. With Clinton and Bush fielding numerous questions on abortion and the Democratic and Republican platforms taking strong opposing positions on the issue, abortion remained salient but was less prominent than in past campaigns.

The election of Bill Clinton signaled a transitional period in presidential abortion politics. Clinton's persistent refrain that abortion should be "safe, legal but rare" is cautiously pro-choice. Although immediately dissolving the antiabortion initiatives of the Reagan-Bush era, Clinton never spoke of the correctness of *Roe* or of a woman's right to control her body; instead, the president phrased his actions in neutral terms, speaking of "protecting vital medical and health decisions from ideological and political debate," and saying, "the American people deserve the best medical treatment in the world."[18] Unlike his Republican predecessors, moreover, Clinton has neither made hard-hitting bully-pulpit speeches on abortion rights nor met with pro-choice groups to discuss his legislative agenda on abortion. Indeed, calling abortion funding a "political football" and recognizing that mandating abortion coverage in federally funded health care would have "sparked a whole reaction,"[19] Clinton's health care plan left the abortion coverage decision to private insurers. Along the same lines, the Clinton administration backed away from absolutist positions on abortion at a 1994 United Nations population conference in Cairo and a 1995 UN conference on women in Beijing.[20] More significantly, Clinton excluded the Hyde Amendment from his budget proposal but was apparently willing to give states leeway to decide whether to fund Medicaid abortions.

Clinton's cautiousness, however, does not portend a return to Jimmy Carter's failed efforts to please both pro-choice and pro-life interests by communicating a mixed message on abortion. Clinton's policies and rhetoric are decidedly pro-choice; it is just that he is unwilling to put the full weight of the presidency behind his pro-choice leanings. This moderation may prove a harbinger of increasing presidential acquiescence to Congress's abortion-related action (which also may be on the wane) and of decreasing presidential attention to abortion and abortion interest groups. At the same time, with the Christian Coalition and other interest groups still making abortion a litmus test issue, the White House—or at least some presidential candidates—may find it difficult to steer clear of abortion-related controversies.[21]

The Lawmaking President

The abortion dispute makes clear that the president plays a large role in defining the legislative agenda. Through congressional testimony, legislative proposals, and especially the veto power, the executive has had a major say in abortion-related lawmaking. Nevertheless, the influence of each administration has varied greatly. Several factors are at play here, including the strength of the president's interest in abortion, the political makeup of Congress (i.e., whether the president and congressional leaders are of the same political party), and, most significantly, the president's choice of a method to affect lawmaking (e.g., either his power of persuasion or his veto power).

When the president recommends legislative initiatives to Congress, the ball is truly in Congress's court. Ronald Reagan, for example, generally was ineffective in his efforts to push through a pro-life legislative agenda. With or without White House cheerleading, Congress was unwilling to approve a constitutional amendment restricting abortion rights, to enact a permanent Hyde Amendment, to forbid federally funded family-planning centers to refer pregnant women for abortions, or to statutorily define a fetus as a legal person. In the end, while prompting legislative hearings and floor debates on his initiatives, Reagan's numerous legislative and constitutional amendment proposals seemed little more than symbolic gestures.

In light of the inherent limits of the power to recommend, it is hardly surprising that the president's influence is more profound when he plays a reactive role, by signing or vetoing enacted legislation and by informing Congress of his support for proposed legislation. George Bush, for example, successfully used his veto power on five abortion-related matters. In three instances, Bush used his veto power defensively, preserving the status quo by blocking congressionally supported programs that he disfavored. Specifically, Congress sought to overturn Reagan administration regulations placing abortion restrictions on international family planning, prohibiting abortion counseling at federally funded family-planning centers, and imposing a moratorium on fetal tissue research. In each instance, Bush refused to yield and successfully vetoed these congressional repeal efforts. By protecting executive-branch initiatives through the veto power, moreover, Bush's vetoes emphasized the potency of the president's power to administer governmental programs.

Bush also made affirmative use of his veto power, by forcing Congress to adopt a presidentially supported program that it had originally disfavored. For example, in its 1980 appropriations package, Congress placed the District of Columbia in the same position as the various states with respect to federal abortion policy by prohibiting the use of federal funds to provide abortions to District of Columbia women. Under President Bush, however, the restrictions tightened: District of Columbia appropriations legislation prohibited expenditure of federal or local funds for abortions except where the life of the mother was endangered.

These new, tougher restrictions brought about a flurry of angry protest from District of Columbia officials, who clamored for statehood with renewed vigor. In 1989 Congress relented and refused to reenact the D.C. funding prohibition as part of its annual District of Columbia Appropriations Act. President Bush vetoed the bill and demanded that Congress reinsert the prohibition. At first, Congress sought to circumvent the veto by enacting legislation that would prohibit the use of federal funds to pay for abortions in the District of Columbia *but* would permit congressionally approved local funds to be used for abortions. Bush would have none of this. Referring to his "deep personal feelings about the tragedy in America of abortion on demand,"[22] Bush again vetoed the District of Columbia Appropriations Act. Recognizing the necessity of getting a spending bill passed, and having failed to override the Bush veto, Congress eventually capitulated and reinserted the prohibition of both federal and city abortion expenditures.

Bush's vetoes set him apart from other presidents. Indeed, Bush (at least through 1995) has been the only president to use his veto power to advance his abortion agenda. Nonetheless, it is clear that the veto power is a potent lawmaking tool. With it, presidents can at least protect the status quo and may be able to force some of their policy preferences on Congress. Presidents, of course, also may affect public discourse and legislative action through their recommendations to and testimony before Congress. A comparison of Reagan's failed legislative campaign and Bush's successful use of the veto, however, suggests that the veto power may be the more significant of the two. In any event, the president—with both the power to place issues before Congress through recommended legislation and the power to veto congressional action that is unacceptable—wields enormous influence in lawmaking. Ironically, in the abortion context, this power has often translated into a legislative stalemate, with Congress refusing to act on the president's initiatives and the president blocking congressional reform efforts.

THE APPOINTMENTS POWER

Executive-branch efforts to shape the abortion dispute through bully-pulpit statements, legislative proposals and testimony, and presidential vetoes pale in comparison to the president's power to shape judicial and regulatory decision-making. The critical power here is the president's authority to appoint federal court judges and executive-branch officials. "The eyes and arms of the principal Magistrate, the instruments of execution,"[23] as James Madison put it, are the individuals selected by the president to put his program into effect.

Judicial appointments, along with court filings, are the most direct ways in which the executive influences constitutional law. Not surprisingly, since *Roe v. Wade* abortion has played a critical part in nearly every Supreme Court appointment. The executive also seeks to reshape abortion rights through its management of the administrative state. With more than five hundred executive-branch appointments requiring Senate confirmation and roughly five thousand presidential positions in all, the president cannot put his agenda in place without a cadre of like-minded individuals running governmental programs. Starting with the Reagan administration, abortion has been a litmus test of sorts for the surgeon general and for political appointees at the Department of Justice and the Department of Health and Human Services.

Judicial Nominations

"The judiciary is a primary player in the formulation of public policy," claimed Reagan Justice Department official Bruce Fein; hence "it would be silly for an administration not to try to affect the direction of legal policy[-making]" through judicial appointments.[24] The distinguishing feature of Reagan's judicial selections is that the president himself singled out abortion when proclaiming that "progress will take place when the federal judiciary is made up of judges who believe in law and order and a strict interpretation of the Constitution."[25] To achieve this end, Reagan pledged to appoint judges "who respect traditional family values and the sanctity of innocent human life . . . [and] who share our commitment to judicial restraint."[26]

To ensure that Reagan's nominees possessed the right judicial tempera-ment, the White House created a Judicial Selection Committee to screen poten-tial nominees. Through day-long committee interviews and painstaking re-views of candidates' speeches, writings, and opinions, three hundred candidates were selected from the more than one thousand interviewed. Among other things, nominees reportedly were asked their personal views on abortion, as well as what their favorite and least favorite Supreme Court decisions were.

Reagan's judicial selection process achieved the desired result. Before the lower federal courts, "Reagan appointees were much more resistant to abortion rights than were the appointees of his predecessor."[27] For example, two staunch critics of *Roe*, law professor John Noonan and former U.S. senator James Buck-ley, were appointed to federal courts of appeal.[28] More strikingly, right-to-life interests vetoed two well-regarded candidates—corporate lawyer Judith Whit-taker (who had supported the Equal Rights Amendment) and Justice Depart-ment official Andrew Frey (who had made donations to Planned Parenthood).

The defining moment in the Reagan administration's campaign to re-shape the judiciary was the July 1987 nomination of Robert Bork to the U.S. Supreme Court. The president nominated Bork to replace judicial moderate Lewis Powell, who had been a swing vote on the sharply divided Court and the justice who often stymied much of the Reagan administration's Court strategy with his decisive votes on abortion, affirmative action, and church-state mat-ters. The Bork nomination, then, threatened to alter fundamental doctrines of the Court. Indeed, Joseph Biden (D-Del.), chair of the Senate Judiciary Com-mittee, suggested that the Bork controversy was more about the loss of Justice Powell than about Bork himself, remarking that if "Bork were about to replace Rehnquist or . . . Scalia, this would be a whole different ball game."[29]

In addition to these high stakes, the Bork nomination was controversial because Bork was the embodiment of all that the Reagan administration said the courts should be. In Reagan's words, Bork shared his "belief in judicial re-straint: that a judge is bound by the Constitution to interpret laws, not make them."[30] For example, Bork condemned *Roe* v. *Wade* as "an unconstitutional decision, a serious and wholly unjustifiable judicial usurpation of State legisla-tive authority."[31]

Bork's opponents, although their principal concern was abortion, decided to focus their attacks on Bork's condemnation of judicially created privacy rights. This decision was purely strategic; the Block Bork Coalition feared that turning the confirmation hearings into a divisive public referendum on abortion would play into White House charges that the Bork opposition was merely a thinly veiled pro-choice special interest group. This strategy was implemented in a full-page advertisement that appeared in the *Washington Post* and other newspapers on 14 September 1987. In it, Planned Parenthood warned that at stake in the Bork nomination were "decades of Supreme Court decisions uphold[ing] your freedom to make your own decisions about marriage and family, childbearing and parenting," and that "if the Senate confirms Robert Bork, it will be too late. Your personal privacy, one of the most cherished and unique features of American life, has never been in greater danger."

Competing reports prepared by the White House, the Justice Department, and Senate Judiciary Committee chairman Joseph Biden served as the opening volley in this debate. The White House report depicted Bork's "judicial philosophy" as the simple demand that, "without a clear constitutional warrant, judges may not displace the considered judgments of elected officials."[32] In contrast, the "Biden Report" argued that Bork's "rejection of constitutional protection[s] against unwarranted intrusions into the intimacies of one's personal life" revealed an unprincipled disregard for "the text, history and tradition of the Constitution."[33] The real battle began on 15 September 1987, when Bork and members of the Senate Judiciary Committee went head to head on the privacy issue. Senator Biden pressed Bork on his assertion that "the economic gratification of a utility company is as worthy of as much protection as the sexual gratification of a married couple, because neither is mentioned in the Constitution."[34] Senator Edward Kennedy (D-Mass.) told Bork that he had "serious questions . . . about placing someone on the Supreme Court that . . . find[s] some rationale not to respect" privacy rights.[35] Bork responded that the founders "banked a good deal upon the good sense of the people" and their elected representatives and asked rhetorically, "Privacy to do what[?] . . . use cocaine in private? Privacy for businessmen to fix prices in a hotel room?"[36]

The Senate Judiciary Committee voted 9 to 5 against Bork's nomination. A cornerstone of the majority report was Bork's refusal to recognize a constitutional right to privacy. For the majority, "the image of human dignity has been associated throughout our history with the idea that the Constitution recognizes 'unenumerated rights.'"[37] Although senators such as Robert Dole (R-Kans.) labeled this privacy attack as "unfair" and "absurd,"[38] the Senate defeated the Bork nomination 58 to 42, in large measure because of the privacy issue.

In the aftermath of his defeat, Bork predicted that a future president who wants "to avoid a battle like mine . . . is likely to nominate men and women who have not written much, and certainly nothing that could be regarded as controversial."[39] Up to a point, Bork is certainly correct. For example, all post-Bork nominees have sworn allegiance to unenumerated privacy rights. Nonetheless, as the political scientist David O'Brien observed, "the process of judicial selection has changed in such fundamental ways that future administrations, whether Democratic or Republican, are sure to follow Reagan's lead in vigorously pursuing their legal policy goals when picking judges."[40]

Nominations to Executive Posts

"The goal of the energetic executive," according to Reagan Justice Department official Terry Eastland, "must be the selection of capable appointees at all levels who are committed to his programs and policies."[41] The appointment of presidential loyalists is necessitated by "the normal politics of Washington [which] militate strongly against even a semblance of managerial cohesion in government."[42] The abortion dispute is proof of these claims. When the White House has emphasized policy cohesion through its appointment of like-minded individuals, the executive has been well equipped to advance its interests. This is the lesson of the Reagan, Bush, and Clinton administrations. In contrast, as seen during the Carter administration, disunity among presidential appointees has led to policy disarray and, with it, executive-branch impotence on the abortion issue.

The Reagan White House not only used judicial appointments but also made vigorous use of appointments to executive posts to pursue its regulatory campaign against abortion. Reagan's regulatory appointees, according to political scientists George Eads and Mike Fix, were "selected for their symbolic value rather than their administrative skills," and "there was no appreciable fear of the damage controversial appointees could generate."[43] A number of Reagan appointees came from the right-to-life movement: OPM head Donald Devine had run the Life Amendment Political Action Committee; Centers for Disease Control director James Mason had opposed abortion rights as head of Utah's state health department; Health and Human Services secretary Richard Schweiker had, as a U.S. senator, sponsored a constitutional amendment to overturn *Roe;* Title X family-planning program head Marjory Mecklenburg had been a founder of the National Right to Life Committee, and her eventual successor Jo Ann Gasper had been editor of the *Right Woman;* and Surgeon General C. Everett Koop had written and lectured against abortion. The Reagan administration also made opposition to abortion a requirement for several key government posts. Charles Fried's nomination for solicitor general, for example, hinged on his willingness to ask the Supreme Court to overturn *Roe* while serving as acting solicitor general.

This policy cohesiveness stands in sharp contrast to the Carter administration, during which top appointees to the Department of Health, Education, and Welfare (HEW) participated in a meeting organized by White House adviser Midge Costanza to protest against Carter's, and his HEW secretary Joseph Califano's, opposition to federal funding of abortion.[44] President Carter did not take kindly to this disunity, insisting "on 'complete loyalty' once an administration decision was made."[45] Nonetheless, Carter often was isolated from his appointees, except for Califano, on the abortion issue. More significantly, Carter was unable to keep his appointees in check. In a remarkable memorandum to the president, Costanza referred to "White House staff members and Agency staff members expressing concern and even anger over your position on abortion" and informed Carter that "in keeping with our policy of openness, I will be holding meetings on the subject."[46]

Carter's sacrificing of policy cohesion on abortion came at a great cost. Hampered in his ability to send a clear message on the issue, Carter was fiercely criticized by both pro-choice and pro-life interests. In contrast, Reagan administration policy cohesiveness helps to explain the effectiveness of Reagan's regulatory efforts. It therefore comes as no surprise that the Bush and Clinton administrations have followed the Reagan model. Bush's appointees have been solidly pro-life and Clinton's pro-choice. For example, Bush and Clinton filled the two cabinet-level positions most involved in the abortion dispute—the positions of attorney general and secretary of health and human services (HHS)—with individuals firmly committed to the administration's policy.

Bush's two attorneys general, Dick Thornburgh (1989–91) and William Barr (1991–93), sought the Court's reversal of *Roe* v. *Wade*, supported pro-life legislative initiatives, and opposed pro-choice initiatives. Clinton's attorney general, Janet Reno, has utilized the same tools to advance her president's social agenda. She made her pro-choice views clear at Senate confirmation hearings and informed abortion rights groups that "you can always count on me to always use my best legal judgments to enhance legal protection for women."[47]

Bush and Clinton's respective appointments of Louis Sullivan and Donna Shalala to head HHS tell a similar story. Sullivan, for example, stood firm against efforts to repeal a Reagan-era ban on fetal tissue research. Shalala expressed diametrically opposite views on the same subjects. She proclaimed her support for fetal tissue research and her desire to lift governmental regulations banning abortion counseling at federally supported family-planning centers. During her first two years on the job, Shalala pursued these and other pro-choice initiatives, supporting the possible opening of the American market for the so-called abortion pill, RU-486.

Bush and Clinton appointments suggest that, as long as abortion remains a high-priority social policy issue, presidents will seek policy cohesion by appointing like-minded individuals in judicial, cabinet-level, and other regulatory appointments. The relative success of the Reagan administration, especially in the aftermath of the disunified Carter administration, makes clear that the appointments power is one of the president's most vital tools in advancing his social policy agenda.

THE EXECUTIVE IN COURT

Judicial appointments tell only part of the story of executive-branch efforts to affect Court decision-making. Through briefs and oral arguments before the lower federal courts and the Supreme Court, the executive has played a highly visible and influential role in the abortion dispute. The starting point for discussing executive-branch advocacy before the courts, not surprisingly, is the election of Ronald Reagan. Prior to Solicitor General Rex Lee's 1982 filing in *Akron* v. *Akron Center for Reproductive Health,* the executive steered clear of cases involving state regulation of abortion. Judicial filings by the Nixon, Ford, and Carter administrations were limited to disputes that directly implicated the federal government.

In *United States* v. *Vuitch,* for example, Nixon's solicitor general Erwin Grisgold successfully defended Congress's policy of allowing abortion in the District of Columbia only when "necessary for the preservation of the mother's life or health," arguing that the "unconditional availability of abortions, unrelated to medical justification would frustrate Congress' intent to restrict abortion access."[48] The Carter administration, through its solicitor general, Wade McCree, defended the constitutionality of the Hyde Amendment in *Harris* v. *McRae.* These filings, while significant, speak as much to the Justice Department's duty to defend the constitutionality of acts of Congress as they do to the White House's position on abortion.

The advent of the Reagan administration changed all that. Possessing "strong pro-life sentiments" and viewing *Roe* v. *Wade* as "an extreme example of judicial overreaching,"[49] the Reagan Justice Department aggressively challenged the Court's abortion jurisprudence. The strategy was twofold: first, as second-term solicitor general Charles Fried put it, "we undertook to get *Roe* overruled";[50] second, the administration viewed the filing of briefs as a way to "stimulate public discourse on an issue."[51]

The Reagan Justice Department's principal avenue was filing amicus curiae briefs in state cases. These lawsuits centered on governmental authority to regulate abortion and therefore directly called into question the Court's reasoning in *Roe* v. *Wade*. Cases stemming from federal action, in contrast, while raising questions about legislative and executive efforts to limit *Roe*, did not call into question the constitutionality of abortion rights. Remarkably, despite the administration's ardent pro-life posturing, the first of these amicus briefs, Rex Lee's filing in *Akron* v. *Akron Center for Reproductive Health* (1983), did not call for the overruling of *Roe*. Described by his successor Charles Fried as "an oddly ambiguous essay, which seemed to accept the premise of *Roe* but urged extreme deference to the legislature in applying it,"[52] Lee's brief asked the Court to substitute for *Roe*'s rigid trimester standard a new standard that would allow a state to "legitimately enact regulations relating to abortion so long as these regulations do not unduly burden the woman's right . . . to choose abortion rather than childbirth."[53]

Lee's tightrope presentation sent shockwaves through both pro-life and pro-choice camps. The *New York Times* disparaged Lee for filing a "political tract . . . [best] suited to the partisan purposes of an Administration eager to appease its disgruntled right wing."[54] Meanwhile, pro-life interests spared no venom in calling for Lee's prompt removal. In a highly publicized tract by James McClellan, of the Center for Judicial Studies, Lee was savaged for not asking the Court to overrule "a single prior decision" and for not "advocat[ing] the Administration's policies."[55] Lee stepped down, complaining, "I'm the Solicitor General, not the Pamphleteer General."[56]

Lee's successor, Charles Fried, had a different take on abortion. As acting solicitor general, Fried argued in *Thornburgh* v. *American College of Obstetricians and Gynecologists* (1986) that *Roe* was "so far flawed and . . . a source of such instability in the law that this Court should reconsider that decision and on reconsideration abandon it."[57] Recognizing that "the Reagan administration made *Roe v. Wade* the symbol of everything that had gone wrong in law, particularly in constitutional law," Fried found it "clear to me that, as Acting Solicitor General, I could not succeed in heading off an anti-*Roe* brief even if I had been convinced that was the right thing to do. I would simply be overruled."[58]

Fried again called upon the Court to "abandon its efforts to impose a comprehensive solution to the abortion question" in *Webster* v. *Reproductive*

Health Services (1989).[59] These efforts nearly succeeded, with a plurality of the Court holding that "the rigid *Roe* framework is hardly consistent with our notion of a Constitution cast in general terms."[60]

Webster set the stage for *Planned Parenthood* v. *Casey.* By this time, George Bush was president and Ken Starr had replaced Charles Fried as solicitor general. Like his predecessor's, Bush's policies were fervently pro-life, and his solicitor general followed the Reagan administration practice of appearing as an amicus in state abortion cases. In *Casey,* Starr filed a brief and argued before the Court that "the Nation's history and tradition do not establish a fundamental right to abortion" and that the Court should not adhere to *Roe* as part of some duty owed to past precedents *(stare decisis).*[61]

In reaffirming abortion rights, *Casey,* of course, rejected the Reagan-Bush campaign to overturn *Roe.* With the election of Bill Clinton, *Roe*'s moorings were further secured by the appointment of pro-choice jurists. The arrival of the Clinton administration, however, hardly marks the demise of executive-branch participation in abortion litigation. In two cases during the 1993–94 term, the Clinton Justice Department joined pro-choice interests in challenging Operation Rescue protesters. In *National Organization for Women* v. *Scheidler* (1993) and *Madsen* v. *Women's Health Clinic* (1994), Clinton's solicitor general, Drew Days, successfully argued that federal racketeering laws apply to Operation Rescue and that a judge may create a buffer zone that prevents abortion protesters from blocking or interfering with public access to an abortion clinic. The Clinton administration was also successful in its 1995 efforts to block Supreme Court review of *Concerned Women for America* v. *Reno,* a First Amendment challenge to federal abortion clinic access legislation.[62]

If the Court hears another state regulation case during Clinton's presidency, there is little doubt that the administration would file an amicus brief defending abortion rights—if nothing else, to stand as a symbolic counterpoint to Reagan-Bush filings. By participating as a vigorous advocate in *all* abortion cases, the Reagan Justice Department set a precedent that is likely to be followed by future administrations, regardless of their views on abortion.

REGULATORY INITIATIVES

In abortion and elsewhere, the most potent weapon in the executive's arsenal is the president's rule-making authority. Through executive orders, agency directives, and regulations, the executive has played an instrumental role in the abortion dispute. Starting with Richard Nixon, all presidents have made use of this authority. More significantly, beginning with the Reagan administration, presidents have made aggressive use of their rule-making authority to accomplish administratively what could not be accomplished through the lawmaking process. For example, after Congress failed to act on a Reagan administration legislative proposal to bar abortion counseling at federally funded family-planning centers, Reagan's secretary of health and human services, Otis Bowen, promulgated regulations that accomplished the same goal.

The key here is that regulatory action does not require formal congressional support. Courts, moreover, are reluctant to overturn regulatory decision-making. Perceiving that "substantial deference is accorded to the interpretation of the authorizing statute by the agency authorized with administering it,"[63] courts only will overturn executive-branch interpretations that are plainly inconsistent with statutory language. Consequently, unless Congress enacts overriding legislation (which is then subject to presidential veto), executive regulations generally have the force of law. In other words, just as Congress can make law by enacting a statute, the president can exercise comparable authority by promulgating regulations.

A Reluctant White House Confronts Abortion

Prior to the Nixon administration, the White House left the abortion dispute to the states. Starting with Richard Nixon's pre-*Roe* directive "that the policy on abortions at American military bases . . . correspond with the laws of the state where those bases are located,"[64] the White House began to confront abortion in its regulatory decision-making.

Aside from its symbolic importance, the Nixon directive is instructive in understanding how a president can translate his policy preferences into regulatory action. Richard Nixon personally was opposed to abortion and, in issuing his directive, spoke about his "personal belief in the sanctity of human life— including the life of the yet unborn" as well as America's "Judeo-Christian heritage."[65] In translating these personal beliefs into public policy, Nixon recognized that, in 1971, most states severely limited abortion access. Consequently, by substituting state-law restrictions for the military's blanket rule allowing abortion, Nixon could restrict abortion access without formally imposing his personal views on military base abortions. The Nixon directive also is significant because it was consistent with the then-existing practice of leaving the regulation of abortion to the states. Indeed, despite pleas from presidential adviser Patrick Buchanan calling for a more aggressive White House role, the only other regulatory matter initiated by the White House was a telephone call from White House chief of staff John Ehrlichman to Nixon appointees in the District of Columbia City Council encouraging them to adopt restrictive antiabortion regulations.[66]

The Ford administration, following its predecessor's lead, was "reluctant to become entangled with such a volatile political issue, one that seemed to be largely outside the scope of national policy-making capabilities."[67] While Watergate had prevented the Nixon administration from gauging *Roe* v. *Wade*'s impact on federal programs, the Ford administration could not duck the abortion issue. Nevertheless, the Ford White House neither promulgated nor repealed abortion-related regulations (although it did conduct an extensive study of "direct and indirect federal funding of abortion services"). Instead, the administration allowed general counsels at affected departments and agencies to implement existing policies within the confines of *Roe*. Pretending that deciphering *Roe*'s impact was solely a question of law and not of policy, Ford informed his secretary of health, education, and welfare, Caspar Weinberger, that there "will probably be some changes in practice based on new legal advice, but not because of a change in policy."[68]

The passage of the Hyde Amendment restricting federal funding for abortions, and other congressional efforts to shape abortion decision-making, forced the executive into action. Charged with the responsibility of implementing this highly politicized legislation, the Carter administration found itself squarely in the middle of the abortion issue. Moreover, Congress had become keenly aware of executive-branch enforcement strategies.

The implementation of the Hyde Amendment fell into the hands of HEW secretary Joseph Califano. Califano, "to assure objectivity, to balance any unconscious bias [he] might harbor, and to reduce [his] vulnerability to changes of personal prejudice, assigned the actual regulation writing to individuals who did not share [his] strong views about abortion."[69] By handing off the drafting of Hyde regulations to HEW attorneys who opposed any restriction on federal funding of abortions, and by deciding not to consult the president about the regulations, Califano learned the hard way that executive-branch rule-making is an inherently political process and not a nonpartisan, objective search for Congress's true intent.

HEW's proposed 1978 regulations specified that a woman's physician could certify the existence of health risks satisfying the exemption for long-lasting physical health damage, and that reporting of rape and incest within sixty days would satisfy the amendment's stipulation that they be "reported promptly." Although the pro-choice *New York Times* complimented "Mr. Califano and his lawyers [for] hav[ing] performed admirably," the HEW regulations came under sharp attack from opponents of abortion funding, including Califano's boss, Jimmy Carter. Carter told Califano that the HEW proposal "permit[ted] too much of a chance for abuse and fraud" and said that he "want[ed] to end the Medicaid mills and stop these doctors who do nothing but perform abortions on demand all day." For Carter, Califano's claim that "what counts is what the Congressional intent is" simply was unsatisfactory.[70]

These skirmishes over Hyde Amendment enforcement reveal the obvious, that the executive has broad discretion in putting Congress's will into effect. That President Carter and his HEW secretary, both of whom opposed abortion funding, found their policy preferences frustrated by agency officials who supported abortion funding highlights the need for the president to appoint to critical decision-making roles individuals who are committed to his agenda. With that said, it is difficult to characterize Hyde Amendment enforcement as a regulatory initiative. The amendment was a congressional initiative, and HEW had no choice but to promulgate regulations administering it.

The Carter administration did play an affirmative role in changing existing policy to match its preferences on the issue of family-planning centers. This set the stage for an epic struggle between Congress, the Supreme Court, and the Reagan, Bush, and Clinton administrations.

Abortion Counseling and Presidential Authority

The battle over abortion-counseling regulations dates back to 1970, when Congress added to Title X, a comprehensive family-planning statute, an explicit prohibition against appropriating funds "where abortion is a method of family planning."[71] The task of developing specific policies and rules to implement this provision devolved upon the executive branch. The Nixon administration interpreted the funding ban "literally," prohibiting "financial support of programs in which abortions are provided." These regulations, promulgated before *Roe,* when the federal abortion controversy was dormant, prompted little reaction. When the Carter administration revised these regulations in 1981, the abortion question had clearly moved to the center stage of American political debate. The Carter administration fueled this debate by mandating that "non-directive counseling" on "pregnancy termination" and other alternative courses of action be given to women "requesting information options for the management of an unintended pregnancy."[72]

The Reagan administration vehemently opposed the Carter regulations. At first, the administration worked with Representative Jack Kemp (R-N.Y.), Senator Orrin Hatch (R-Utah) and others to legislatively prohibit recipients of family-planning funding from referring pregnant women for abortions. That measure failed, so the administration elected to override the Carter scheme through its own regulatory initiatives. On 30 July 1987, Reagan briefed right-to-life leaders about "steps that I believe represent powerful examples of what can be done now to protect the lives of unborn children," including "a restriction on the use of Federal funds for activities that advocate abortion."[73]

On 1 September 1987, proposed regulations were published. The Reagan proposal placed three controversial restrictions on funded clinics: (1) that they maintain complete physical and financial separation of federally funded activities and abortion-related activities; (2) that they not encourage, promote, or advocate abortion as a method of family planning; and (3) that they refuse to provide abortion counseling or referrals.[74] The impact of this proposal was tremendous, affecting over one-third of the total public family-planning funds (approximately $150 million per year)[75] and 3,900 clinics serving 4.3 million people.[76]

The Reagan proposal immediately was challenged in court, and the case quickly worked its way to the Supreme Court. In its Supreme Court brief and oral arguments, the Bush administration picked up where the Reagan administration had left off. Relying principally on *Harris* v. *McRae*, the government contended that the right to an abortion need not be subsidized by the state and that the regulations did not amount to an unconstitutional obstacle to the exercise of that right. The Supreme Court agreed, upholding the regulations in its May 1991 *Rust* v. *Sullivan* decision. Noting that "the government may 'make a value judgment favoring childbirth over abortion, and . . . implement that judgment by the allocation of public funds,'" the Court concluded that "the Government has not discriminated on the basis of viewpoint; it has merely chosen to fund one activity to the exclusion of the other."[77]

The Bush administration was gratified by *Rust* (especially since Bush appointee David Souter had cast the fifth and decisive vote). Congress, however, sought to overturn the regulation through a bill that would have required Title X clinics to provide a pregnant woman with counseling on all of her options, including abortion. The sponsors of the bill, which was introduced in January 1991 by Senator John Chafee (R-R.I.) and forty-five Senate co-sponsors, viewed the Reagan regulations' denial of "quality health care" to "low-income pregnant women" as "bizarre and cruel."[78]

This legislative repeal effort ultimately stalled, however. Congress then turned to the appropriations process by approving a rider that prohibited federal funding of the Reagan regulations. On 19 November 1991 President Bush vetoed the appropriations bill containing the rider. He argued that physicians were free to give a woman "complete medical information about her condition" and that the regulations were necessary to ensure that the federal family-planning program not be entangled with abortion.[79] The Bush veto sparked sharp congressional debates, but the override effort failed in the House of Representatives by 12 votes. The vote was 276 to 156.[80]

Bush's victory, however, was only to last as long as his administration. On 22 January 1993 Bill Clinton repealed the rule. Taking a swipe at the Reagan and Bush administrations for "contraven[ing] the clear intent of" Congress, which had "passed legislation to block the Gag Rule's enforcement but failed to override Presidential vetoes,"[81] Clinton suggested that he was duty bound to repeal the rule. But by pointing to the "clear intent" of the 1991 Congress, Clinton never confronted the issue of whether the Reagan-Bush rule was consistent with the desires of the Congress that had enacted Title X in 1970.

From Reform to Repeal: Foreign Aid, Fetal Tissue, and the Abortion Pill

The saga of Title X abortion-counseling restrictions reveals both the power and the ephemeral nature of executive-branch rule-making. Congress could not, and the courts would not, undo this Reagan-Bush initiative. With a single stroke of the pen, however, Bill Clinton was able to suspend the so-called "gag rule." This same scenario played itself out with Reagan-Bush regulatory initiatives prohibiting abortion counseling by organizations receiving United States Agency for International Development (USAID) funds, imposing a moratorium on federally funded fetal tissue research, and establishing an import and testing ban on the abortion pill RU-486. In each instance, the Reagan and Bush administrations promulgated the rule and successfully fended off legislative repeal and court challenges. In each instance, the Clinton administration lifted the Reagan-Bush restriction.

The USAID restriction is the first of these Reagan-Bush initiatives, predating and perhaps setting the stage for analogous Title X restrictions on family-planning counseling. Responding to pro-life objections to USAID recipients' use of USAID and private funds to support abortion research and to provide abortion-related services, the Reagan administration decided to announce dramatic changes in U.S. policy at an August 1984 International Conference on Population being held by the United Nations in Mexico City. In accord with its new policy, known as the "Mexico City Policy," the White House extended the narrowly drawn USAID abortion-funding prohibition into a policy barring all U.S. aid to international family-planning organizations that provided information on abortions.

The Mexico City Policy was subject to judicial and legislative challenge. In the courts, first the Reagan and later the Bush administration successfully fended off a challenge against the regulation of the use of private funding.[82] A fierce battle also was fought in Congress, where George Bush twice invoked his veto power to preserve the Mexico City Policy. While the policy persevered under Bush, its fate was sealed after the 1992 election. Bill Clinton repealed these "unwarranted" and "excessively broad anti-abortion conditions," claiming that "they have undermined efforts to promote safe and efficacious family planning programs in foreign nations."[83]

Hitting much closer to home, the Reagan administration in 1988 launched its most controversial antiabortion initiative by placing a moratorium on the funding of research using aborted fetal tissue. Denying funding to an NIH-approved experiment that would have transplanted human fetal tissue into the brain of a patient with Parkinson's disease, assistant HHS secretary Robert Windom cited unresolved "ethical and legal" questions. In November 1989 the moratorium was extended indefinitely—this time by Bush's secretary of health and human services, Louis Sullivan. While recognizing that the use of aborted fetal tissue "could potentially produce health benefits," Sullivan contended that "providing women the additional rationalization of directly advancing the cause of human therapeutics cannot help but tilt some already vulnerable women toward a decision to have an abortion."[84]

Sullivan's actions spurred Congress into action. The House, by a 274-to-144 margin, and Senate, by a vote of 87 to 10, approved legislative proposals to overturn the NIH ban. President Bush, as expected, vetoed the bill. One day after the veto, lawmakers in the House launched a vigorous, emotionally charged override attempt. Representative Jolene Unsoeld (D-Wash.) spoke for many others when she blasted the Bush veto as "unbelievable. . . . This President who promised to be kinder and gentler would condemn the American people to be prisoners of right-wing religious zealots fixated on women's reproductive organs."[85] Strong words, *but* the House came up fourteen votes short of the required two-thirds supermajority; the final vote was 271 to 156. With the election of Bill Clinton, the fetal tissue research debate lost almost all importance. On 22 January 1993, Clinton lifted the ban on fetal tissue research.

Medical research was again at issue in the controversy involving RU-486, popularly known as the abortion pill. In June 1989 the FDA issued an "Import Alert" banning the importation of RU-486 and directing seizure of the drug and all other unapproved abortifacient drugs.[86] In Congress, a counterattack launched in November 1990 took the form of a series of three hearings relating to RU-486 which were initiated by Representative Ron Wyden (D-Ore.) in the

Committee on Small Business's Subcommittee on Regulation, Business Opportunities, and Energy. In 1991 two pieces of legislation relating to RU-486 were introduced, and Representative Wyden held another subcommittee hearing.

The RU-486 controversy came to a head in 1992 when Leona Benten, a young social worker, attempted to enter the United States with a single dose of RU-486 that she intended to use to terminate her pregnancy. The FDA seized and detained the drug, and Benten became the center of a legal maelstrom. The U.S. District Court for the Eastern District of New York ordered the drug returned to Benten. The district court also denied the government's motion for a stay pending appeal, but the U.S. Court of Appeals issued a temporary stay, and Benten appealed to the U.S. Supreme Court to vacate the stay. While Benten awaited a decision by the Supreme Court, Representative Patricia Schroeder (D-Colo.) introduced legislation to compel the return of Benten's RU-486. Benten, however, lost before both Congress and the Court: Schroeder's bill failed, and the Supreme Court denied Benten's application to vacate the stay.[87] When she was unable to regain her dose of RU-486, Leona Benten obtained a surgical abortion.

The 1992 election of Bill Clinton heralded a new era for RU-486. Rescinding the Import Alert, Clinton directed HHS secretary Donna Shalala to "promptly assess initiatives by which the Department of Health and Human Services can promote the testing, licensing, and manufacturing in the United States of RU-486."[88] In response to this mandate, Shalala and FDA commissioner David Kessler began a dialogue with RU-486's French manufacturer, Roussel-Uclaf, which ultimately led Roussel to donate its patent on the drug without remuneration. At a 16 May 1994 press conference that included Shalala, Kessler, and pro-choice congressional leaders, it was announced: "Now this drug is going to be regulated on the basis of medical science and not politicized science."[89]

Clinton administration counteractivism has nullified the regulatory initiatives of Clinton's two Republican predecessors. In dismantling these initiatives, Clinton has certainly demonstrated the ease with which the White House can keep its regulatory house in order, especially as compared to efforts to check executive-branch rule-making through either the courts or Congress. The Clinton administration, however, has not launched regulatory initiatives of its own. Instead, Clinton administration rule-making marks a return to the pre-Reagan era: when Congress enacts or amends a statute, the administration will promulgate regulations; when Congress is silent, the administration is silent, too.

CONCLUSION

The executive's reputation for being a strong, single-minded participant in the abortion dispute is ill-deserved. The source of nearly all executive-branch initiatives on this issue is Ronald Reagan, and while George Bush was willing to fall on his sword to preserve these initiatives, no other president has been willing to vigorously use all his powers to advance his abortion agenda. Richard Nixon, Gerald Ford, and Jimmy Carter launched few abortion-related initiatives, preferring, instead, to let the states and federal courts resolve most aspects of this divisive issue. Furthermore, Bill Clinton, although sometimes perceived as a pro-choice activist, has limited his activism to nullifying Reagan-Bush initiatives. This pattern is likely to continue. With the Supreme Court carving out a middle-ground position on abortion in *Planned Parenthood* v. *Casey*, the White House has little to gain by staking out a hard-line position on abortion.

Nevertheless, since Reagan, presidents have articulated a clear position on the rightness or wrongness of *Roe*. Whereas Congress, because of party affiliations and the unlikelihood of unifying 535 members, cannot speak with a single voice, presidents are empowered to take advantage of the bully pulpit that is unique to their office. Carter did not take advantage of this bully pulpit. His regulatory appointees often disagreed with his moderately pro-life positions, and the end result was policy discord that wound up alienating both pro-choice and pro-life interests. Ronald Reagan and his regulatory appointees, in contrast, spoke in harmony and set the tone for future administrations.

The question then becomes, how will the executive make use of its power? It is important to recognize the extraordinary range of options available to the executive in the face of a Supreme Court decision with which it disagrees. The White House may recommend antiabortion legislation (and constitutional amendments) to Congress, appoint judges and federal officials who oppose *Roe*, file briefs and argue cases, condition approval of legislation on the inclusion of antiabortion language, and promulgate and implement regulations.

Deciphering why some administrations make fuller use of these powers than others is quite another matter. One explanation, suggested by presidential scholar Terry Eastland, is that most presidents are risk averse; they "hoard popularity for the sake of reelection," even though "opinion polls, and reelections are not the measure of a strong presidency."[90] There is a kernel of truth here. Richard Nixon sometimes was advised to jump into and at other times was urged to stay away from the abortion fray, for no reason other than political gain. Gerald Ford's 1976 election campaign also looked at the abortion issue in such pragmatic terms. Bill Clinton's characterization of abortion as a "political football" in the health care debates also fits this pattern.

Likewise, Ronald Reagan and George Bush aggressively pursued the abortion issue, in part for political gain. The impetus for Reagan's July 1987 meeting with right-to-life leaders and the accompanying announcement of his abortion-counseling policy, for example, was the desire to soothe relationships between the president and his pro-life political allies in the wake of the dismissal of pro-life activist Jo Ann Gasper. More strikingly, George Bush's opposition to *Roe* originated when he became Ronald Reagan's 1980 running mate. Prior to that time, Bush had distinguished himself from Reagan by supporting *Roe*.

That Reagan and Bush sought political advantage through the vigorous pursuit of their antiabortion agenda, of course, does not mean that moral conviction played no role in their decision-making. Nonetheless, with the Supreme Court's *Casey* decision, it appears less likely that future administrations will so stridently advance their views on abortion. While Ronald Reagan's defeat of Jimmy Carter points to the importance of the president and his appointees' sharing a cohesive vision on the abortion issue, the policies and practices of the Clinton administration suggest that the executive will pursue its abortion agenda in less obvious and less vigorous ways than did the Reagan and Bush administrations. Rather than engage in divisive rhetoric or initiate pro-choice initiatives comparable to its predecessors' pro-life initiatives, the Clinton administration is advancing its agenda through pro-choice appointments, through the dismantling of Reagan-Bush programs, and through its day-to-day administration of the regulatory state.

Clinton's strategy, while more subtle than that of his predecessors, is hardly a harkening back to the pre-Reagan era. Unlike Nixon and Ford, for example, Clinton does not maintain that a president's personal views on abortion should not translate into federal abortion policy. Moreover, with the exponential growth of post-*Roe* legislative and executive abortion initiatives, presidents simply cannot avoid playing a significant role in the administration of these programs.

Clinton's approach also may prove to be the model for future administrations. The *Casey* decision, while it may not completely bridge the gap between pro-choice and pro-life interests, is far less divisive than *Roe*. Consequently, there is little political incentive for the executive to risk alienating significant portions of the electorate by aggressively pursuing a hard-line abortion policy.

8 / What the Abortion Debate Teaches Us about American Politics

THE ABORTION DISPUTE REVEALS THAT the shaping of constitutional values is a dynamic process in which the courts, the executive, and the legislature at both the federal and state level engage in a dialogue with each other. The Supreme Court has moderated *Roe*'s stringent trimester standard thanks to judicial appointments made by the president and confirmed by the Senate, amicus filings by the solicitor general and by congressional interests, and state legislators whose willingness to legislatively challenge *Roe* has created repeated opportunities for the Court to fine-tune its abortion doctrine. With *Webster* and *Casey*, the Court recognizes that state legislatures and courts likely will play the pivotal role in defining the reaches and limits of abortion rights. These decisions, moreover, shifted to Congress and the White House the decision to nationalize more extensive abortion rights through the Freedom of Choice Act and other legislative proposals.

Congress and the White House also have shaped abortion rights and participated in a dialogue with the courts and each other through legislative enactments and administrative rule-making. Congress puts into law a vision of constitutional meaning whenever it enacts abortion-related legislation; the executive participates through the president's signing (or refusing to sign) this legislation and through the Justice Department's defending (or refusing to defend) these measures; and the courts, finally, adjudicate constitutional challenges to these enactments. Administrative rule-making follows a similar interactive course. Agency heads engage in constitutional interpretation when promulgating regulations; the executive defends these regulations in court and fends off congressional attacks through testimony and—if need be—the veto power. Congress also participates in rule-making through its confirmation of agency heads, oversight of governmental programs, and amicus filings in court, and occasionally through legislation to moderate disfavored initiatives. The courts, finally, have entered the fray through decisions concerning the scope of executive power to interpret vague statutory language.

The dialectic between courts, agencies, and lawmakers appears never-ending. The Supreme Court's approval of legislative and executive action does not put an end to elected-branch involvement. Congress expressed its displeasure with the Court's approval of the Reagan-Bush family-planning rule in *Rust* v. *Sullivan* by statutorily prohibiting the rule's implementation, only to have the president successfully veto that statute. With the election of Bill Clinton, moreover, Congress moderated abortion-funding restrictions; and the Clinton administration repudiated Reagan- and Bush-era regulations. These policy reversals, especially Clinton administration actions, are rooted in elected officials' changing constitutional values in addition to their political leanings.

States, too, need not approve Supreme Court decision-making that validates their lawmaking authority. In the wake of *Webster* and *Casey,* five states expressed disapproval of those decisions by liberalizing their abortion statutes. Furthermore, state courts regularly interpret state constitutional provisions as providing greater protections than are offered by the U.S. Constitution.

This dynamic is pervasive. It clearly shows the judiciary to be one part of a constitutional dialogue that involves all of government. The abortion dispute is instructive for other reasons. Two decades of repeated volleys between the executive, legislative, and judicial branches of both state and federal government reveal a great deal about the American governmental and political processes. Prior chapters have focused principally on the powers of elected government to either support or oppose the Supreme Court's abortion jurisprudence. This chapter will shift the focus away from the identification of elected-government authority and towards the lessons the abortion dispute teaches us about American politics. Specifically, this chapter will extend earlier chapters' studies of Congress, the executive, and the states, by examining in greater detail the seriousness with which elected government approaches constitutional issues; the reasons why elected government regularly makes use of some but not all of its powers to shape constitutional disputes; and the impact of single-issue politics on political institutions. While some of these issues have been considered before, this chapter will provide a fuller and more focused treatment of elected-branch constitutional interpretation and especially abortion's impact on the governmental process.

THE SERIOUSNESS WITH WHICH ELECTED BRANCHES
UNDERTAKE INTERPRETATION

Does elected government take seriously its responsibility as constitutional interpreter? After all, lawmakers and regulators might simply pursue whatever policies serve their political interests, leaving constitutional questions to the courts. Alternatively, lawmakers and regulators could invest great time and energy in determining what is and is not constitutional. The abortion dispute suggests that the truth lies somewhere in between. Sorting out why some but not all matters are given serious attention is useful in understanding both the abortion dispute and the American system. This is an inquiry that applies with equal force to the Congress, the executive, and the states.

Before turning to the specifics of abortion-related constitutional interpretation, a confession is in order. While it is relatively simple to ascertain the number of constitutional experts testifying at congressional hearings, the frequency with which elected officials invoked the Constitution in defending or attacking bills or regulations, and the like, it is next to impossible to ascertain whether these constitutional pronouncements are part of a forthright search for constitutional truth or, instead, whether the Constitution is being used as a smoke-screen for overriding policy concerns. Yet, in certain instances, it does seem likely that elected government is concerned about the constitutionality of its endeavors. When legislators or regulators moderate their proposals in the face of constitutional objections, for example, it seems likely that these adjustments are intended to shore up the constitutional foundations of their work-product (although such adjustments may simply be intended to help ensure a bill's passage or a regulation's promulgation by undermining opponents' attacks). More striking are instances where pro-life or pro-choice legislators either defend the constitutionality of measures they oppose or, alternatively, reject on constitutional grounds abortion measures that match their policy preferences (although these episodes are so rare that they border on nonexistent).

Most of the time, however, the sincerity of elected-branch proclamations is harder to gauge. For example, it is hardly surprising that pro-choice legislators and regulators claim that human life legislation is unconstitutional and that the Freedom of Choice Act is constitutional, despite the fact that both measures are rooted in Congress's authority to enforce the Fourteenth Amendment. For similar reasons, pro-lifers' alternating invocations of the First Amendment, either to support abortion-counseling regulations or to oppose clinic access legislation, are suspect. Nonetheless, in spite of the speculativeness of the undertaking ahead, some tentative conclusions can be reached about the seriousness with which elected branches undertake constitutional interpretation. The focus of attention here will be Congress and the executive.

Congress and the Constitution

The most visible, most observed, and most criticized elected-branch player is Congress. Committee hearings and reports, floor debates, and amicus filings call attention to the seriousness with which Congress approaches the task of constitutional interpretation. Congress has made variable use of these tools in its consideration of abortion-related issues. Little to no attention was paid to constitutional concerns when Congress enacted the Hyde Amendment and the Adolescent Family Life Act. In contrast, constitutional concerns have figured prominently in constitutional amendment proposals, court-stripping proposals, the Human Life Act, the Freedom of Choice Act, and clinic access legislation.

AFLA and the Hyde Amendment support Owen Fiss's observation that legislators are uninterested in the "search for the meaning of constitutional values, but instead see their primary function in terms of registering the actual, occurrent preferences of the people."[1] AFLA and the Hyde Amendment each raised serious constitutional concerns—AFLA because it favored religions that disapprove of abortion, and the Hyde Amendment because it limits the availability of abortions. In each instance, these challenges were sustained by lower federal courts only to be overturned by bare five-member majorities of the Supreme Court.[2] Congress, however, appeared indifferent to constitutional concerns when enacting these measures.

AFLA originated in the Senate Labor and Human Resources Committee. Hearings held in March 1981 featured the testimony of economists, physicians, child psychologists, and sociologists but no constitutional scholars.[3] Likewise, the committee report makes no mention of constitutional issues.[4] Indeed, when AFLA was reauthorized in 1984, Congress seemed little concerned with the fact that a constitutional challenge had been launched against the measure. Subcommittee chair Jeremiah Denton (R-Ala.) simply noted that "the courts will have to decide whether the law as passed by Congress is constitutional. The task before the subcommittee and the Congress is to oversee the activities of the current act and to see that the intent of the law is being carried out."[5]

Congress did not hold hearings or prepare a report when it enacted the Hyde Amendment. Introduced on the House floor, the amendment was subject to prolonged, fierce, and emotional debate. While amendment supporters occasionally criticized *Roe* as "mistaken and immoral," and opponents suggested that Congress's refusal "to pay for something guaranteed by the Constitution" is itself unconstitutional, these references were rare and never rose above the level of rhetoric.[6] Constitutional concerns figured more prominently when the Hyde Amendment went before the Supreme Court. A bipartisan coalition of more than two hundred members of Congress, including members who had voted against the amendment, filed an amicus brief defending Congress's right not to spend money under the appropriations power.[7]

In contrast to AFLA and the Hyde Amendment, constitutional concerns played a highly visible role in early 1980s attacks on *Roe*. Republican control of both the White House and the Senate after the 1980 election empowered pro-life forces. Human life legislation, court-stripping proposals, and constitutional amendment proposals were all under active consideration by the Senate Judiciary Committee in 1981. In each case, there were extensive hearings dominated by constitutional law experts. Committee and subcommittee reports, too, were replete with citations to this expert testimony as well as Supreme Court decisions and law review articles.[8] Unlike the Labor and Human Resources Committee's handling of AFLA, the Senate Judiciary Committee's behavior seemed to show a keen interest in separation of powers and in constitutional interpretation concerns.

Differences between these two committees are to be expected. Unlike AFLA, where Congress used funding as a mechanism for abortion regulation, the early 1980s proposals directly challenged both the correctness of *Roe* and the propriety of judicial involvement in the abortion dispute. Constitutional concerns could not be easily brushed aside in this context.

Moreover, the Judiciary Committee's variable treatment of court stripping, human life legislation, and constitutional amendment proposals supports its reputation as a "Committee of Lawyers" that reacts to constitutional questions "in a very judicial, courtlike fashion."[9] For example, in studies comparing the Senate and House judiciary committees (virtually all of whose members are lawyers) to other congressional committees, political scientists—including Roger Davidson, Larry Evans, and Mark Miller—have found that the judiciary committees are far more aware of Supreme Court rulings and, correspondingly, far less willing to enact legislation that is inconsistent with Court decision-making. Exemplifying Richard Fenno's claim that "committees differ," a "good legal argument [not power] wins on Judiciary"; and judiciary committees "consume a substantial amount of time debating the constitutionality of the legislation that they approve."[10] Furthermore, through Supreme Court confirmation hearings, Senate Judiciary Committee members are called upon to interrogate nominees and constitutional experts about vagaries in constitutional doctrine and judicial philosophy.

All of this is not to say that the judiciary committees are not results-oriented in their approach to constitutional interpretation. When the Republicans controlled the Senate and the White House in the early 1980s, the House Judiciary Committee dedicated itself to blocking Reagan's conservative social agenda. Indeed, since 1976 the House Judiciary Committee has steered clear of pro-life efforts to moderate or reverse *Roe* through legislation or constitutional amendment. During the Bush presidency, moreover, Democratic leadership in both House and Senate Judiciary Committees fought off a constitutional amendment proposal on flag burning by embracing a clearly unconstitutional statutory alternative.

Conservative Republicans on Judiciary also have played fast and loose with constitutional interpretation. For example, when the Senate Judiciary Committee was considering highly controversial and constitutionally suspect human life legislation, constitutional law experts were initially excluded from Republican-controlled hearings. After several protesters were arrested for disrupting hearings dominated by pro-life medical witnesses, "extensive and exhaustive hearings [were arranged] so that all points of view ultimately and finally [were] heard."[11] Despite these blemishes, the House and Senate Judiciary Committees have invested significant time and effort exploring the constitutionality of proposed abortion-related measures.

Early 1980s attacks on *Roe* exemplify these committees' reputation as "committee[s] of lawyers." Court-stripping proposals, which were savaged as an inappropriate and unconstitutional interference with a co-equal branch by most constitutional experts and by Reagan's attorney general William French Smith, never emerged from committee. Proposed human life legislation also raised questions about Congress's constitutional authority to respond to court decisions. Subcommittee chair Senator John East (R-N.C.) believed that Congress was constitutionally empowered to find that life begins at conception and to enforce that finding through legislation; Orrin Hatch (R-Utah), although strongly opposed to *Roe*, concluded that Congress's authority under section 5 of the Fourteenth Amendment does not include the establishment of substantive rights; Max Baucus (D-Mont.) argued that Congress can establish rights but cannot statutorily overturn Supreme Court decisions. East, Hatch, and Baucus all made the assessment of Congress's authority the centerpiece of their remarks, and made ample references to case law and the testimony of constitutional experts.

The Human Life Act never made it to the floor of Congress; the full Senate Judiciary Committee, instead, focused its efforts on a proposed constitutional amendment to return the abortion issue to the states. This alternative was favored for three reasons. First, it is beyond dispute that Congress may initiate a constitutional amendment to overturn a Supreme Court decision. Second, unlike statutory court-stripping and human life proposals, which are easily characterized as legislative powergrabs, constitutional amendment proposals express disapproval of *Roe* without challenging judicial independence. Third, "without actually moving to outlaw abortion," the federalism amendment enabled Congress to "demonstrate their concern about *[Roe]*, while at the same time disposing of this troublesome issue by throwing it back to the states."[12]

Constitutional concerns figured prominently in Senate consideration of the federalism amendment. Subcommittee hearings included several constitutional experts who discussed both the soundness of *Roe* and the appropriateness of checking the court through a constitutional amendment.[13] The Judiciary Committee, which voted 10 to 7 to report the amendment out, likewise addressed these constitutional interpretation and structure-of-government concerns in its report.[14] Floor debates on the amendment, although varied, also considered the correctness of *Roe* as a matter of constitutional interpretation.

Constitutional concerns also have played a large role in Congress's consideration of post-*Webster* pro-choice initiatives, especially the Freedom of Choice Act and the Freedom of Access to Clinic Entrances Act. Not only were constitutional concerns canvassed at congressional hearings and discussed in committee reporters but FOCA and FACE sponsors (up to a point) heeded constitutional objections and modified their handiwork to meet some of these criticisms.

FOCA's original sponsors, anticipating the Supreme Court's eventual overturning of *Roe*, sought to codify abortion rights under Congress's authority to enforce the Fourteenth Amendment. Because it did not explicitly recognize the rights of parents to participate in the abortion decision or the power of states to refuse to pay for abortions, however, the bill was attacked by President Bush and others for "going well beyond even *Roe* versus *Wade*."[15] FOCA's exclusive reliance on section 5 of the Fourteenth Amendment also proved problematic, since pro-choice legislators had earlier condemned human life legislation for using section 5 to balance fetal interests against a woman's right to choose. FOCA sponsors responded to these two charges. First, while not answering all of the Bush administration's criticisms, they modified the bill to recognize parental rights and state funding authority. Second, the Commerce Clause was listed as an additional source of congressional authority to enact

FOCA. Indeed, as was true with the 1964 Civil Rights Act's public accommo-dations provisions, the Commerce Clause eclipsed section 5 as the principal justification for the measure. Committee reports, sponsor statements, and pro-FOCA constitutional experts spoke first of Congress's commerce authority.

FACE also underwent significant changes in response to constitutional objections raised by opponents of the act. The original version of FACE, while imposing penalties on any person who intimidates, interferes with, or physi-cally obstructs access to abortion services, never included a definition section defining the terms "interfere with," "intimidates," and "physical obstruction." FACE critics, including constitutional experts Michael McConnell and Michael Paulsen, said that these undefined terms were "imprecise and unconstitution-ally overbroad, [and] could be construed to include much entirely lawful con-duct."[16] FACE sponsors took some of these criticisms to heart and amended the statute by including a definitions section. While some sponsors claimed that this modification was superfluous,[17] other members cited the change in the defini-tions sections as critical to their vote. Senator David Durenberger (R-Minn.), for example, explained that the committee "had made several important changes to the bill since its introduction in March 1993 that had gone a long way toward addressing [his] concerns and the concerns of some of [his] colleagues."[18]

FACE, FOCA, and the antiabortion initiatives of the early 1980s demon-strate Congress's awareness of the critical importance of constitutional inter-pretation to abortion-related issues. Critics of Congress are unimpressed by this constitutional exegesis. Paul Brest, for example, argues that the legislative history of the Human Life Bill reveals that constitutional complications are typically raised by bill opponents as "rhetorical stratagems" and that propo-nents sought to stack the hearing with pro-life witnesses and eventually drafted a "Subcommittee report [which] reads more like an advocate's brief than a judicial opinion."[19] The fact remains, however, that many abortion opponents disapproved of human life legislation and court-stripping legislation as a con-stitutionally inappropriate substitution of legislative for judicial authority. Along the same lines, abortion rights supporters defended the Hyde Amend-ment as a constitutionally permissible exercise of the appropriations power.

The Executive and the Constitution

Measuring the seriousness of executive-branch interpretation of the Con-stitution is quite a different matter from discerning Congress's seriousness. Part of the problem is that, unlike Congress, the executive often is obligated to ad-vance a constitutional argument. When a lawsuit is filed challenging the constitutionality of congressional or executive action, for example, Justice Department attorneys have no choice but to file a brief defending governmental conduct. Similarly, when Justice Department officials are asked to share their views about the constitutionality of proposed legislation with Congress, the executive must articulate its constitutional views. Some conclusions, however, can be reached both about the executive's approach to these tasks and about the executive's interest in constitutional analysis on other abortion-related measures.

Before Congress, executive-branch witnesses seem quite willing to spin their interpretations of statutory language and Supreme Court precedent to suit their policy preferences. Bush's attorney general William Barr, for example, criticized FOCA sponsors' claims that the act did no more than codify Court-recognized abortion rights.[20] Barr and his assistant attorney general John Harrison also challenged FOCA on constitutional grounds. Harrison testified before Congress "that there is considerable doubt whether Congress can enact the proposed ban on State anti-abortion legislation [FOCA] under section 5 of the Fourteenth Amendment" and "that the basic principle of federalism . . . would be severely damaged by the enactment of legislation of this kind."[21] The testimony about FACE by Clinton's attorney general, Janet Reno, paralleled Barr and Harrison's approach in style, if not ideology. Reno defended FACE against opponents' claims that the statute would criminalize abortion clinic protests by narrowly construing provisions of the act. Reno also defended FACE against First Amendment objections, saying, "It does not target conduct on the basis of its expressive content."[22]

Policy preferences undoubtedly played a large role in Reno, Harrison, and Barr's testimony. Partisanship, however, is not the only factor at play in Justice Department testimony. Legal positions at odds with policy preferences, while sometimes obscured by predominant policy objectives, are nonetheless expressed. Reagan's attorneys general William French Smith and Edwin Meese both found court-stripping proposals designed to nullify abortion and school prayer decisions unconstitutional. Likewise, Janet Reno's FACE testimony noted that, while the Commerce Clause provided Congress with ample authority to enact clinic access legislation, Congress's power to enact FACE "pursuant to Section 5 of the Fourteenth Amendment is less clear."[23] Moreover, the Justice Department sometimes admits that disfavored legislation may well be constitutional. This is precisely what occurred with FOCA. John Harrison specifically recognized that Supreme Court Commerce Clause decisions "gave Congress broad power, and that at least some legislation concerning abortion could be grounded in that power."[24] Although Harrison and Reno's constitutional confessions played a less prominent role than did other parts of their testimony, it seems clear that Justice Department testimony is not exclusively animated by policy preferences.

Beyond its efforts to influence congressional decision-making, the executive, through amicus curiae briefs and judicial appointments, also has sought to transform Supreme Court doctrine. For the Reagan administration, *Roe* epitomized "everything that had gone wrong in law, particularly constitutional law."[25] Amicus curiae briefs attacking *Roe,* and the appointment of Robert Bork and judges unwilling "to create new constitutional rights out of thin air,"[26] advanced the administration's vision of judicial authority in a democratic society.

Too much should not be read into the Reagan administration experience, however. Reagan's philosophy of judging matched his social agenda so closely that policy concerns undoubtedly played a pivotal role in the development and articulation of his judicial philosophy. Reagan, moreover, did not always follow his own script. His nomination of Sandra Day O'Connor, for example, had very little to do with ideology. The appointment, instead, was largely a by-product of his stated commitment to appoint the first woman to the Supreme Court. Needless to say, presidents who were less ideological have been less committed to advancing a judicial philosophy through their Supreme Court appointments. George Bush's nomination of David Souter and Bill Clinton's selection of Stephen Breyer, for example, had as much to do with ease of confirmation as with constitutional principle. However, it would be wrong to dismiss an administration's vision of the Court's role in government as nothing more than a smokescreen to hide its social agenda. The Reagan administration, at least, proved willing to spend some political capital and to open itself up to academic and editorial criticism for articulating its judicial philosophy.

When promulgating regulations, the executive is cautious in interpreting its authority under the Constitution. The debate within the Reagan administration over abortion-counseling regulations is a good example of this caution. Although pro-life interests within the White House's domestic policy shop sought a blanket prohibition of the awarding of federal funding to organizations that perform abortions, attorneys for the Office of Legal Counsel and the White House Counsel's Office feared that this proposal would not withstand judicial attack. Instead, they narrowed the funding ban—prohibiting the use of federal funds to support abortion counseling *but* allowing fund recipients to use private funds to perform abortions at separate facilities. This caution paid off; a bare five-member Supreme Court majority approved the restrictions.

Rule-making's special status is due to the fact that it is consequential and discretionary. In contrast, congressional testimony is less consequential and

Justice Department briefs and arguments less discretionary. Specifically, when defending an existing law or regulation in court, the executive has no choice but to advance whatever constitutional theory will support that government policy. Moreover, when presenting its views before Congress, the executive is not the principal decision-maker but is one (albeit the most important) of several interests presenting their views. In plain terms, only when crafting regulations is the executive fully accountable for the content of governmental action.

Whatever one's assessment of the seriousness with which Congress and the executive undertake constitutional interpretation, it is remarkable that the undisputed benchmark of seriousness is fidelity to Supreme Court decision-making. The judiciary committees are understood to take constitutional interpretation seriously because they are keenly interested in whether the Court will uphold their actions and are therefore willing to moderate the legislation they produce. Much the same can be said of executive-branch action. Justice Department testimony and rule-making takes constitutional interpretation seriously when it honors the parameters established by the Supreme Court. Indeed, even efforts to change Court decision-making through judicial nominations and briefs are premised on the belief that it is Court decision-making that matters.

This view is so prevalent that neither executive-branch officials nor legislators take and defend constitutional positions at odds with those taken by the Supreme Court. When Bush administration officials testified against FOCA, for example, they never forthrightly called upon Congress to embrace a theory of federalism at odds with Supreme Court pronouncements. Within Congress, only John East spoke of Congress's authority to independently interpret the Constitution, but his subcommittee report on human life legislation nonetheless emphasized Supreme Court decision-making.

Court rulings are sufficiently open-ended that they present plenty of fodder for both pro-choice and pro-life forces. Indeed, Supreme Court decisions were invoked by both supporters and opponents of every bill, amendment, and regulation referred to in this section. The fact remains, however, that both sides of any given issue perceive that their constitutional arguments will be taken seriously only if those arguments are built around Court doctrine.

ELECTED GOVERNMENT'S RESPONSES TO COURT ABORTION RULINGS

Patterns of congressional and White House responses to *Roe* have emerged over the past twenty years. Congress and the executive make use of different types of powers at different moments (i.e., before judicial action, during adjudication, and after judicial action). Moreover, congressional and White House actions also speak to elected government's willingness (or unwillingness) to address the correctness of *Roe* v. *Wade*. Congressional opposition to *Roe* has been expressed principally in prohibitions of funding, many of which must be reenacted every year. Constitutional amendments, court stripping, and statutory repeal have been rejected. When Congress acts to support abortion rights, moreover, it typically acts to rein in either the executive, for a regulation it disapproves; or the courts, for a statutory interpretation that it disfavors. Constitutional amendments or statutory language asserting the correctness of *Roe* have been eschewed. Since Ronald Reagan's 1980 election, the presidency has made use of all the weapons available to it to advance its pro-choice or pro-life positions. Judicial and administrative appointments, legislative initiatives, the veto power, rule-making, and the bully pulpit head the list of these presidential tools. But in the 1990s the vigor of presidential advocacy appears to have been moderated by *Planned Parenthood* v. *Casey*'s embrace of a middle-ground approach to abortion regulation.

Congress's mixed approach and its heavy reliance on appropriations-based policy-making are quite understandable. Appropriations measures are preferred to constitutional amendments and direct statutory repeals because they are easier to enact. In addition to earmarking or threatening to cut off an agency's funds, Congress frequently expresses policy preferences through limitations riders introduced on the House or Senate floor while an appropriations bill is under consideration. These riders have had tremendous impact. Military activities in Southeast Asia, public funding of abortion, air bags for automobiles, foreign assistance to Nicaraguan Contras, tax exemptions for discriminatory schools, religious activities in public schools, and public funding of school desegregation are but some of the areas affected by such riders.

Take the case of the Hyde Amendment. Antiabortion forces, unable to get proposals for statutes and constitutional amendments out of committee, turned their attention to appropriations-based policy-making. Since appropriations must be enacted every year, antiabortion forces were able to compel a majority vote in favor of or opposed to Medicaid funding. That Congress would approve such a funding ban is hardly surprising. A ban on public funding leaves the individual's right to abortion intact and hence appears to be a moderate response. Congress's decision not to finance an activity that many find morally reprehensible does not necessarily call into question the correctness of *Roe;* instead, the decision not to appropriate funds is part and parcel of Congress's power of the purse. It is also—because of the single-year nature of appropriations—a decision with a limited shelf life and great opportunity for repeated fine tuning. Direct legislative repeals, in contrast, are uncompromising, and thus the political costs of supporting such measures are great. Congress, on issues as sharply divisive as abortion, has strong incentives not to prompt the ire of losers by making decisions that are too decisive or too final.

Congress's management of the administrative state also reveals the prevalence of appropriations-based policy-making. Due to an "increasing tendency for legislatures to prescribe administrative organization, procedures, and programs in greater detail,"[27] Congress often asserts control over federal departments and agencies through the "purse strings" of government. Unlike other types of oversight, which usually rely on the *threat* of direct action, appropriations *are* direct action. As the Senate Committee on Governmental Affairs concluded: "Appropriations oversight is effective precisely because the statutory controls are so direct, unambiguous, and virtually self-enforcing. . . . The dollar figures in appropriations bills represent commands which cannot be bent or ignored except at extreme peril to agency officials."[28] In the abortion context, Congress turned to the appropriations process to check perceived executive abuses. Lawmakers approved appropriations riders to block Reagan administration abortion-counseling, international family-planning, and fetal tissue research initiatives (only to be thwarted by Bush vetoes).

This recourse to the appropriations process epitomizes Congress's penchant to duck the ultimate question of whether *Roe* was rightly or wrongly decided. Legislation to reverse Reagan-era antiabortion initiatives follows a similar pattern. Designed to check a too-aggressive executive, these measures are classic exercises of Congress's oversight authority. Along the same lines, when Congress passes a law revising the Supreme Court's declaration that civil rights protections do not extend to pregnancy discrimination or, in response to the Supreme Court's *Bray* v. *Alexandria Women's Health Clinic* decision, enacts legislation on abortion clinic access, it is simply checking what it perceives to be the Court's misinterpretation of statutory language. In both instances, Congress was playing a reactive role, one in which the political costs of acting are kept to a minimum. For similar reasons, Congress has rejected constitutional amendments, human life legislation, and the Freedom of Choice Act. Recognizing that the decisional costs of a direct affirmation or repudiation of *Roe* are much greater than those of indirect measures, Congress has avoided absolutist approaches to the abortion dispute.

White House decision-making has been calibrated much differently than has congressional decision-making. Rather than play a reactive role, Reagan, Bush, and (albeit to a lesser extent) Clinton all have been activists. Reagan's antiabortion speeches and regulatory agenda, Bush's defense of that agenda in court and through the veto, and Clinton's immediate dismantling of Reagan-Bush programs exemplify the White House's commitment to vigorous and strident leadership on the abortion question. This activism—like Congress's decision to minimize decisional costs—is pragmatic. Unwilling to alienate both pro-choice and pro-life interests with a Carteresque middle-ground strategy, the White House aligns itself with one or the other set of interest groups in the abortion dispute.

Starting with the 1980 election of Ronald Reagan, for example, every president has subscribed to a substantive theory of abortion rights and has been willing to back up that theory with Supreme Court filings and arguments. While the theories of pro-choice and pro-life administrations are incompatible with each other, the singular nature of the presidency now demands that the executive embrace one theory or the other. On questions of presidential authority, moreover, pro-choice and pro-life administrations have advanced similar arguments. The Reagan, Bush, and Clinton administrations all have endorsed broad executive-branch authority to interpret vague legislative mandates. By promulgating, defending in court, and repealing executive-initiated regulations, these administrations have broadly construed their rule-making authority.

Congress's tendency to be reactive and diffuse, in contrast to the competing executive tendency to endorse one or the other side, is critically important in understanding the abortion dispute. The executive's comparative advantage here, however, now appears ready to give way to political pragmatism. In the wake of *Casey*, the benefits of a hard-line position on abortion are less apparent. More precisely, since the Court has committed itself to and public opinion strongly supports a middle-ground approach to state regulatory authority, the White House must carefully consider the risks of both making waves in calm seas and diverting scarce resources away from other policy areas.

INSTITUTIONAL CONCERNS

The abortion dispute has exacted a heavy price from all three branches of the federal government. Specifically, abortion's dominance as a single-issue concern has subordinated competing and otherwise relevant concerns that influence decision-making by Congress and the executive. Abortion's dominance has also altered public perceptions of the Supreme Court, if not the Court's perception of itself. Without doubt, as the political scientist Gilbert Steiner put it, "any tendency to engage in the abortion dispute in a manner that distorts the functioning of government institutions is . . . deplorable, perhaps intolerable."[29] Nonetheless, the abortion controversy has created just such distortions in function.

The nomination and confirmation of federal court judges, especially Supreme Court justices, is the most obvious example of how the abortion issue displaces other concerns. Since Ronald Reagan, presidents have been under great pressure to use support or opposition to abortion as a "litmus test" in the judicial selection process. Reagan-era judicial nominees "were asked directly about their views on abortion"; one appeals court nominee was withdrawn after it became known that he had contributed to Planned Parenthood;[30] and pro-life interests vetoed the planned nomination of federal appeals court judge Patrick Higgenbotham to the Supreme Court because in one of his opinions—albeit reluctantly—he recognized *Roe* to be the law of the land.[31] The Clinton administration appears no different. Candidate Bill Clinton stated "that a judge ought to be able to answer a question in a Senate hearing, 'Do you or do you not support the right to privacy, including the right to choose'" and asserted that those he appointed to the Supreme Court "will be strong supporters of *Roe* v. *Wade*."[32] With respect to his Supreme Court nominee Ruth Bader Ginsburg, Clinton commented that her writings suggested that she was pro-choice, and that was "the important thing."[33]

The abortion issue has, on occasion, dominated other areas of executive-judicial relations. Abortion, for example, played a prominent role in the staffing of the Justice Department's Office for Legal Policy (charged with judicial selection) and the solicitor general's office. Rex Lee resigned as solicitor general after Reagan's first term, in part, because of his unwillingness to respond to administration-condoned interest group pressure and ask the Supreme Court to overturn *Roe* and other disfavored rulings. More striking, the nomination of Charles Fried to succeed Lee was made contingent on Fried's seeking *Roe*'s reversal as acting solicitor general.[34]

Abortion likewise has affected legislative-judicial relations, becoming the pivotal issue in Senate Judiciary Committee confirmation hearings. Starting with the 1981 nomination of Sandra Day O'Connor, committee questioning and reports bespeak an obsession with right-to-privacy concerns. "The harsh reality," as Senate majority leader George Mitchell (D-Maine) put it in 1991, "is that the politics of abortion now dominates the process of filling vacancies to the Supreme Court."[35] Since the Bork nomination, the Judiciary Committee has made clear to nominees that a willingness to embrace the right to privacy and a respect for *stare decisis* is a prerequisite for the job. While the 1994 confirmation of Stephen Breyer suggests that abortion's dominance may be on the wane, there is reason to think that future nominees will be asked to profess allegiance to *Roe* itself or to proclaim their willingness to preserve *Roe* under the doctrine of *stare decisis*.

Abortion also has proven surprisingly critical to Congress's annual enactment of the federal budget. Technically, House and Senate rules preclude substantive policy-making through appropriation bills. This distinction between authorizations and appropriations is designed to ensure both that fiscal policy concerns dominate debates over the budget and that committees with expertise in particular areas screen authorization legislation in those areas. The Hyde Amendment reveals the limits of the appropriations-authorizations distinction and, with it, the impossibility of confining appropriations to fiscal policy matters. First enacted in 1976, the Hyde Amendment has proven a permanent and destabilizing force in appropriations policy-making. Debate over the fiscal year 1977 rider lasted eleven weeks, with dozens of compromise proposals on the floor. The fiscal year 1978 stalemate was worse, lasting more than five months. Debates over the Hyde Amendment and other abortion-related riders remain contentious. In 1989 the appropriations process was delayed by skirmishes between the White House and Congress over the sweep of abortion-funding prohibitions. In 1993, amidst procedural maneuvering and acrimony, Congress passed and President Clinton signed a modified Hyde measure.

The disruption caused by these battles demonstrates the potentially debilitating impact of appropriations-based policy initiatives on Congress's ability to perform essential legislative functions. Congress is well aware of these costs. As early as a 1946 report by the Joint Committee on the Organization of Congress, Congress is on record opposing appropriations riders because they obstruct and retard the debate on appropriations.[36] Hyde-type riders are problematic for other reasons. As initially proposed, the first Hyde Amendment would have prohibited the use of funds "to perform abortions except where the life of the mother would be endangered if the fetus were carried to term."[37] The chair upheld a point of order on this: because the administrative agency would have taken on a new duty by ascertaining whether the mother could safely carry the fetus to term, the amendment constituted substantive legislation in an appropriations bill, a practice forbidden by House rules.[38] A point of order also was sustained on a subsequently offered amendment that would have prohibited funding "except where a physician has certified the abortion is necessary to save the life of the mother."[39] To avoid such problems, the amendment was modified: "None of the funds appropriated under this Act shall be used to pay for abortions or to promote or encourage abortions."[40] Representative Hyde, regretful that he had to omit the exception for therapeutic abortions, claimed that he had been "forced into this position today by points of order."[41]

Abortion, finally, has transformed interest group advocacy before the Supreme Court. When *Roe* was argued, ten amicus briefs were filed; when *Webster* was argued, that number had risen eightfold, to seventy-eight.[42] Moreover, the justices today—as Justice Scalia bemoaned in *Webster*—are subject to "carts full of mail from the public, and streets full of demonstrations, urging us—their unelected and life-tenured judges . . . —to follow the popular will."[43] This assault on the Court as an institution, whether healthy or unhealthy, is profound. It may well explain why *Casey* began its opinion with the admonition that "liberty finds no refuge in a jurisprudence of doubt."[44]

CONCLUSION

The abortion dispute reveals a great deal about the American governmental and political process. Abortion, among other things, highlights the institutional tugs and pulls that help explain elected-government decision-making; the seriousness with which elected government approaches constitutional interpretation; and the impact of single-issue politics on the political process. What is especially striking about each of these inquiries is the profound role that Supreme Court decisions and the Court's status as a coequal branch of the federal government have played in defining abortion politics. Outside of Reagan's regulatory initiatives (where court rulings played an instrumental but ancillary role), the Supreme Court has set the tone of elected-government decision-making. When the Court reaffirmed abortion rights in *Casey*, executive and legislative decision-making was affected dramatically. The Clinton administration, recognizing *Casey*'s popularity, became less strident and more reactive in advancing its pro-choice agenda. Along the same lines, Congress's tendency to avoid absolutist responses took hold, and freedom-of-choice legislation suffered a fatal blow. Congress also played a reactive role in enacting pregnancy discrimination and clinic access legislation—responding to disfavored Court interpretations of statutory language.

Supreme Court decision-making also has proven the benchmark for elected government in its assessment of the constitutionality of its conduct. Dominating consideration of clinic access, human life, and freedom-of-choice legislation, for example, were committee hearings and reports sorting out the constitutionality of these proposals under existing Court doctrine. Elected-government disapproval of Court doctrine, moreover, is typically expressed in efforts to get the Court to reverse its own decision-making. The Reagan and Bush administrations, while seeking to transform Court doctrine, likewise viewed Court decision-making as decisive. Through amicus curiae filings and Supreme Court appointments, these pro-life administrations sought to create circumstances in which the Court itself would overturn *Roe*. In so doing, abortion put a stranglehold on the appointments and confirmation process.

The Court has played an instrumental role in defining elected-government action. However, Court action has not proven decisive in several key respects. Elected government, while unwilling to pursue certain alternatives out of respect for the Court, nonetheless is willing to challenge the Court. Funding bans, judicial appointments, and state laws testing the parameters of *Roe* all express disapproval of Court decision-making. In a few instances, moreover, elected government has approved antiabortion legislation without consideration of the constitutionality of its actions. The Hyde Amendment and the Adolescent Family Life Act are two prominent examples.

9 / Converging Values
The Evolution of Court and Elected-Government Views on Abortion

SUPREME COURT ABORTION DECISIONS have been extraordinarily consequential. Not only has access to comparatively safe and affordable abortions improved but elected-government attitudes towards abortion rights have undergone a dramatic shift. In the two decades since *Roe*, abortion rights have become institutionalized and are no longer vulnerable to possible shifts in judicial decision-making. The Supreme Court, too, has undergone a dramatic transformation in the years since *Roe*. Gone is the stringent trimester standard responsible for the invalidation of most post-*Roe* legislation. In its place, the undue burden test recognizes that elected government plays an important role in defining the parameters of the abortion right.

Shifts in judicial and elected-government attitudes make clear that the courts and elected government shape constitutional values and each other. Court decisions, while shaping both the content and the process of elected-government action, nonetheless must operate within the confines of political action. By the same token, elected-government action cannot stray too far from the constitutional norms set forth in Supreme Court decisions.

ELECTED-GOVERNMENT ATTITUDES TOWARDS THE JUDICIARY

The Supreme Court, while it does not have the last word on the abortion dispute, is a critical part of the dynamic that defines the reaches and limits of the abortion right. What role the Court plays in shaping abortion rights is another matter. Common sense suggests a positive correlation between the respect accorded *Roe* and the judiciary's influence in defining the abortion issue. Along the same lines, common sense suggests a positive correlation between changes in abortion rates following *Roe* and the decision's impact. What then if abortion rates had not changed after *Roe*, or if elected government sought to undermine the decision through massive legislative and administrative resistance? Would this mean that *Roe* was inconsequential or that elected government does not take seriously Court edicts? These questions figure largely in the abortion dispute's relevance to an understanding of American political institutions.

Measuring Roe's Impact

Roe was controversial from the start. Rather than a modest extension of a well-accepted right to use contraceptives, *Roe* marked a radical departure, and ultimately resulted in the overturning of forty-six state laws. Indeed, in an opinion that now seems remarkable, the American Civil Liberties Union concluded in February 1967 that restrictive abortion laws "are not so unreasonable as to be unconstitutional," for "society could decide . . . to place such a value on the life of the unborn child as to render abortion possible only in a narrow range of circumstances."[1] Furthermore, that nineteen states had liberalized criminal statutes governing abortion in the decade preceding *Roe* does not undermine the case's significance. Abortion reform efforts, while on the rise, typically involved exempting abortions performed because of rape, incest, and medical necessity from criminal abortion statutes, and did not seek more far-reaching repeals of criminal abortion statutes. Moreover, immediately before *Roe*, reform initiatives had suffered surprising defeats in several states.

Roe also made a difference. While political scientist Gerald Rosenberg and others have called *Roe*'s impact into question,[2] pointing to statistics showing that the rate of legal abortions rose more dramatically in the years before *Roe* (300%—from 193,500 in 1970 to 586,800 in 1972) than in the two years after *Roe* (52%—from 586,800 in 1972 to 898,600 in 1974),[3] these statistics ultimately are unpersuasive. Imagine, as law professor Peter Schuck does, what would have happened if *Roe* had gone the other way. "The abortion rate might have increased at a lower rate or even declined. . . . Indeed, had *Roe* upheld state criminalization of abortion, the burden of political inertia would have strongly, probably decisively, favored the pro-life forces."[4] In the end, statistics revealing the prevalence of pre-*Roe* abortions do no more than demonstrate that the rise of abortions is attributable to much more than a single Supreme Court decision.

Several other factors also support the conclusion that *Roe* is consequential. First, *Roe* helps explain the rise in the number of legal abortions from

586,800 in 1972 to 1,553,900 in 1980.[5] *Roe*'s checking of state power enabled market mechanisms to make abortions more affordable and accessible. For example, the number of women who could not obtain an abortion dropped from more than 1 million in 1973 to less than six hundred thousand in 1977.[6] In freeing the market (especially in authorizing nonhospital abortions), *Roe* also helped diminish the psychological costs of the abortion procedure. Second (and relatedly), *Roe* has spurred changes in access to abortion in the most restrictive states (due to increased availability) and among poor women (due to increased affordability). Third, the abortion procedure has become safer as a consequence of *Roe*. From 1963 to 1973, the abortion death rate was roughly 5.7 per million persons, and criminal procedures accounted for 75 percent of abortion deaths from 1940 to 1972.[7] The number of maternal deaths fell from the pre-*Roe* figure of 57 per year to 6 in 1974, 3 in 1976, and none in 1979.[8] Fourth, in the five years following the Court's decision, *Roe* helped precipitate a "dramatic decline in . . . numbers of newborns abandoned for adoption and rates of illegitimate births."[9]

The key to this impact is the availability of safe and economical abortion providers. Correspondingly, *Roe* is less important in jurisdictions where there are no abortion providers. For this reason, Gerald Rosenberg argues that the refusal of many hospitals to perform abortions suggests that *Roe* would have been ineffective had the Court approved hospital-only abortions. None of this suggests that the Court is ineffective, however. The Court *did* authorize nonhospital abortions, thereby staving off potential implementation problems. More important, *Roe* created its own implementing market by creating a need for nonhospital abortion providers, and those providers soon appeared. As Rosenberg recognizes: "In the wake of the Court decisions there was a sharp increase in the number of abortion providers."[10] This self-implementing characteristic distinguishes *Roe* from *Brown*. In *Brown*, the Court decision did not create its own market mechanism; instead, external incentives (federal funding prohibitions) were required to secure compliance from southern states that otherwise preferred one-race schools.

Roe's reliance on market forces, however, does not ensure that abortion rights will be fully realized throughout the nation. Abortion is a disfavored medical procedure, and consequently, abortion services tend to be performed by very few physicians at very few clinics in the most populous counties. Most strikingly, only 17 percent of the nation's 3,135 counties have abortion facilities.[11] Furthermore, in 1990, according to the *Washington Post*, "300 clinics and physician's offices . . . perform about half of the 1.6 million abortions performed every year in the United States."[12] Correlatively, "at U.S. medical schools, only a quarter of ob/gyn residency programs require abortion training, and another quarter don't offer it at all."[13] That abortion services are concentrated, of course, does not negate *Roe*'s extraordinary impact. It simply highlights inherent limits in market mechanisms in guaranteeing constitutional rights.

Roe's self-executing nature also helps explain the rise of the "right-to-life" movement and, with it, antiabortion regulation and legislation. Having won a devastating victory at the time when it seemed the war had only just begun, the pro-choice movement has not needed to try to pass legislation guaranteeing a woman's right to choose. In other words, because the costs of continued lobbying exceeded the benefits, the pro-choicers slipped back into the category of "the unorganized or relatively less-organized members of society" who "do not find it cost effective to resist having their wealth taken away."[14] The pro-life movement, however, had every reason to remain organized. Because religious organizations formed the backbone of the movement, it had a ready-made organizational structure; thus its lobbying costs were lower than those of the pro-choice movement. Furthermore, the pro-lifers' objective, the protection of unborn children, was far from accomplished, so their movement still could hope to obtain benefits from its lobbying activities.

With pro-choice forces securing an unqualified, constitutionally guaranteed right to first-trimester abortions, pro-life forces therefore came to dominate the political marketplace: the greater *Roe*'s practical and symbolic importance, the more vociferous the antiabortion movement became. If one measures a case's impact by the strength of the opposition, *Roe*'s landmark status is assured. Between 1973 and 1989, forty-eight states passed 306 abortion measures. Congress and the White House too were extraordinarily active, if less prolific, during this period—debating more than five hundred abortion bills and numerous regulatory initiatives. This degree of activity in the face of *Roe*'s stringent trimester approach is staggering.

Just as *Roe* transformed the political marketplace in 1973, *Webster* v. *Reproductive Health Services* had a similarly profound effect in 1989. As Cass Sunstein observed, "the Court's partial retreat from *Roe* [in *Webster*] may well have galvanized the women's movement in a way that will have more favorable and fundamental long-term consequences for sexual equality than anything that could have come from the Court."[15] Specifically, pro-choice interests, such as NARAL and NOW, experienced unprecedented growth in revenues, membership, and political clout. Most significantly, in contrast to the 1973–89 period, only three states (Pennsylvania, Utah, and Louisiana) sought to capitalize on *Webster* by enacting meaningful abortion restrictions.

Webster clearly changed the political landscape of abortion politics without prompting significant changes in abortion rights. Rather than suggesting that court opinions are of little consequence, however, this state of affairs bespeaks the importance of judicial action. By changing the calculus of antiabortion proposals, *Webster* made right-to-life initiatives less likely to succeed. Instead, the *Roe*-created status quo has become the governing norm—despite the fact that *Roe* had earlier invalidated forty-six state laws. In fact, the Supreme Court's 1992 reaffirmation of *Roe* in *Planned Parenthood* v. *Casey* was explicitly grounded in the *stare decisis* effect of *Roe*. While *Casey* also reaffirmed *Webster*'s repudiation of the "rigid" trimester test, its adherence to *Roe*'s "central holding" further reveals the transformative power of judicial edicts. This transformation of the status quo involves not just judicial action but also market conditions, elected government, and interest groups, but the judiciary is certainly a partner in this dynamic process.

Abortion Rights as a Commodity in the Political Marketplace

Supreme Court abortion decisions also offer telling evidence of elected-government attitudes towards the Court. To be sure, most elected-government action has sought to limit abortion rights. At the same time, no federal and virtually no state action has directly challenged Supreme Court edicts. The Hyde Amendment, AFLA, and family-planning and fetal tissue regulations do not contradict *Roe* and its progeny. In contrast, proposals that sought to nullify *Roe*—human life legislation, court-stripping efforts, and constitutional amendments—have been rejected by Congress. And only a handful of states have played a leadership role in enacting stringent abortion laws. Most states wait to see if the courts will approve these "challenger" state initiatives.[16] Furthermore, most challenger state action is not clearly at odds with Court decisions but tests the limits of these decisions. For example, *Roe* did not explicitly address parental or spousal consent, public funding, hospital-only abortions, waiting periods, and the like. State action on those subjects engages the judiciary in a dialogue on the sweep of abortion rights; it does not necessarily challenge Court authority.

The possibility that elected-government output may not measure elected-government preferences also suggests that too much should not be read into elected-government resistance to *Roe*. Many elected officials were quietly pleased by *Roe*. John Hart Ely, for example, speaks of "the sighs of relief as this particular albatross was cut from the legislative and executive necks."[17] That an avalanche of abortion restrictions were enacted may only mean that legislators saw no disadvantage in responding to pro-life interest groups, for pro-choice concerns were content to leave it to the courts to protect their interests. In a sense, federal and state efforts to limit abortion rights paid homage to a judiciary that would toe the line and provide whatever constitutional protections were appropriate.

Roe's transformation of the political marketplace, in other words, was rooted in the belief that the Supreme Court would vigorously defend abortion rights. That public opinion polls reflected popular support for limited abortion rights did not matter; interest group pressures were able to push legislative majorities to support abortion restrictions. By legalizing abortion, therefore, *Roe* eliminated the demand for pro-choice legislation while causing the demand for pro-life legislation to grow. At the same time, *Roe* also increased the supply of pro-life legislation. Before the decision, the benefit the pro-choicers obtained from a legislative victory was offset by the loss the pro-lifers sustained, and vice versa. But *Roe* eliminated nearly all negative externalities associated with pro-life laws. By writing abortion rights into the Constitution, the Court assured pro-choicers that they could not lose the benefits they had won. Legislators voting on pro-life bills no longer had to worry that their pro-choice constituents might complain. Instead, they could vote for the bills so that the pro-life activists would obtain a legislative benefit, while *Roe* ensured that pro-choice citizens would not suffer any measurable loss.

Despite the efforts of pro-life groups to pass laws that might give the Supreme Court an opportunity to limit *Roe*, between 1973 and 1989 the Court decided only a single major issue in these groups' favor, when it permitted states to refuse to fund poor women's abortions through Medicaid.[18] *Webster,* by threatening the rights of middle- and upper-class women, changed this political dynamic and revealed a general contentment among federal and state legislators with the status quo *Roe* had created. Instead of a new wave of abortion regulation, legislative inaction followed in *Webster*'s wake. Many legislators would have preferred that the Court retain control over abortion and not return the issue to elected government. This reaction is not surprising, for legislators knew that pro-choice forces were "going to take names and kick ankles." As a result, the *Roe*-created status quo became the governing norm, despite the fact that *Roe* had earlier invalidated forty-six state laws. In 1994, for example, no state introduced legislation to outlaw abortion. Of equal significance, all abortion regulation measures adopted in the years following *Casey* have involved restrictions approved by the Court: waiting periods, informed consent, and parental notification.

Elected-government perceptions about the judicial role and the respect owed to Supreme Court decisions figures prominently in the story of abortion politics. The dialogue that takes place between the courts and federal and state government is highly nuanced. For example, rather than legislatively respond to family-planning regulations before the *Rust* v. *Sullivan* decision, Congress deferred to the Supreme Court in the hopes that it could avoid the issue altogether. When the Court upheld the regulations, legislative repeal efforts targeted both the Court, for its decision, and the White House, for its support of that decision. This dialogue reveals much more than the temporary nature of Supreme Court decisions. Elected government has chosen certain types of limited responses and rejected more confrontational approaches. That is telling— as is the fact that federal and state officials, while supporting measures at odds with abortion rights, may well have preferred that the Court maintain control over this issue.

Musings about the Future: Prospective Overruling and Legislative Reliance

Roe skewed the political process. By minimizing the costs of enacting antiabortion legislation (since pro-choice interests could look to the courts for protection) and by creating a market for pro-life legislation (since most existing abortion restrictions were nullified by the decision), *Roe* prompted a tidal wave of abortion restrictions. What then of state laws unconstitutional under *Roe* and its pre-*Webster* progeny but constitutional today under the Court's more relaxed standards? Would the majority's will be furthered or frustrated by enforcement of these measures? On the one hand, a majority of legislators voted for these measures. On the other hand, according to Ruth Bader Ginsburg, Gerald Rosenberg, and others, pro-choice legislative repeal efforts (cut short by *Roe*) might have resulted in the repeal or moderation of many abortion restrictions.

Despite general contentment with *Casey*, judicial solutions to this dilemma might well produce the next wave of abortion litigation.[19] Courts may (but need not) revive formerly invalidated statutes under the view that, had the legislature changed its position, it would have rescinded the statute. Since the pre-*Roe* abortion reform movement had only limited success in liberalizing antiabortion laws and next to no success in repealing those laws, there is little reason to conclude that these laws would have been invalidated but for *Roe*. As Guido Calabresi observed, the "burden of inertia" favors existing laws.[20] Information costs, the comparative ease of blocking legislation in committee or on the legislative floor, and the risk of a gubernatorial veto are but some of the reasons that existing laws are infrequently repealed.

There is a tremendous irony here. *Roe,* as the post-*Webster* experience reveals, made abortion rights an accepted (if not beloved) part of our political culture. Nonetheless, since the revival decision hinges on how the world would look absent *Roe,* it may nonetheless be appropriate to validate majoritarian decision-making through the revival of unpopular legislation. Were courts to force pro-choice groups to overcome the "burden of inertia," the pre-*Roe* abortion wars would be fought again—but this time according to post-*Roe* sensibilities. Alternatively, by emphasizing "the fair treatment of those who based their behavior on [*Roe* and other] judicial interpretations,"[21] the courts may honor the emerging post-*Casey* sensibility and place the onus on right-to-life groups to reenact abortion restrictions. In either event, the courts will frame the abortion dispute through a ruling grounded in *Roe*'s impact on majoritarian politics and in elected-branch attitudes towards the judiciary.

JUDICIAL ATTITUDES TOWARDS ELECTED GOVERNMENT

Just as the courts shape elected government, elected government also shapes the courts. Through the post-*Roe* period, the Supreme Court validated elected-government efforts to limit abortion rights. At the federal level, the Court approved several legislative and regulatory initiatives and struck none down. By emphasizing Congress's power of the purse and the deference owed to executive-branch statutory interpretations, the Court upheld abortion funding restrictions in *Harris* v. *McRae* (1980); federally supported adoption counseling by religious organizations in *Bowen* v. *Kendrick* (1988); and regulations forbidding family-planning centers to discuss abortion in *Rust* v. *Sullivan* (1990). These decisions make clear that the elected branches play a vital role in the abortion dispute.

The 1992 case *Planned Parenthood* v. *Casey* is a culmination of these interchanges between the Court and elected government. After five abortion-dominated Supreme Court confirmation hearings and hundreds of thousands of abortion protesters marching each year at its steps, the Court formally reconsidered and moderated *Roe.* Remarkably, because it reaffirmed the "central holding" of *Roe* on *stare decisis* grounds,[22] *Casey* never considered the correctness of *Roe.* At the same time, *Casey* gutted *Roe*'s stringent trimester standard and replaced it with a government-friendly "undue burden" test. This finessing of the *Roe* issue, without doubt, is tightrope walking at its finest (or most pernicious, depending on your perspective). Rather than hand pro-choice or pro-life interests an overwhelming victory, *Casey* sought to find a middle ground between two irreconcilable poles.

Casey is a remarkable decision. At one level, the Court seems to be beside itself in self-doubt. Acknowledging that it can neither appropriate funds nor command the military to enforce its orders, the Court recognizes that its power lies "in its legitimacy, a product of substance and perception that shows itself in the people's acceptance of the Judiciary."[23] In other words, as psychologists Tom Tyler and Gregory Mitchell observed, the Court seems to believe "that public acceptance of the Court's role as interpreter of the Constitution—that is, the public belief in the Court's institutional legitimacy—enhances public acceptance of controversial Court decisions."[24] This emphasis on public acceptance of the judiciary seems to be conclusive proof that the outcome in *Casey* cannot be divorced from the case's explosive social and political setting.

Casey, however, goes to great lengths to declare that "social and political pressures," far from being relevant, must be resisted. Otherwise, anarchy will rule the day, for our nation will have forsaken its commitment "to the rule of law."[25] Beyond this rule-of-law claim, *Casey* invokes judicial supremacy to defend the Court's authority to settle the abortion dispute. Calling on the "contending sides of a national controversy to end their national division,"[26] *Casey* implores the public to rise to the occasion by submitting to the Court. In a statement showing remarkable arrogance, the Court suggests that the American people's "belief in themselves . . . as a people is not readily separable from their understanding of the Court invested with the authority to . . . speak before all others for their constitutional ideals."[27] Under this vision, as the law professor Robert Nagel perceptively put it, America's commitment to the rule of law "requires widespread habits of mind that conceive of the announced law as authoritatively settled even as it evolves."[28]

There is a bitter irony here. Willing to link legitimacy and public perception but unwilling to admit sensitivity to social and political forces, the Court effectively looks for an escape hatch by declaring itself supreme. Whereas in *Roe* the Court concealed efforts to dictate elected-government action behind high-sounding rhetoric about the judicial task being "free of emotion and predilection,"[29] the *Casey* decision concealed by subterfuge the Court's desire to soothe competing interests. What is remarkable is the Court's linkage of legitimacy with judicial supremacy. The Court feels compelled to play the "last-word" game, but that game appears tinged with concern for public acceptance.

Casey then brings the last-word debate full circle. From its opening salvo—"Liberty finds no refuge in a jurisprudence of doubt"[30]—to its formal release, where each member of the *Casey* plurality took turns reading from the opinion in open Court, *Casey* was treated as a monumental event designed to quiet the abortion dispute. These theatrics signal the Court's sensitivity to public opinion and its recognition that social and political forces would define the decision's future. Nonetheless, the Court thought it necessary to counterbalance its sensitivity to social and political influences by asserting, in dramatic fashion, that the rule of law hinges on judicial supremacy. In plain terms, judicial finality appears to be little more than a shibboleth; *but* it is the Court's shibboleth.

CONCLUSION

The Court and elected government have influenced each other over the course of the abortion dispute. Without question, the Court has set the parameters of elected-government decision-making. State legislators have been extremely sensitive to trends in Court decision-making. Just as *Roe* prompted a flood of antiabortion legislation, *Webster* and *Casey* have placed a virtual hold on state lawmaking.

Court decision-making too has clearly been affected by social and political influences. *Casey*'s moderation of *Roe* seems directly linked to political challenges to the rigid trimester standard. Of equal significance, the Court's reaffirmation of abortion rights is a testament to the Court's perception that its institutional legitimacy is hinged to its refusal to overrule a decision under political fire.

The story of abortion rights is ultimately one of tension and cooperation. Elected government and the courts have pushed and influenced each other quite a bit in the two decades since *Roe*. With each branch giving up some ground to the other, battles have been fierce—but less fierce than they otherwise might have been. Indeed, in 1996 the gap between the attitudes of elected government and judicial attitudes has narrowed to the point of being almost nonexistent.

10 / The Interactive Constitution

"THERE IS A MAGNETIC ATTRACTION TO the notion of an ultimate constitutional interpreter," wrote Walter Murphy, "just as there is a magnetic pull to the idea of some passkey to constitutional interpretation that will, if properly turned, always open the door to truth, justice, and the American way."[1] But just as finality "is not the language of politics,"[2] constitutional decision-making too is a never-ending process. The abortion dispute is testament to the fact that constitutional decision-making is part and parcel of an ongoing political process.

The proposition that elected government actively participates in the shaping of constitutional values is hardly novel. One hundred years ago, James Bradley Thayer wrote of Congress's role in interpreting the Constitution.[3] In 1921, Justice Cardozo reminded us that judges are attentive to "the great tides and currents which engulf" the rest of us.[4] And today, a growing number of legal academics and political scientists are examining the propriety, quality, and influence of elected-branch interpretations.[5]

The assertion, made in this book's introduction, that landmark Supreme Court decisions can only be understood in their political context has been amply demonstrated in this study. To begin with, no branch of government has the power to unilaterally reorder society. The executive, legislative, and judicial branches are engaged in an ongoing dialogue, with each branch checking (and perhaps educating) the others. "Our government," as Alexander Bickel put it, "consists of discrete institutions, but the effectiveness of the whole depends on their involvement with one another, on their intimacy, even if it often is the sweaty intimacy of creatures locked in combat."[6]

By preventing any branch of government from dominating the others, this interactive process shows that constitutional values emerge from an ongoing dialogue. This book's case studies reinforce this message. Whether the issue is abortion, desegregation, the legislative veto, or the rights of religious parents, the courts and elected government shape each other. While this conclusion seems anything but pathbreaking, it nonetheless runs against the grain of three of the most visible models of judicial authority.

One model, judicial supremacy, sees the Supreme Court as the dominant voice in constitutional decision-making. Embraced by the Supreme Court (which, with false modesty, once deemed itself "infallible only because we are final"),[7] undergraduate, graduate, and law schools perpetuate this model. Specifically, by focusing almost exclusively on Court decisions, the constitutional law class hardly ever considers elected-government action. Countering judicial supremacy's emphasis on the Court's power to uphold or invalidate governmental action, Robert McCloskey, Robert Dahl, Richard Funston, and other political scientists emphasize that "the salient fact, whatever the explanation, is that the Court has seldom lagged far behind or forged far ahead of America."[8] This majoritarian model, rather than claiming that the Court is without power, argues that the Court is unlikely to make meaningful use of the power it possesses. Outside of transitional periods, "in which the Court is a holdover from the old coalition," the Court will not thwart the dominant political alliance that "it is inevitably part of."[9] In stark contrast to the judicial supremacy and majoritarian models, a third model, which calls into question the power of courts to alter bureaucratic and institutional practices, has been proposed by Gerald Rosenberg, Cass Sunstein, and other progressive academics. Pointing to severe limitations in the design of American courts, these scholars label the judiciary a "hollow hope" that rarely makes a difference. Meaningful reform, instead, is accomplished through social movements and elected-branch initiatives.

Without question, some Court decisions are inconsequential. It is also true that the courts often follow dominant political trends. Finally, elected government has sometimes abided by the demands of a judiciary that trumps majoritarian preferences. What none of these models takes into account, and what this study demonstrates, is that constitutional decision-making is an ongoing dynamic fueled by both judicial and nonjudicial forces.

DO COURTS MATTER?

That there are instances where court opinions do not bind elected government cannot be denied. Supreme Court decisions limiting religious observance in the public schools and prohibiting the legislative veto, for example, have been disregarded. The public-school cases demand that objecting students bear the fiscal and emotional toll of challenging school systems that would prefer to heed religious belief in preference to Supreme Court decisions. This price is quite high, and consequently many religious practices remain unchallenged. The legislative veto is a more dramatic, more surprising case, for the affected parties are Congress and the White House rather than "backwater" school systems. Nonetheless, following the Supreme Court's 1983 repudiation of this device in *Immigration and Naturalization Service* v. *Chadha,* more than three hundred new legislative vetoes have been enacted and countless informal arrangements have been made between oversight committees and governmental agencies. The explanation for this widespread disobedience is that neither Congress nor the White House "wants the static model of separated powers offered by the Court."[10] That the Court repudiated the legislative veto hardly matters. With both sides benefiting from legislative vetoes, market forces have simply driven legislative veto arrangements underground.

The legislative veto and religion cases share a common feature. Neither decision creates incentives for compliance. Compliance, instead, is a by-product of the implementing community. Consequently, when the implementing community resists, the judicial impact is muted. In other instances, however, elected government acts affirmatively in the face of a decision that is not self-implementing. When a federal appeals court directed the Federal Communications Commission to take race into account in broadcast-licensing decisions, for example, the commission not only complied with that decision but embraced other policy initiatives to increase the number of minority broadcasters.[11] More significantly, federal desegregation efforts prompted southern school desegregation in the wake of widespread resistance to *Brown.*

Judicial influences are more pronounced when incentives for enforcement are a natural outgrowth of the opinion. Employers now incorporate Title VII employment discrimination rulings into their hiring and promotion practices in order to avoid litigation costs. Likewise, health care providers responded to the extraordinary demand for nonhospital abortions in the wake of *Roe* by opening abortion clinics. Elected government may strengthen these self-implementing decisions. For example, employment discrimination litigation pursued by the Equal Employment Opportunity Commission and the Department of Justice quickened the pace of Title VII compliance. Elected government may also oppose self-implementing decisions, as occurred when antiabortion funding restrictions prevented some poor women from seeking an abortion. Yet, unlike non-self-implementing decisions, in which governmental resistance is extremely significant, self-implementing decisions can withstand governmental attack. Witness the abortion decision: despite the approval of the abortion-funding ban in *Harris* v. *McRae,* abortion rates have remained stable.

Court decisions may also overcome the inertia that sometimes stalls legislative reform efforts. For example, when *Roe* was decided, a vigorous right-to-life movement successfully blocked pro-choice legislative reform efforts in Michigan, North Dakota, and elsewhere. Although 64 percent of Americans supported abortion rights at that time, pro-life forces proved that a "small but intense minority can exercise political influence disproportionate to its numbers when a diffuse and silent majority does not organize to fight back."[12] *Roe*'s recognition of abortion rights therefore validated majority preferences while it invalidated the laws of forty-six states.

Roe did more than place public opinion polls ahead of legislative majorities. *Roe* also changed the political culture of abortion. States that had been willing to validate minority preferences by enacting abortion restrictions at the behest of pro-life interest groups reversed course after the Supreme Court, in *Webster* and *Casey,* signaled its willingness to approve such restrictions.

This phenomenon—of elected government acclimating to and embracing restrictive judicial norms—is not limited to abortion. The 1991 Civil Rights Act approved disparate-racial-impact proofs of employment discrimination, a measure that would not have been adopted by the 1964 Congress.[13] Congress's change of heart was a direct result of a 1971 Supreme Court decision, *Griggs* v. *Duke Power,* which recognized disparate-impact proofs. In 1991, however, *Griggs* was a nullity—effectively overruled by a 1989 Supreme Court decision. Although *Griggs* was a judicial creation, it was also—by 1991—a cornerstone of employment discrimination litigation. The 1991 Civil Rights Act, by formally embracing disparate-impact proofs, validated judicially created norms.

The 1993 Religious Freedom Restoration Act follows a similar pattern. After the Supreme Court's 1990 *Employment Division* v. *Smith* decision reversed the longstanding judicial practice of subjecting *all* governmental conduct that burdens religious exercise to exacting judicial review, Congress stepped in to statutorily mandate the Court's preexisting practice. Finding that "laws 'neutral' towards religion may burden religious exercise as surely as laws intended to interfere with religious exercise," Congress explicitly condemned *Smith* in order "to restore" demanding judicial review of any and all burdens on religious exercise.[14] For Congress, *Smith* ran headlong into legislative expectations of vigorous protections for religious exercise, expectations created by longstanding judicial practices.

Supreme Court decisions also serve as a benchmark for lawmakers and administrators in sorting out the constitutionality of proposed legislation and regulations. For example, while *Chadha*'s legislative veto holding has been largely ignored, its demand that legislation be passed by both houses of Congress and be presented to the president has played a large role in congressional debates and hearings regarding the line item veto. Since Congress does not separately enact each line item contained in an appropriation bill, the Senate Judiciary Committee and the Justice Department's Office of Legal Counsel have both concluded that, under *Chadha*, a statutory item veto may well be unconstitutional. Supreme Court decisions likewise dominated congressional consideration of legislation criminalizing flag desecration. In the wake of a Supreme Court decision striking down a Texas law that criminalized flag burning, Congress struggled with the question of whether it should seek to penalize flag desecration through a statute or a constitutional amendment. In choosing a statute, lawmakers relied heavily on First Amendment scholars who argued that a flag-burning statute was consistent with Supreme Court norms.

Courts matter. They matter a lot. Sometimes their orders set in motion market mechanisms that guarantee their effectiveness. Sometimes the threat of judicial action prompts either settlement or a legislative initiative. Courts' opinions influence legislative deliberations and change the status quo. Occasionally, courts trump agencies and interpose their normative views into the law. It may be that these influences sometimes result in unwise policy decisions and sometimes exceed the proper judicial role in our system of separated powers, but they *are* judicial influences nonetheless.

SOCIAL AND POLITICAL INFLUENCES ON SUPREME COURT DECISION-MAKING

Law, as Morris Raphael Cohen wrote in 1933, is anything but a "closed, independent system having nothing to do with economic, political, social, or philosophical science."[15] As this study reveals, courts cannot be separated from the social and political influences that permeate all aspects of constitutional decision-making. Supreme Court justices are well aware of political concerns when devising their opinions. John Marshall saw *Marbury* v. *Madison* as an opportunity to strengthen the Federalist judiciary at the expense of his political rivals, the newly elected Jeffersonians. By holding that the executive was subject to lawsuit and that acts of Congress may be struck down by the courts, Marshall adroitly advanced this political agenda. Political concerns also figured prominently in Earl Warren's efforts at crafting a unanimous opinion in *Brown* v. *Board of Education*. Fearing massive resistance to a divided opinion, Warren purposefully weakened the content of *Brown* to forge a unanimous opinion. Specifically, the Court left it to southern district judges to take "local conditions" into account and fashion whatever remedy they deemed appropriate. In a similar vein, Harry Blackmun's suggestion that the Court issue a press release to accompany *Roe* v. *Wade* was a preemptive strike designed to limit the political repercussions of an unpopular decision.

Politics is also informative in assessing Supreme Court doctrine. For example, one measure of *Garcia* v. *San Antonio Metropolitan Transit Authority*'s claim that states' rights concerns are adequately represented in Congress is the legislation that Congress passed in response to *Garcia*.[16] On the one hand, because it held that states and municipalities were subject to federal wage and hours legislation, *Garcia* was seen as a major blow to states' rights advocates. On the other hand, responding to complaints that *Garcia* subjected states and localities to tens of millions of dollars in overtime claims, Congress enacted legislation to moderate the impact of overtime judgments, thus protecting states' interests.

A more direct connection between politics and Court doctrine is the way in which political judgments frame constitutional disputes. Congress's choice to ground the public accommodations section of the 1964 Civil Rights Act in the Commerce Clause as well as the Fourteenth Amendment allowed the Court to treat constitutional challenges to the 1964 act as commerce cases. Similarly, the use of the Commerce Clause in both clinic access and proposed freedom-of-choice legislation enabled the Court to treat pro-choice legislative initiatives as commerce cases.

Politics, moreover, contributes to the ultimate meaning of Court action. The institutional dynamics that made the legislative veto so popular before *Immigration and Naturalization Service* v. *Chadha* explain why the device continues to be used, so often that more than three hundred legislative vetoes were put into place in the decade after *Chadha*. The limits of *Brown*'s eventual delegation of remedial authority to southern district court judges are illustrated by the fact that mid-1960s elected-branch action caused the implementation of more desegregation in 1965 than had occurred in the decade following *Brown*. Likewise, the limits of *Roe*'s trimester standard are highlighted by countless legislative and administrative initiatives at variance with the decision.

Politics, finally, matters because the Supreme Court often will moderate its decision-making as part of a constitutional dialogue that takes place between the Court and elected government. Congress ultimately persevered in challenging the Court's 1918 rejection of the Commerce Clause as the basis for child labor legislation. Executive and legislative action to express disapproval of *Roe*

v. *Wade* through funding restrictions was approved by the Court in both *Harris* v. *McRae* and *Rust* v. *Sullivan*. More strikingly, *Planned Parenthood* v. *Casey* validated elected-government opposition to the trimester standard by replacing it with a more permissive "undue burden" test. These post-*Roe* decisions, by recognizing that elected government plays an important and appropriate role in the abortion arena, reduced the pressure on elected government to respond to *Roe* through the more drastic techniques of constitutional amendment or court stripping.

Political influences, while critical, tell only part of the story. The Court is also sensitive to social conditions as well as to its own institutional legitimacy. Obscenity and sodomy prosecutions have been upheld, in part, because the law "is constantly based on notions of morality." Likewise, the Court emphasized "expectations that society is prepared to honor" in rejecting a marijuana grower's claim that aerial surveillance flights violated his right to privacy. Indeed, as the Supreme Court's emphasis on history and tradition in its privacy cases makes clear, "the thinking of many authoritative jurists, eminent scholars, and important politicians converges on the ideas that the Constitution protects implied rights and that these rights should be defined in significant part by judicial examination of our traditions."[17]

Closely connected to this emphasis on tradition is the fact that the Court also speaks of its legitimacy being tied to public opinion. The post-*Roe* cases, especially *Casey*, call attention to this sensitivity to public opinion. Fearing that "to overrule *Roe* under fire" would make the Court appear like a lap dog to elected government, *Casey* ruled that "to reexamine a watershed decision would subvert the Court's legitimacy."[18] As a result, the Court upheld *Roe* on *stare decisis* grounds, revealing that social attitudes may figure prominently in constitutional decision-making.

The nexus between legitimacy and public opinion hardly begins with the *Casey* decision. Writing in the *Federalist Papers*, Alexander Hamilton reminded those who feared a too-powerful Supreme Court that "the judiciary . . . may be truly said to have neither FORCE nor WILL but merely judgment."[19] Implicit in this statement, as de Toqueville recognized in the 1840s, is that the judicial power "is enormous, but it is the power of public opinion. [Judges] are all powerful so long as the people respect the law; but they would be impotent against neglect or contempt of the law."[20] For the Supreme Court justice Robert Jackson, writing in 1951, "long-sustained public opinion does influence the process of constitutional interpretation. . . . The practical play of the forces of politics is such that judicial power has often delayed but never permanently defeated the persistent will of a substantial majority."[21] "In a political system ostensibly based on consent," as Walter Murphy and Joseph Tannenhaus recognized in their 1990 study on the Court and public opinion, "the Court's legitimacy—indeed, the Constitution's—must ultimately spring from public acceptance . . . of its various roles."[22]

All of this brings us to the crucial question: How independent is the Court? Taken at face value, *Casey*'s middle-ground approach, as well as its emphasis on legitimacy and public acceptance, supports the claim of Robert Dahl, Richard Funston, and others that the Supreme Court is molded by popular opinion.[23] Dahl's landmark 1957 study found that the Court was hardly ever successful "in blocking a determined and persistent lawmaking majority on a major policy."[24] Rather, with the appointments-confirmation process enabling the elected branches to place on the Court individuals whose political philosophies comport with majoritarian preferences, Dahl concludes that the "policy views dominant on the Court are never long out of line with the policy views dominant among the lawmaking majorities of the United States."[25] Funston's 1975 study builds upon this theme. Arguing that only "during transitional periods" will the Court "perform the counter-majoritarian function ascribed to it by traditional theory,"[26] Funston concludes that the Court is typically a yea-saying branch. "The hypothesis, in other words, is that, as Mr. Dooley so cryptically puts it 'the Supreme Court follows the election returns.'"[27]

There is little doubt that the Court is sensitive to politics. The abortion dispute, however, stands as a counterexample to Dahl and Funston's broader claims about judicial compliance with lawmaking majorities. To begin with, by invalidating legislative decision-making, the Court has spoken as a countermajoritarian voice throughout the abortion controversy. *Roe* v. *Wade* struck down forty-six state laws. From *Roe* to *Webster,* the Court withstood an onslaught of state antiabortion measures, striking most of them down and extending its reasoning in *Roe*. Although the Court approved federal and state efforts to limit abortion through appropriations bans and other indirect restrictions, it never backed away from its conclusion that a woman has a constitutionally protected right to terminate her pregnancy. *Casey,* while limiting *Roe,* nonetheless reaffirms *Roe*'s "central holding." In so doing, *Casey* invalidated a spousal notification provision that has wide public support.[28] Indeed, the Court's countermajoritarian role underlies *Casey*'s invocation of legitimacy theory. Arguing that public confidence in the Court would be undermined if *Roe* were overruled under political fire, *Casey* suggests that the Court's institutional legitimacy is, at least in part, a by-product of its willingness to invalidate governmental action. For this reason, three of the Court's five Reagan-Bush appointees broke ranks with the judicial philosophy of the presidents who appointed them.

Casey, while exceptional, does not stand alone. Within days of its *Casey* decision, the Court again embraced legitimacy concerns in *Lee v. Weisman.* Refusing to overturn a controversial 1971 decision, *Lemon v. Kurtzman,* which severely limited governmental involvement in religion, the Court ruled that the city of Providence, Rhode Island, was not justified in its practice of inviting members of the clergy to give invocations and benedictions at middle-school graduation ceremonies. That the Reagan and Bush administrations had repeatedly sought the overruling of *Lemon* did not matter. It also did not matter that the Court had openly questioned *Lemon,* refusing to apply it in cases involving legislative chaplains or access by religious groups to public facilities. Refusing to "accept the invitation of . . . the United States to reconsider our decision in *Lemon,*"[29] the Court resisted overturning a longstanding controversial precedent under political fire. As in *Casey,* the Court apparently saw its institutional legitimacy as tied to public perceptions of its independence.

CONCLUSION

A permanent feature of our constitutional landscape is the ongoing tug and pull between elected government and the courts. Focusing on the abortion dispute, this book has demonstrated that the dialogue that takes place between the Court and elected government is constructive. Today, twenty-three years after *Roe,* the prospects of executive-legislative-judicial equilibrium on the abortion issue seem better than at any time since the controversy emerged in the 1960s. At the federal level, no branch of government is at war with another, and public policy generally matches public opinion. Unpopular Reagan-Bush initiatives on fetal tissue research, family-planning counseling, and the like have been repealed and are unlikely to return. In contrast, restrictions on abortion funding, which are acceptable to the courts and remain popular with Congress and much of the nation, persist. State action, although more variable, is generally stable, and since *Webster* it has been the exception, not the rule. Indeed, state lawmaking virtually ground to a halt with *Casey.* Of equal significance, states accept *Casey* and no longer are pursuing measures that would outlaw abortion altogether.

The Supreme Court seems quite comfortable with, and is in part responsible for, the current state of affairs. Court doctrine has both shaped and been shaped by elected-branch decision-making. *Roe* nationalized abortion rights at a time when state reform efforts, while on the rise, could not guarantee success. Yet the Court has given way on restrictions on abortion funding, as well as on

Reagan-era rule-making and other elected-branch counterinitiatives. Furthermore, although the Court rejected efforts to overturn *Roe,* the "undue burden" test advanced by Reagan's solicitor general Rex Lee now seems the governing standard in state regulation cases.

The abortion dispute then reveals the fallacy of judicial supremacy, Dahl and Funston's majoritarian arguments, and progressive critiques of an inconsequential Court. Without question, social and political forces "set the boundaries for judicial activity and influence the substance of specific decisions, if not immediately then within a few years."[30] Yet, by "placing issues on the agenda of public opinion and of other public institutions [and] providing an imprimatur of legitimacy to one side or another,"[31] Court action affects majoritarian preferences, and judicial decisions serve as a benchmark in constitutional deliberations undertaken by elected government. More strikingly, *Casey's* noneventful aftermath reveals that *Roe* shaped political attitudes towards abortion rights.

The emerging equilibrium on abortion rights will not end this dispute, however. Pro-choice and pro-life interests are too polarized and too powerful for there to be a common ground on abortion. Abortion battles, however, may become less fierce and less destabilizing. With public opinion and public policy in rough accord, there is little reason for elected government or the courts to disrupt this awkward balance. Justice Scalia's hope of "compromises satisfying a sufficient mass of the electorate that this deeply felt issue will cease distorting our democratic process" may be realized after all.[32]

That this compromise came about through the "sweaty intimacy of creatures locked in combat" makes clear that no branch of government can dominate constitutional decision-making. The rigidity of *Roe* (let alone *Dred Scott,* the child labor case, and other regressive decisions!) makes clear that judicial supremacy yields unworkable solutions, not a more equitable world. "Government by lawsuit," as Justice Robert Jackson warned, "leads to a final decision guided by the learning and limited by the understanding of a single profession—the law."[33] Alexander Bickel puts the matter more directly—"doubt[ing] the Court's capacity to develop 'durable principles'" and therefore doubting "that judicial supremacy can work and is tolerable."[34]

Complex social policy issues are ill suited to the winner-take-all nature of litigation. Emotionally charged and highly divisive issues are best resolved through political compromises that yield middle-ground solutions, rather than through an absolutist and often rigid judicial pronouncement. Witness the ongoing controversy over the separation of church and state. On one side of the divide, separationists claim that government may only employ secular means to achieve secular ends. On the other side, revisionists claim that the prohibition against the establishment of religion only bars the establishment of a national religion by the federal government.

Strict adherence to either separationist or revisionist thinking leads to unacceptable results. Strict compliance with separationist thinking would place religion at a positive disadvantage compared to secular world-views or cultural expressions. Separationist theory, if carried to its logical extreme, would require the removal of "In God We Trust" from our currency, and the words "under God" from our Pledge of Allegiance; an end to the purchase or display of some of the great works of art at our publicly funded museums; an end to tax exemption for religiously affiliated institutions as well as churches; and the elimination of chaplains from the armed services and religion from the curriculum of our state universities. Revisionists, by ignoring the dangers inherent in close church-state entanglement, commit similar errors. Application of their theory would allow the states to limit public funds, public employment opportunities, and so on, to the sect of its choosing without violating the Establishment Clause.

The practical difficulties of validating either separationist or revisionist positions highlight the dilemma that courts face in resolving constitutional disputes. Were court decisions to have last-word status, this dilemma would be far worse. Because winner-take-all litigation does not favor middle-ground approaches, politically workable solutions often require elected-government intervention. Along these lines, decisions such as *Roe* and *Chadha* point to the risks of overly rigid judicial interpretations and thus to the need for social and political forces to moderate Court decision-making.

The adversarial model has also failed because of the high costs of enforcement. When the state loses in court, its regulatory scheme is, of course, without effect. When the state wins in court, however, it faces a dilemma. The battle between fundamentalist parents and state educators exemplifies this problem. Religious educators and parents often profess that they would rather go to jail than comply with regulatory demands that violate their religious beliefs. Tremendous pressure is placed on the state through this steadfast resistance. Sanctions such as the padlocking of churches, the jailing of ministers and parents, and the termination of parental rights can be successful only if there is widespread public support.

Courts, for the most part, are sensitive to these *realpolitik* concerns. *Casey*'s moderation of *Roe* is a particularly vivid illustration of this phenomenon. Judicial handling of school desegregation tells a similar tale. For example, *Brown* is testament not just to the reaches but also to the limits of judicial action.

By taking into account potential resistance to its decision, the Court in *Brown* engaged in the type of interest-balancing that has set political parameters on judicial intervention in equal educational opportunity. Noting that "some achievable remedial effectiveness may be sacrificed because of other social interests" and that "a limited remedy" may be chosen "when a more effective one is too costly to other interests,"[35] the Court recognized that victims' rights must be balanced against a broad spectrum of competing policy concerns. Specifically, aside from victims' rights, the Court in *Brown* valued local control of public school systems, and judicial restraint.

School desegregation is revealing for other reasons. During the Nixon and Reagan administrations, the Court and elected government fought a pitched battle over busing. That battle has now abated. In 1991 and again in 1992, the Supreme Court, as it did with abortion, has recognized greater state and local controls over public schools.[36] And as in the case of abortion, moreover, the Court has limited a controversial hard-line position rather than disavowing it. Thus an equilibrium of sorts has been achieved. Specifically, by empowering district court judges to take local circumstances into account in sorting out whether a school system has satisfied its desegregation obligations, the Rehnquist Court has emphasized concerns for local control and judicial restraint at the expense of victims' rights. At the same time, these Court rulings neither require nor encourage district court judges to terminate school desegregation injunctions. Along these lines, while the Rehnquist Court rejected district court efforts to include suburban school systems in a Kansas City desegregation order, the Court did not interfere with intrusive district court orders that required the building of state-subsidized housing in Yonkers and imposed a statewide tax levy to support desegregation in Kansas City.[37]

Attaining an equilibrium with regard to school desegregation and abortion required all branches and all levels of government to do battle with one another. This dynamic process yielded a very nuanced, very delicate (if not very deliberate) compromise. That this interactive process may appear a bit too much like the making of sausage helps to explain Barbara Craig and David O'Brien's characterization of the abortion dispute as an "illustrative . . . [and] disappointing reflection" of the American system.[38] Nevertheless, our system is one, as Justice Ginsburg rightly observed at her confirmation hearing, where courts "do not guard constitutional rights alone. Courts share that profound responsibility with Congress, the President, the states, and the people."[39]

That courts sometimes start these constitutional dialogues is indisputable. Without *Brown* or *Roe*, equal educational opportunity and abortion rights would mean very different things today. *But* it is equally indisputable that workable approaches to school desegregation and abortion rights require elected-government participation, sometimes supporting and at other times opposing Court action. Religious liberty tells a similar tale, with the Supreme Court leaving it to elected officials to fill the void created by Court decisions. The stories of the federal minimum wage and the legislative veto also make clear that Court decisions must operate within and therefore will be redefined by a political culture. *Garcia* and especially *Chadha* have been limited by subsequent executive and congressional action. In all those instances, the Supreme Court has helped to shape but has never dominated the social and political forces that surround its decisions.

"The genius of the system lies in the very tension itself, and in our ability to combine active democracy, constitutional principles, and judicial judgment."[40] Whether or not, as Earl Warren put it, "the day-to-day job of upholding the Constitution . . . [rests] on the shoulders of every citizen,[41] "we reject Supremacy in all three branches because of the value placed upon freedom, discourse, democracy, and limited government."[42] This repudiation of supremacy, while amply supported in this book, is nonetheless elusive. It rejects the notion of an ultimate constitutional interpreter in favor of a dynamic process. As the last-word debate reveals, there is a strong appeal to locate within government an ultimate constitutional interpreter.

This search is futile. The struggle over judicial supremacy, for example, is governed more by ephemeral political concerns than by principle. Abraham Lincoln and Edwin Meese rejected judicial supremacy because they opposed Supreme Court rulings. Indeed, Meese's progressive critics have done an about-face on this very issue. With the advent of the Rehnquist Court, progressives have increasingly turned their attention away from the courts and towards elected government, claiming that the judiciary is disinclined to advance progressive causes and heralding majoritarian reform as producing "more lasting, legitimate, and fundamental change."[43] Borrowing a line from conservative attacks against an imperial judiciary, progressives now speak of judicial intervention "dwarf[ing] the political capacity of the people . . . [by] deaden[ing] its sense of moral responsibility."[44]

The interactive process described in this book is neither progressive nor regressive. On certain issues, abortion being a prime example, rights have been moderated. At other times, however, progressive causes have been advanced. Child labor and civil rights legislation grounded in the Commerce Clause are two vivid examples. More significant than the outcomes it produces, this interactive process is an accurate portrayal of constitutional decision-making. The give-and-take between elected government and the courts permeates all of constitutional decision-making.

Vigorous interchange between the Court, elected government, and the public also results in more vibrant and durable constitutional interpretation. The quality of constitutional decision-making is a by-product of the seriousness of interpretation. Consequently, the more actors are interpreting the Constitution and butting heads with each other, the better. In addition to these advantages, interactive constitutional interpretation "moralizes the process of government" and hence is more democratic.[45] Both progressives and conservatives should prefer this type of dialectic to some constitutional philosopher king specifying what is constitutional truth.

Notes

Chapter 1. Introduction

1. Gerald N. Rosenberg, *The Hollow Hope: Can Courts Bring About Social Change?* (Chicago: University of Chicago Press, 1991), 2. Rosenberg's study, as discussed below, seeks to refute this depiction.

2. *Webster* v. *Reproductive Health Services*, 492 U.S. 490, 535 (1989) (Scalia, J., concurring in the judgment).

3. Robert H. Bork, *The Tempting of America* (New York: Free Press, 1990), 116.

4. Rosenberg, *Hollow Hope*, 201, 342.

5. See Bob Woodward, "The Abortion Papers," *Washington Post*, 22 Jan. 1989, D1, D2.

6. Harry Blackmun, memorandum, quoted in David Garrow, *Liberty and Sexuality* (New York: Macmillan, 1994), 587.

7. Ibid., 585, 587.

8. *Roe v. Wade*, 410 U.S. 113, 116 (1973).

9. *Thornburgh* v. *American College of Obstetricians and Gynecologists*, 476 U.S. 747, 759, 771 (1986).

10. *Planned Parenthood of Southeastern Pennsylvania* v. *Casey*, 112 S.Ct. 2791, 2854 (1992) (Blackmun, J., concurring in part and dissenting in part).

11. Ruth Bader Ginsburg, "Speaking in a Judicial Voice," *New York University Law Review* 67 (Dec. 1992): 1185, 1198 (emphasis added).

12. Ibid., 1208.

13. Ruth Bader Ginsburg, "Some Thoughts on Autonomy and Equality in Relation to Roe v. Wade," *North Carolina Law Review* 63 (Jan. 1985): 375, 381.

14. William J. Clinton, "The President's News Conference," *Weekly Compilation of Presidential Documents* 29 (15 June 1993): 1081. (Hereafter this publication is cited as *Weekly Comp.*)

15. Cass R. Sunstein, "Three Civil Rights Fallacies," *California Law Review* 79 (May 1991): 751, 766; Michael Kinsley, "The New Politics of Abortion," *Time* 134 (17 July 1989): 96.

16. Rosenberg, *Hollow Hope*, 184.

17. David Garrow, "History Lesson for the Judge: What Clinton's Supreme Court Nominee Doesn't Know about Roe," *Washington Post*, 20 June 1993, C3.

18. Kathleen M. Sullivan, "Law's Labor," *New Republic*, 23 Mar. 1994, 42, 44. For

1972 polling data, see George H. Gallup, *The Gallup Poll: Public Opinion, 1972–1977* (Wilmington, Del.: Scholarly Resources, 1978), 1:54.

19. Robert A. Dahl, "Decision-Making in a Democracy: The Supreme Court as a National Policy Maker," *Journal of Public Law* 6 (fall 1957): 279, 285.

20. Robert G. McClosky, *The American Supreme Court* (Chicago: University of Chicago Press, 1960), 224.

21. See Laurence H. Tribe, *Abortion: The Clash of Absolutes* (New York: Wharton, 1990); Kristen Luker, *Abortion and the Politics of Motherhood* (Berkeley: University of California Press, 1984).

22. Amy Gutmann, "No Common Ground," *New Republic*, 22 Oct. 1990, 43.

23. Kinsley, "Politics of Abortion," 96.

24. Guttman, "No Common Ground," 43.

25. Barbara Hickson Craig and David M. O'Brien, *Abortion and American Politics* (Chatham, N.J.: Chatham House, 1993), xv.

CHAPTER 2. JUDICIAL REVIEW OR JUDICIAL SUPREMACY?

1. Ruth Marcus, "Constitution Confuses Most Americans: Public Ill-Informed on U.S. Blueprint," *Washington Post*, 15 Feb. 1987, A13.

2. Edwin Meese, "The Law of the Constitution," *Tulane Law Review* 61 (Apr. 1987): 983; Michael Kinsley, "Meese's Stink Bomb," *Washington Post*, 2 Oct. 1986, A19; Anthony Lewis, "Law or Power?" *New York Times*, 27 Oct. 1986, A23. Lawrence Tribe and Eugene Thomas are quoted in Stuart Taylor Jr., "Liberties Union Denounces Meese," ibid., 24 Oct. 1986, A17.

3. *Marbury v. Madison*, 5 U.S. (1 Cranch) 137, 177 (1803).

4. *The Works of James Buchanan*, ed. John B. Moore (Philadelphia: Lippincott, 1910), 10:106.

5. *Cooper v. Aaron*, 358 U.S. 1, 18 (1958).

6. *Planned Parenthood of Southeastern Pennsylvania v. Casey*, 112 S.Ct. 2791, 2815 (1992).

7. Harold Burton, "The Cornerstone of Constitutional Law: The Extraordinary Case of Marbury v. Madison," *American Bar Association Journal* 36 (Oct. 1950): 807.

8. Marshall to Samuel Chase, 23 Jan. 1804, in Albert Beveridge, *The Life of John Marshall* (New York: Houghton Mifflin, 1919), 3:177.

9. Earl Warren, "Chief Justice Marshall: The Expounder of the Constitution," *American Bar Association Journal* 41 (Aug. 1955): 687.

10. *Annals of Congress*, 1st Cong., 1st sess., 439.

11. *Writings of Thomas Jefferson*, ed. Albert Bergh (Washington, D.C.: Thomas Jefferson Memorial Association, 1903–4), 11:215.

12. Ibid., 14:659.

13. *House of Representatives Report No. 86*, 26th Cong., 1st sess., 1840.

14. *New York Times Co. v. Sullivan*, 376 U.S. 254, 276 (1964).

15. *A Compilation of the Messages and Papers of the Presidents, 1789–1897*, ed. James D. Richardson (Washington, D.C.: Government Printing Office, 1896–99), 3:144. For a detailed discussion of the politics surrounding *McCulloch* and its aftermath,

see Paul Brest and Sanford Levinson, *Processes of Constitutional Decisionmaking,* 3d ed. (Boston: Little, Brown, 1992), 9–57.

16. *Dred Scott* v. *Sandford,* 60 U.S. 383, 451 (1856).

17. Abraham Lincoln, 10 July 1858, quoted in Brest and Levinson, *Constitutional Decisionmaking,* 212.

18. Stephen Douglas, 17 July 1858, quoted in Brest and Levinson, *Constitutional Decisionmaking,* 212.

19. *The Collected Works of Abraham Lincoln,* ed. Roy P. Basler (New Brunswick, N.J.: Rutgers University Press, 1990), 3:267.

20. Ibid., 2:401.

21. *Papers of the Presidents, 1789–1897* 7:3210.

22. *Collected Works of Lincoln* 2:516.

23. *Papers of the Presidents, 1789–1897* 7:3210.

24. Alexander Bickel, *The Least Dangerous Branch: The Supreme Court at the Bar of Politics* (New Haven: Yale University Press, 1962), 4.

25. *Lochner* v. *New York,* 198 U.S. 45 (1905).

26. House Committee on Labor, *To Prevent Interstate Commerce in the Products of Child Labor,* 64th Cong., 1st sess., 1916, H.R. Rept. 46, pt. 1:7.

27. *Hammer* v. *Dagenhart,* 247 U.S. 251, 276 (1918).

28. *Congressional Record,* 65th Cong., 3d sess., 1918, 57, pt. 1:609 (remarks of Sen. Thomas Hardwick, 18 Dec. 1918). (Hereafter, *Congressional Record* is cited as *Cong. Rec.*)

29. *Child Labor Tax Case,* 259 U.S. 20, 37 (1922).

30. Franklin D. Roosevelt, *The Public Papers and Addresses of Franklin D. Roosevelt* (New York: Random House, 1935), 4:205–10.

31. Ibid., 6:51–57.

32. Charles Evans Hughes to Sen. Burton K. Wheeler, in Senate Committee on the Judiciary, *Reorganization of the Federal Judiciary,* 75th Cong., 1st sess., 1937, S. Rept. 711, app. C, 38. Hughes claimed that the proposal was at odds with the Constitution's demand that the judicial power be vested in a single Supreme Court.

33. Ibid., 14.

34. Owen Robert, *The Court and the Constitution* (Port Washington, N.Y.: Kennikat Press, 1951), 61. Congress's enactment of legislation providing full pay for justices who retired also facilitated the replacement of *Lochner*-era justices with New Deal justices. See Louis Fisher and Neal Devins, *Political Dynamics of Constitutional Law* (St. Paul, Minn.: West, 1992), 87–88.

35. Senate Committee on the Judiciary, Subcommittee to Investigate the Administration of Internal Security Act and Other Internal Security Laws, *Limitation of Appellate Jurisdiction of the U.S. Supreme Court,* 85th Cong., 1st sess., 1957, S. 2646.

36. Ibid., 574.

37. *Cong. Rec.,* 85th Cong., 2d sess., 1958, 104, pt. 4:4423.

38. Abram Chayes, "Foreword: Public Law Litigation and the Burger Court," *Harvard Law Review* 96 (Nov. 1982): 4.

39. "Text of the 1984 Republican Party Platform," in *Congressional Quarterly Almanac* (1984), 40:41B, 55B.

40. William French Smith, "Urging Judicial Restraint," *American Bar Association Journal* 68 (Jan. 1982): 59, 60.
41. Senate Committee on the Judiciary, *Nomination of Edwin Meese III*, 98th Cong., 2d sess., 1984, S. Hrg. 98-1255, 185–86.
42. Meese, "Law of the Constitution," 982.
43. "Why Give That Speech?" *Washington Post*, 29 Oct. 1986, A18.
44. Meese, "Law of the Constitution," 986.
45. Ibid., 1004.
46. Senate Committee on the Judiciary, *Nomination of Justice William Hubbs Rehnquist*, 99th Cong., 2d sess., 1986, S. Hrg. 99-1067, 187.
47. William H. Rehnquist, *Grand Inquests: The Historic Impeachments of Justice Samuel Chase and President Andrew Johnson* (New York: Morrow, 1992), 278.
48. Senate Committee on the Judiciary, *Nomination of Anthony M. Kennedy*, 100th Cong., 1st sess., 1987, S. Hrg. 100-1037, 222–23.
49. Ruth Bader Ginsburg, "Speaking in a Judicial Voice," *New York University Law Review* 67 (Dec. 1992): 1198.
50. Senate Committee on the Judiciary, *Nomination of Ruth Bader Ginsburg*, 103d Cong., 1st sess., 1993, S. Exec. Rept., pt. 2:103–6.
51. *Brown* v. *Allen*, 344 U.S. 443, 540 (1953).
52. Charles Evans Hughes, *Addresses and Papers of Charles Evans Hughes* (New York: Putnam's Sons, 1908), 139–40.

Chapter 3. Constitutional Interpretation by Elected Government

1. Herbert Weschler, "Toward Neutral Principles of Constitutional Law," *Harvard Law Review* 73 (Nov. 1959): 6.
2. *Baker* v. *Carr*, 369 U.S. 186, 217 (1962).
3. *Goldwater* v. *Carter*, 444 U.S. 996, 1004 (1979).
4. Louis Fisher, *Constitutional Dialogues: Interpretation as Political Process* (Princeton: Princeton University Press, 1988), 102.
5. Alexander M. Bickel, "The Passive Virtues," *Harvard Law Review* 75 (Nov. 1961): 49.
6. Gerald Gunther, "The Subtle Vices of the 'Passive Virtues'—A Comment on Principle and Expediency in Judicial Review," *Columbia Law Review* 64 (Jan. 1964): 17.
7. William O. Douglas, *The Court Years, 1939–1975: The Autobiography of William O. Douglas* (New York: Random House, 1980), 113.
8. Philip Ellman and Norman Silber, "The Solicitor General's Office, Justice Frankfurter, and Civil Rights Litigation, 1946–1960: An Oral History," *Harvard Law Review* 100 (Feb. 1987): 840.
9. *Brown* v. *Board of Education of Topeka*, 347 U.S. 483, 495 (1954).
10. *Rogers* v. *Belley*, 401 U.S. 815, 837 (1971) (dissent).
11. *Mitchell* v. *W. T. Grant Co.*, 416 U.S. 600, 636 (1974) (dissent).
12. David F. Pike, "The Court Packing Plans," *National Law Journal* 5, no. 51 (29 Aug. 1983): 1.

13. Henry J. Abraham et al., "Judicial Selection: The Reagan Years," in *Judicial Selection: Merit, Ideology, and Politics* (Washington, D.C.: National Legal Center for the Public Interest, 1990), 33.

14. Stephen J. Wermiel, "Confirming the Constitution: The Role of the Senate Judiciary Committee," *Law and Contemporary Problems* 56 (autumn 1993): 121.

15. Ibid., 122. The principle of *stare decisis* calls upon the Court to respect precedent (to ensure stability in our legal system) and to distinguish precedent-based judicial decision-making from elected-government policy-making.

16. W. John Moore, "In Whose Court?" *National Journal* 23 (5 Oct. 1991): 2400.

17. National Abortion Rights Action League (NARAL), "Supreme Court Alert" (27 June 1991).

18. Robin West, "The Aspirational Constitution," *Northwestern Law Review* 88 (fall 1993): 241.

19. Owen Fiss, "The Forms of Justice," *Harvard Law Review* 93 (Nov. 1979): 9.

20. Abner J. Mikva, "How Well Does Congress Support and Defend the Constitution," *North Carolina Law Review* 61 (Apr. 1983): 610.

21. Ibid., 588, 609–10. With respect to nonlawyer members of Congress, this contention is supported by (albeit dated) empirical analysis. See Donald G. Morgan, *Congress and the Constitution* (Cambridge: Harvard University Press, 1966).

22. Paul Brest, "Congress as Constitutional Decisionmaker and Its Power to Counter Judicial Doctrine," *Georgia Law Review* 21 (1986): 59.

23. Louis Fisher, "Constitutional Interpretation by Members of Congress," *North Carolina Law Review* 63 (May 1985): 746.

24. Mark C. Miller, "Congress and the Constitution: A Tale of Two Committees," *Seton Hall Constitutional Law Journal* 3 (fall 1993): 317.

25. Richard Wolf, "Topic: The Flag Amendment. Don't Let Hysteria Hurt Flag's Meaning," *USA Today*, 12 July 1989, 9A (interview with Chairman Edwards).

26. Leslie Goldstein, "The ERA and the U.S. Supreme Court," *Law and Political Studies* 1 (1987): 145.

27. Jane Mansbridge, *Why We Lost the ERA* (Chicago: University of Chicago Press, 1989), 47.

28. *National Defense Authorization Act for Fiscal Years 1988 and 1989*, Public Law 100-180, 101 Stat. 1019, 1087 (1987).

29. *Religious Freedom Restoration Act of 1993*, Public Law 103-141, 107 Stat. 1488 (1993).

30. *Zurcher* v. *Stanford Daily*, 436 U.S. 547, 567 (1978).

31. *Cong. Rec.*, 96th Cong., 2d sess., 1980, 126, pt. 20:26564 (statement of Rep. Robert Kastenmeier).

32. *Staggers Rail Act of 1980*, Public Law 96-448, 94 Stat. 1895 (1980).

33. David A. Strauss, "Presidential Interpretation of the Constitution," *Cardozo Law Review* 15 (Oct. 1993): 114.

34. *Nominations of Edward H. Levi to be Attorney General of the United States: Hearings before the Senate Committee on the Judiciary*, 94th Cong., 1st sess., 1975, 7; Cornell Clayton, *The Politics of Justice* (Armonk, N.Y.: Sharpe, 1992), 143–45 (describing Bell's confirmation hearing); *Confirmation Hearings of Federal Ap-*

pointments: Hearings before the Senate Committee on the Judiciary, 102d Cong., 1st sess., 1991, pt. 2:142.

35. Jeremy Rabkin, "At the President's Side: The Role of the White House Counsel in Constitutional Policy," *Law and Contemporary Problems* 56 (autumn 1994): 63, 97. For a fuller treatment of the relationship of the White House staff to the president, see Bradley H. Patterson Jr., *The Ring of Power: The White House Staff and Its Expanding Role in Government* (New York: Basic Books, 1988).

36. Senate Committee on Commerce, *Civil Rights—Public Accommodation: Hearings before the Senate Committee on Commerce,* 88th Cong., 1st sess., 1963, 28 (testimony of Attorney General Robert Kennedy).

37. S. Rept. 152, 101st Cong., 1st sess., 1989, 24 (minority views; quoting Barr).

38. Ronald Reagan, "Veto of Fairness in Broadcasting Act of 1987," *Weekly Comp.* 23 (29 June 1987): 715.

39. George Bush, "Statement on the Flag Protection Act of 1989," *Weekly Comp.* 25 (26 Oct. 1989): 1619.

40. Ronald Reagan, "Statement on Signing H.J. Res. 372 into Law," *Weekly Comp.* 21 (11 Dec. 1985): 1491.

41. *Rust* v. *Sullivan,* 500 U.S. 173 (1991).

42. Role of the Solicitor General, 1 Op. Off. Legal Counsel 228, 231 (1977).

43. See H. W. Perry, *Deciding to Decide: Agenda Setting in the United States* (Cambridge: Harvard University Press, 1991), 128–33.

44. See Brief for the United States, *City of Akron* v. *Akron Center for Reproductive Health,* 462 U.S. 416 (1983).

45. See Norman Silber, "The Solicitor General's Office, Justice Frankfurter, and Civil Rights Litigation, 1946–1960: An Oral History," *Harvard Law Review* 100 (Feb. 1987): 817, 842 (interviewing Philip Ellman).

46. See Victor S. Navasky, *Kennedy Justice* (New York: Athenaeum, 1971), 287–90.

47. See Lincoln Caplan, *The Tenth Justice: The Solicitor General and the Rule of Law* (New York: Knopf, 1987), 34; Rebecca Mae Salokar, *The Solicitor General: The Politics of Law* (Philadelphia: Temple University Press, 1992), 73–74.

48. For one account, see Joseph Califano, *Governing America: An Insider's Report from the White House and the Cabinet* (New York: Simon and Schuster, 1987), 237–43; for a slightly different account, see Griffin Bell and Ronald J. Ostrow, *Taking Care of the Law* (New York: Morrow, 1992), 28–32.

49. Caplan, *Tenth Justice,* 54–59, 139–44; Charles Fried, *Order and Law: Arguing the Reagan Revolution—A Firsthand Account* (New York: Simon and Schuster, 1991), 27–35.

50. See Linda Greenhouse, "Bush Reverses U.S. Stance against Black College Aid," *New York Times,* 22 Oct. 1991, B6.

51. See Joan Biskupic, "For Solicitor General's Office, New Directions in Old Cases," *Washington Post,* 22 Feb. 1994, A1.

52. Brief for the United States, 14, *Federal Communications Commission* v. *Pacifica Foundation,* 438 U.S. 726 (1978).

53. Brief for the Federal Communications Commission, 16, *Metro Broadcasting* v. *Federal Communications Commission,* 497 U.S. 547 (1990); Brief for the United

States as Amicus Curiae, 8, *Metro Broadcasting* v. *Federal Communications Commission*, 497 U.S. 547.

54. Earl Black, *Southern Governors and Civil Rights: Racial Segregation as a Campaign Issue in the Second Reconstruction* (Cambridge: Harvard University Press, 1976), 299.

55. Gerald Rosenberg, *The Hollow Hope: Can Courts Bring About Social Change?* (Chicago: University of Chicago Press, 1991), 78.

56. *Michigan* v. *Long*, 463 U.S. 1032 (1983).

57. *Prune Yard Shopping Center* v. *Robins*, 447 U.S. 74, 81 (1980).

58. *Wisconsin* v. *Constantineau*, 400 U.S. 433, 440 (1971) (Burger, J., dissenting).

59. *People* v. *Disbrow*, 127 Cal. Rptr. 360, 368–69 (1976).

60. California Constitution, art. 1, sec. 24.

61. For an overview of these and other decisions, see Louis Fisher, "How the States Shape Constitutional Law," *State Legislatures* 14 (Aug. 1989): 37.

62. Robert H. Jackson, "The Supreme Court in the American System of Government," reprinted in Mark W. Cannon and David M. O'Brien, *Views from the Bench* (Chatham, N.J.: Chatham House, 1985), 20.

CHAPTER 4. CONSTITUTIONAL DIALOGUES

1. *Brown* v. *Board of Education of Topeka*, 347 U.S. 483, 495 (1954).

2. Robert Bork, *The Tempting of America: The Political Seduction of the Law* (New York: Free Press, 1990), 74, 77.

3. Alexander Bickel, *The Supreme Court and the Idea of Progress* (New Haven: Yale University Press, 1978), 132.

4. *Cong. Rec.*, 88th Cong., 2d sess., 1964, 110, pt. 7:8614 (statement of Sen. John Sparkman).

5. *Civil Rights Act of 1964*, Public Law 88-352, 78 Stat. 241 (1964).

6. *Elementary and Secondary Education Amendments of 1966*, Public Law 89-750, 80 Stat. 1191 (1966).

7. Gary Orfield, *The Reconstruction of Southern Education: The Schools and the 1964 Civil Rights Act* (New York: Wiley-Interscience 1969), 5.

8. *Elementary and Secondary Education Amendments of 1966*, 1209.

9. *Swann* v. *Charlotte-Mecklenburg County Board of Education*, 402 U.S. 1 (1971).

10. H.R. 13915, 92d Cong., 2d sess., 1972.

11. *Education Amendments of 1972*, Public Law 92-318, 86 Stat. 235, 371–72 (1972).

12. Ibid., 354–71.

13. Speech by William Bradford Reynolds, assistant attorney general for civil rights, before the Delaware Bar Association, Feb. 1982, 9.

14. *Omnibus Reconciliation Act of 1981*, Public Law 97-35, 95 Stat. 357 (1981).

15. Neal Devins and James Stedman, "New Federalism in Education: The Meaning of the Chicago School Desegregation Cases," *Notre Dame Law Review* 59 (1984): 1243, 1256–57.

16. *Board of Education* v. *Dowell*, 498 U.S. 237, 247 (1991).

17. *National League* v. *Usery*, 426 U.S. 833, 852 (1976).

18. *Public Papers of the Presidents of the United States: Richard Nixon, 1969–1974* (Washington, D.C.: Government Printing Office, 1973), 749.

19. Ibid., 638.

20. *Federal Register* 44, no. 247 (21 Dec. 1979): 75628–30.

21. Working Group on Federalism of the Domestic Policy Counsel, "The Status of Federalism in America" (Nov. 1986).

22. *Garcia v. San Antonio Metro Transit Authority,* 469 U.S. 528, 555 (1985).

23. Edwin Meese, "The Attorney General's View of the Supreme Court: Toward a Jurisprudence of Original Intent," *Public Administration Review* 45 (Nov. 1985): 701–2.

24. Bureau of National Affairs, Federal Contracts Report 1058 (1986); Exec. Order 12112, sec. 3(a) (1987).

25. *Fair Labor Standards Amendments of 1985,* Public Law 99-150, 99 Stat. 787 (1985).

26. *Cong. Rec.,* 99th Cong., 1st sess., 1985, 131, pt. 21:28984 (remarks of Sen. Howard Metzenbaum).

27. *New York v. United States,* 112 S.Ct. 2408 (1992).

28. *United States v. Lopez,* 115 S.Ct. 1624 (1995).

29. *Immigration and Naturalization Service v. Chadha,* 462 U.S. 919, 967 (1983) (dissent).

30. Griffin Bell and Ronald J. Ostrow, *Taking Care of the Law* (New York: Morrow, 1982), 95.

31. William French Smith, *Law and Justice in the Reagan Administration* (Stanford, Calif.: Hoover Institution Press, 1991), 221.

32. Louis Fisher, "The Legislative Veto: Invalidated, It Survives," *Law and Contemporary Problems* 56 (autumn 1993): 273, 292.

33. Ibid., 284.

34. Bell and Ostrow, *Taking Care of the Law,* 94.

35. Smith, *Reagan Administration,* 221.

36. George Bush, "Statement on Signing the Treasury, Postal Service, and General Government Appropriations Act, 1992," *Weekly Comp.* 27 (28 Oct. 1991): 1525.

37. Fisher, "Legislative Veto," 288.

38. Stephen Breyer, "The Legislative Veto after *Chadha,*" *Georgetown Law Journal* 72 (Feb. 1984): 785, 793.

39. *Public Papers of the Presidents of the United States: Ronald Reagan, 1984* (Washington, D.C.: Government Printing Office, 1987), 2:1056.

40. James M. Beggs, NASA administrator, to House and Senate Appropriations Committee, 9 Aug. 1984, reprinted in Louis Fisher and Neal Devins, *Political Dynamics of Constitutional Law* (St. Paul, Minn.: West, 1992), 142.

41. Secretary of State James Baker to House Speaker Jim Wright, 28 Apr. 1989, reprinted in Fisher and Devins, *Political Dynamics,* 142.

42. Robert Pear, "Unease Is Voiced in Contra Accord," *New York Times,* 26 Mar. 1989, A1.

43. David Hoffman and Ann Devroy, "Bush Counsel Contests Contra Aid Plan," *Washington Post,* 26 Mar. 1989, A5.

44. Fisher, "Legislative Veto," 292.

45. *State* v. *Faith Baptist Church*, 301 N.W.2d 571 (Neb.), *appeal dismissed*, 454 U.S. 803 (1981).

46. Neal Devins, "Fundamentalist Christian Educators v. State: An Inevitable Compromise," *George Washington Law Review* 60 (1992): 818, 828–29.

47. *State* v. *Faith Baptist Church*, 301 N.W.2d 571 (Neb.), 577, 580.

48. "The Report of the Governor's Christian School Panel," 26 Jan. 1984, 27.

49. Ibid., 1.

50. Ibid., 21.

51. Nebraska Revised Statutes, sec. 79-1701 (1990).

CHAPTER 5. THE MAKING AND UNMAKING OF *ROE* V. *WADE*

Keith Finch, a 1992 graduate of the College of William and Mary, Marshall-Wythe School of Law, played a significant role in the drafting of this chapter.

1. Eva R. Rubin, *Abortion, Politics, and the Courts*, rev. ed. (New York: Greenwood Press, 1987), 12.

2. Marian Faux, *Roe v. Wade: The Untold Story of the Landmark Supreme Court Decision That Made Abortion Legal* (New York: Macmillan: 1988), 53.

3. James C. Mohr, *Abortion in America: The Origin and Evaluation of a National Policy* (New York: Oxford University Press, 1978), 35.

4. Reva Siegel, "Reasoning from the Body: A Historical Perspective on Abortion Regulation and Questions of Sexual Protections," *Stanford Law Review* 44 (Jan. 1992): 261, 283.

5. Ibid., 286.

6. Kristen Luker, *Abortion and the Politics of Motherhood* (Berkeley: University of California Press, 1986), 26.

7. David Garrow, *Liberty and Sexuality: The Right to Privacy and the Making of Roe v. Wade* (New York: Macmillan, 1994), 288.

8. Lawrence H. Tribe, *Abortion: The Clash of the Absolutes* (New York: Norton, 1990), 37–38; Garrow, *Liberty and Sexuality*, 306–10.

9. Garrow, *Liberty and Sexuality*, 562.

10. Ibid., 547.

11. Barbara Hickson Craig and David M. O'Brien, *Abortion and American Politics* (Chatham, N.J.: Chatham House, 1993), 177.

12. Albert M. Pearson and Paul M. Kurtz, "The Abortion Controversy: A Study in Law and Politics," *Harvard Journal of Law and Public Policy* 8 (spring 1985): 427.

13. Marlene Gerber Fried, "Transforming the Reproductive Rights Movement: The Post-Webster Agenda," in *From Abortion to Reproductive Freedom: Transforming a Movement*, ed. Marlene Gerber Fried (Boston: South End Press, 1990), 1, 5.

14. Debra W. Stewart and Jeanne Bell Nicholson, "Abortion Policy in 1978: A Follow-up Analysis," *Publius* 9 (winter 1979): 161, 165.

15. Tribe, *Abortion*, 145–46.

16. Lee Epstein and Joseph F. Kobylka, *The Supreme Court and Legal Change: Abortion and the Death Penalty* (Chapel Hill: University of North Carolina Press, 1992), 211.

17. Rubin, *Abortion, Politics, and the Courts*, 113. For a book-length treatment of the

subject see Michele McKeegan, *Abortion Politics: Mutiny in the Ranks of the Right* (New York: Free Press, 1992).

18. Michael Margolos and Kevin Neary, "Pressure Politics Revisited: The Anti-Abortion Campaign," *Policy Studies Journal* 8 (spring 1980): 698, 702–3.

19. Ibid., 705–6.

20. Ibid., 706.

21. Ibid., 710.

22. On this subject, see Thomas R. Morris, "States before the U.S. Supreme Court: State Attorneys General as Amicus Curiae," *Judicature* 70 (Feb.–Mar. 1987): 298.

23. Oral argument transcript reprinted in *Seventy-Five Landmark Briefs and Arguments of the Supreme Court of the United States,* ed. Philip B. Kurkland and Gerhard Casper (Arlington, Va.: University Publications of America, 1975), 796.

24. Compare *Roe v. Wade,* 410 U.S. 113, 163 (1973), to *City of Akron v. Akron Center for Reproductive Health,* 462 U.S. 416 (1983).

25. For a perceptive treatment of this topic, see Glen Halva-Neubauer, "Abortion Policy in the Post-*Webster* Age," *Publius* 20 (summer 1990): 27.

26. Cynthia Gorney, "Taking Aim at Roe v. Wade," *Washington Post Magazine,* 9 Apr. 1989, 18.

27. See Susan Behuniak-Long, "Friendly Fire: Amicus Curiae and Webster v. Reproductive Health Services," *Judicature* 74 (Feb.–Mar. 1991): 261.

28. Brief for Appellants, 9, *Webster* v. *Reproductive Health Services,* 492 U.S. 490 (1989).

29. Brief of the Attorneys General of Louisiana et al., as Amicus Curiae, 11, *Webster* v. *Reproductive Health Services,* 492 U.S. 490.

30. Brief of the Attorney General of California et al. and Amicus Curiae, 11, *Webster* v. *Reproductive Health Services,* 492 U.S. 490.

31. Brief of the Amicus Curiae on behalf of 608 State Legislators from 32 states, 9, *Webster* v. *Reproductive Health Services,* 492 U.S. 490.

32. *Webster* v. *Reproductive Health Services,* 492 U.S. 490, 518. A plurality decision is one in which a majority of the Court approves a particular outcome but is divided on the reasoning that supports that outcome.

33. *Webster* v. *Reproductive Health Services,* 492 U.S. 490, 521.

34. Press conference of the National Right to Life Committee, Federal News Service (3 July 1989), available on LEXIS.

35. Press conference on the *Webster* v. *Reproductive Health Services* decision, Kate Michelman, executive director, National Abortion Rights Action League, Federal News Service (3 July 1989), available on LEXIS.

36. *State Reproductive Health Monitor* 1 (Dec. 1990): i.

37. William Schneider, "Wrong Way for Women's Movement," *National Journal* 31 (5 Aug. 1989): 2018. By contrast, in 1985 only 50 percent of respondents said they supported *Roe,* and only 55 percent opposed a constitutional amendment banning abortion. Schneider, "Wrong Way," 2018.

38. R. W. Apple Jr., "Limits on Abortion Seem Less Likely," *New York Times,* 29 Sept. 1989, A1.

39. Catherine Whitney, *Whose Life? A Balanced, Comprehensive View of Abortion from Its Historical Context to the Current Debate* (New York: Morrow, 1991), 126.

40. Carol Matlack with Maya Weber, "Abortion Lobbyists Striking a Vein of Gold," *National Journal* 11 (16 Mar. 1991): 632.

41. See ibid.

42. Ibid.

43. See, e.g., Robert Shogan and David Lauter, "Bush Abortion Position Draws Fire from GOP Politics," *Los Angeles Times,* 9 Nov. 1989, A1.

44. See Debra L. Dodson and Lauren D. Burnbauer, *Election 1989: The Abortion Issue in New Jersey and Virginia* (New Brunswick, N.J.: Eagleton Institute of Politics, Rutgers, 1990), 42–59.

45. Ibid., 45.

46. Dan Balz and Maralee Schwartz, "Abortion: From Forefront to Periphery," *Washington Post,* 3 Nov. 1990, A1; Holly Idelson, "Budget, Jobs, and Abortion Are Big Issues in States," *Congressional Quarterly Weekly Report* 48 (8 Sept. 1990): 2840.

47. Joe Frost, "Americans in the Center Focus on Abortion Fight," *New Orleans Times Picayune,* 11 Sept. 1991, A3.

48. William E. Schmidt, "Onetime Abortion Foe Isn't So Sure Anymore," *New York Times,* 4 Dec. 1989, A18.

49. Gorney, "Taking Aim at Roe v. Wade," 18.

50. Marcia Coyle, "Is the Court Avoiding the Big Question?" *National Law Journal* 12 (9 July 1990): 1.

51. Quoted in Linda Feldmann, "States Stitching Patchwork Quilt of Abortion Laws," *Christian Science Monitor,* 7 Nov. 1990, 8.

52. Jeffrey Schmalz, "Abortion Access Stands in Florida," *New York Times,* 12 Oct. 1989, A23.

53. Rochelle Sharpe, "Shock of Passage May Awaken Activists," *Idaho Statesman,* 23 Mar. 1990, A4.

54. Cecil Andrus, text of speech, *Idaho Statesman,* 31 Mar. 1990, A4.

55. Renee Villeneuve, "GOP Adversary Trio Say Andrus Waffles," *Idaho Statesman,* 31 Mar. 1990, A3.

56. *Idaho Statesman,* 29 Mar. 1990, 9A.

57. The president's veto operates in similar ways. See Chapter 7, below.

58. Ed Anderson, "Roemer Vetoes Bill on Abortion," *New Orleans Times-Picayune,* 15 June 1991, A1.

59. Buddy Roemer, interview by Peter Jennings (ABC television broadcast, 1 Nov. 1990).

60. Ed Anderson, "Legislature Bans Abortion," *New Orleans Times-Picayune,* 19 June 1991, A1.

61. "In Search of a Compromise on Abortion," *U.S. News and World Report,* 6 Nov. 1989, 31.

62. "Casey 'Satisfied' with 1989, Confronted Tough Issues Like Abortion," *United Press International,* 20 Dec. 1989, BC Cycle.

63. *Planned Parenthood of Southeastern Pennsylvania* v. *Casey,* 112 S.Ct. 2791, 2803 (1992).

64. Ibid., 2820.

65. NBC / Wall Street Journal Poll, *Wall Street Journal,* 22 May 1992; NBC / Wall Street Journal Poll, ibid., 23 Oct. 1992, A1.

66. Robert J. Blenda, John Benson, and Karen Donelan, "The Public and the Controversy over Abortion," *JAMA*, 15 Dec. 1993, 2871.

67. Bruce Fein, "Jurisprudence of Popular Opinion?" *Washington Times*, 7 July 1992, F1.

68. *State Reproductive Health Monitor* (Alan Guttmacher Institute), 4, no. 4 (Dec. 1993): i.

69. *State Reproductive Health Monitor* (Alan Guttmacher Institute), 5, no. 2 (May 1994): ii.

70. *Prune Yard Shopping Center* v. *Robins*, 447 U.S. 74, 75 (1980).

71. *American Academy of Pediatrics* v. *Van de Kamp*, 263 Cal. Rptr. 46, 51 (1989).

72. Ibid., 51.

73. Florida Constitution, art. 1, sec. 23.

74. *In Re T. W.*, 551 S.2d 1186, 1191–92 (Fla. 1989).

75. Bobby Welch, interview on "The New Civil War" (ABC television broadcast, 1 Nov. 1990).

76. Leander Shaw, chief justice of the Florida Supreme Court, comments on "The New Civil War" (ABC television broadcast, 1 Nov. 1990).

77. Craig and O'Brien, *Abortion and American Politics*, 77.

78. Halva-Neubauer, "Abortion Policy," 49.

79. Robin Toner, "Abortion Right Goes On, State by State," *New York Times*, 21 Jan. 1991, A18.

Chapter 6. Congress and Abortion

1. *Cong. Rec.*, 93d Cong., 1st sess., 1973, 119, pt. 28:37113.

2. *House Committee on Appropriations, Conference Report: Making Appropriations for the Departments of Labor and Health, Education, and Welfare, and Related Agencies*, 93d Cong., 2d sess., 1974, H.R. 1489; reprinted in *Cong. Rec.*, 93d Cong., 2d sess., 1974, 120, pt. 27:36928, 36933.

3. Peg O'Hara, "Congress and the Hyde Amendment . . . How the House Moved to Stop Abortions," *Congressional Quarterly* 38 (19 Apr. 1980): 1038.

4. *Cong. Rec.*, 94th Cong., 2d sess., 1976, 122, pt. 16:20410.

5. Ibid., 20410 (remarks of Rep. Henry Hyde).

6. Ibid., 20411 (remarks of Rep. Daniel Flood).

7. Ibid., 20412 (remarks of Rep. Robert Bauman).

8. Public Law 95-205, 95 Stat. 1460 (1977).

9. *Health and Human Services Appropriation Bill*, 103d Cong., 1st sess., 5 Jan. 1993, Public Law 103-12.

10. *Cong. Rec.*, 101st Cong., 1st sess., 1989, 135, daily ed. (2 Aug. 1989): H4928.

11. *Cong. Rec.*, 101st Cong., 1st sess., 1989, 135, daily ed. (11 Oct. 1989): H6915–16.

12. See Robert Marshall Wells, "House Passes Labor-HHS Bill, but Senate Outlook Unclear," *Congressional Quarterly Weekly Report* 53 (7 Aug. 1995): 2364; Dan Morgan, "Abortion Foes Prevail in House Panel Votes," *Washington Post*, 21 July 1995, A1.

13. See Morgan, "Abortion Foes Prevail."

14. Brief for Appellees, 171, *Harris* v. *McRae*, 448 U.S. 297 (1980).

15. Brief for Amici Curiae, 11–12, *Harris* v. *McRae,* 448 U.S. 297.

16. *McRae* v. *Califano,* 491 F.Supp. 630, 742 (E.D.N.Y. 1980).

17. Brief of Rep. Jim Wright et al., 29, 6, *Harris* v. *McRae,* 448 U.S. 297.

18. Ibid., 14.

19. *Harris* v. *McRae,* 448 U.S. 297, 318.

20. Ibid., 325.

21. Brief of Sen. Bob Packwood et al., 3, *Thornburgh* v. *American College of Obstetricians and Gynecologists,* 476 U.S. 747 (1986).

22. Brief Amicus Curiae of the Center for Judicial Studies and Certain Members of Congress in Support of Appellants, *Webster* v. *Reproductive Health Services,* 492 U.S. 490 (1989).

23. Brief of Center for Judicial Studies, 15, 18.

24. Brief for Rep. Don Edwards et al., as Amicus Curiae in Support of Petitioners, 27, *Planned Parenthood of Southeastern Pennsylvania* v. *Casey,* 112 S.Ct. 2791 (1992).

25. Ibid., 2.

26. Brief Amicus Curiae of Hon. Henry H. Hyde et al., in Support of Respondents, 1, *Planned Parenthood* v. *Casey,* 112 S.Ct. 2791.

27. *Pregnancy Discrimination Act,* 92 Stat. 2076 (1978).

28. Compare "Aid for Pregnant Girls Set," *New York Times,* 7 Nov. 1982; with "Defeat of 'The Chastity Law,'" *Washington Post,* 2 May 1987.

29. *Bowen* v. *Kendrick,* 487 U.S. 589 (1988).

30. Senate Judiciary Committee, *The Human Life Bill,* 97th Cong., 1st sess., 1981, S. 158.

31. Susan R. Burgess, *Contest for Constitutional Authority: The Abortion and War Powers Debates* (Wichita: University Press of Kansas, 1992), 46.

32. Senate Judiciary Committee, *The Human Life Bill: Hearings before the Subcommittee on Separation of Powers of the Senate Judiciary Committee,* 97th Cong., 1st sess., 1981, 157–68.

33. The letter is reprinted in *Cong. Rec.,* 97th Cong., 2d sess., 1982, 128, pt. 16:21185.

34. *Cong. Rec.,* 97th Cong., 1st sess., 1982, 127, pt. 6:7360–61 (statement of Rep. Charles Dougherty).

35. Senate Judiciary Committee, *Human Life Bill,* 21.

36. Ibid., 423.

37. Ibid., 36 (separate remarks of Sen. Orrin Hatch).

38. Senate Committee on the Judiciary, *Report on the Human Life Federalism Amendment,* 97th Cong., 2d sess., 1982, S. Rept. 97-465. Conservative Republicans still support this approach. See Nat Hentoff, "Situational Ethics on Abortion," *Washington Post,* 6 Aug. 1994, A19.

39. *Webster* v. *Reproductive Health Services,* 492 U.S. 490 (1989).

40. See Committee on Labor and Human Resources, *Freedom of Choice Act of 1992,* 102d Cong., 2d sess., 1992, S. Rept. 102-321.

41. Ibid.

42. See, e.g., *Cong. Rec.,* 101st Cong., 2d sess., 1990, 136, daily ed. (12 July 1990): E2311 (statement of Rep. Don Edwards).

43. Senate Labor and Human Resources Committee, *The Freedom of Choice Act of 1992: S. Rep. No. 321,* 102d Cong., 2d sess., 1992, 48.

44. See letter from Attorney General William P. Barr to Sen. Edward M. Kennedy, 1 July 1992, 16 U.S. Op. Off. Legal Couns. 1 (1992). The Bush Justice Department's opposition to FOCA is discussed in Chapter 8.

45. Beth Donovan and Charles Mantesian, "Candidates Try to Mold *Casey* to Match the Voter's Moods," *Congressional Quarterly* 50 (4 July 1992): 1955.

46. *Bray v. Alexandria Women's Health Clinic,* 113 S.Ct. 753 (1993).

47. *Freedom of Access to Clinics' Entrances Act of 1993,* 103d Cong., 1st sess., 1993, H.R. Rept. 103-306, 6.

48. Ibid., 27 (dissenting views).

49. Ibid., 27.

50. Ibid., 26–27.

51. Ibid., 11–12. See also *Freedom of Access to Clinic Entrances Act of 1993: Hearing before the Committee on Labor and Human Resources,* 103d Cong., 1st sess., 12 May 1993, S. Hrg. 103-128, 17–19 (statement of Attorney General Janet Reno).

52. William J. Clinton, "Remarks on Signing the Freedom of Access to Clinics Act of 1994," *Weekly Comp.* 30 (26 May 1994): 1165.

53. Senate Judiciary Committee, *Nomination of Anthony M. Kennedy to Be Associate Justice of the Supreme Court of the United States: Hearings before the Senate Committee on the Judiciary,* 100th Cong., 1st sess., 1987, S. Hrg. 100-1037, 164.

54. Senate Judiciary Committee, *Nomination of David H. Souter to Be Associate Justice of the Supreme Court of the United States: Hearings before the Senate Committee on the Judiciary,* 101st Cong., 2d sess., 1990, S. Hrg. 101-1263, 53–54.

55. Senate Judiciary Committee, *Nomination of Judge Clarence Thomas to Be Associate Justice of the Supreme Court of the United States: Hearings before the Senate Committee on the Judiciary,* 102d Cong., 1st sess., 1991, S. Hrg. 102-1084, pt. 1:127.

56. "Excerpts from Senate Hearing on Ginsburg Nomination to the Supreme Court," *New York Times,* 22 July 1993, A20.

57. Senate Judiciary Committee, *Nomination of David Souter,* 54.

58. Senate Judiciary Committee, *Nomination of Clarence Thomas,* 98 (statement of Sen. Patrick Leahy).

59. Ibid.

60. *Cong. Rec.,* 102d Cong., 1st sess., 1991, 137 (15 Oct. 1991): 14705.

61. Charles Fried, *Order and Law: Arguing the Reagan Revolution—A Firsthand Account* (New York: Simon and Schuster, 1991), 36.

62. Joseph A. Califano Jr., *Governing America* (New York: Simon and Schuster, 1981), 59.

63. See Laurie McGinley and Rick Wartzman, "Foster's Bid to Be Surgeon General Ends in Defeat amid Divisions over Abortion," *Wall Street Journal,* 23 June 1995, A5.

64. See ibid.; Colette Fraley, "Foster Clears One Hurdle, Hopes for Floor Vote," *Congressional Quarterly Weekly Report* 53 (31 May 1995): 1508.

65. Quoted in *Cong. Rec.,* 97th Cong., 1st sess., 1981, 127, pt. 21:27517 (statement of Sen. Slade Gordon).

66. *Cong. Rec.,* 97th Cong., 1st sess., 1981, 127, pt. 21:27522 (statement of Sen. Carl Levin).

67. *Cong. Rec.*, 97th Cong., 1st sess., 1981, 127, pt. 21:27517 (statement of Sen. Slade Gordon).

68. Quoted in *Cong. Rec.*, 103d Cong., 1st sess., 1993, 139, daily ed. (15 July 1993): S8796 (statement of Sen. Don Nickels).

69. *Cong. Rec.*, 103d Cong., 1st sess., 1993, 139, daily ed. (7 Sept. 1993): S10981 (statement of Sen. Edward Kennedy).

70. Ted Weiss, chairman, Human Resources and Intergovernmental Relations Subcommittee of the United States House of Representatives, to Louis Sullivan, M.D., secretary, Department of Health and Human Services, 13 Nov. 1989, obtained through Freedom of Information Act request.

71. For an extended discussion of Bush's use of the veto power to further pro-life objectives, see Chapter 7.

72. Neil A. Lewis, "The Supreme Court: The Hearing," *New York Times*, 13 July 1994, A1.

CHAPTER 7. THE EXECUTIVE AND ABORTION

1. Republican party platform, 1984, reprinted in *Congressional Quarterly* 42, no. 34 (25 Aug. 1984): 2076. Republican moderates have urged the dropping of this abortion plank from the 1996 party platform. See David Broder, "Lobbyist Takes Over GOP," *Washington Post*, 30 Jan. 1993, A1.

2. Democratic party platform, 1984, reprinted in *Congressional Quarterly* 42, no. 34 (25 Aug. 1984): 207.

3. Richard Nixon, "Statement about Policy on Abortion at Military Base Hospitals in the United States," 3 Apr. 1971, in *Public Papers of the Presidents of the United States* (Washington, D.C.: Government Printing Office, 1972), 127; George McGovern, speech at Freemont, Neb., 6 May 1972, *Congressional Quarterly* 30, no. 35 (2 Sept. 1972): 2222.

4. Richard Nixon to Cardinal Cooke, 1992, in *Federal Abortion Politics*, ed. Neal Devins (New York: Garland, 1995), vol. 2, pt. 1, pp. 30–31; Patrick Buchanan to President Nixon, memorandum, 6 Sept. 1973, in ibid., vol. 2, pt. 1, p. 40.

5. Jim Cannon to Phil Buchen, memorandum re abortion, 6 Jan. 1976, in Devins, *Federal Abortion Politics*, vol. 2, pt. 1, p. 103.

6. President Gerald R. Ford to the Most Reverend Joseph L. Bernadin, *Weekly Comp.* 12 (10 Sept. 1976): 1327.

7. James Carter, "President's News Conference of July 12, 1977," in *Public Papers of the Presidents: Jimmy Carter, 1977* (Washington, D.C.: Government Printing Office, 1978), 2:1237.

8. "Mr. Carter's Cruel Abortion Plan," *New York Times*, 13 June 1977, A28.

9. *Cong. Rec.*, 96th Cong., 2d sess., 6 Feb. 1980, 126, pt. 2:2214 (remarks of Rep. Philip Crane).

10. Republican party platform, 1980, reprinted in *Congressional Quarterly* 38, no. 29 (19 July 1980): 200.

11. Ronald Reagan, *Abortion and the Conscience of the Nation* (Nashville: Nelson, 1984), 19.

12. Ibid., 15.

13. Ronald Reagan, "Remarks by the President in Briefing for Right to Life Leaders," *Weekly Comp.* 23 (30 July 1987): 882.

14. Terry Eastland, *Energy in the Executive* (New York: Free Press, 1992), 26 (quoting Hamilton).

15. Ethan Bronner, "Bush Position Has Shifted Greatly," *Boston Globe,* 26 Oct. 1989, A26.

16. George Bush, "Remarks to Participants in the March for Life Rally," *Weekly Comp.* 25 (23 Jan. 1989): 110.

17. George Bush, "National Sanctity of Human Life Day, 1992," Proclamation 6397, *Federal Register* 56 (20 Dec. 1991): 66775.

18. Bill Clinton, "Remarks on Signing Memorandums on Medical Research and Reproductive Health and an Exchange with Reporters," *Weekly Comp.* 29 (22 Jan. 1993): 85.

19. Bill Clinton, "Remarks in the ABC News Nightline Town Meeting in Tampa, Florida," *Weekly Comp.* 29 (23 Sept. 1993): 1850.

20. See John Lancaster, "Vatican Envoy Praises Gore's 'Positive' Statements on Abortion," *Washington Post,* 6 Sept. 1994, A13; George Archibald, "U.S. Delegates to Conference Offer Boost to Motherhood," *Washington Times,* 7 Aug. 1995, A8.

21. See Thomas S. Edsall, "Dole Rebuffs Gramm Call to Take Antiabortion Vow," *Washington Post,* 9 Sept. 1995, A1.

22. George Bush, "Message to the House of Representatives Returning without Approval of the District of Columbia Appropriations Act of 1990," *Weekly Comp.* 25 (20 Nov. 1989): 1801.

23. Quoted in Charles C. Thatch Jr., *The Creation of the Presidency, 1775–1789: A Study on Constitutional History* (Baltimore: Johns Hopkins Press, 1969), 152–53.

24. David M. O'Brien, *Judicial Roulette: The Report of the Twentieth Century Task Force on the Appointment of Federal Judges* (New York: Twentieth Century Fund / Priority Press, 1988), 53.

25. Ronald Reagan, "Message to the National Convention of the Knights of Columbus," *Weekly Comp.* 22 (5 Aug. 1986): 1049.

26. Republican party platform, 1984, reprinted in *Congressional Quarterly* 42, no. 34 (25 Aug. 1984): 2076

27. Steven Alumbaugh to C. K. Rowland, "The Links between Platform-Based Appointment Criteria and Trial Judges' Abortion Judgements," *Judicature* 24 (Oct.–Nov. 1990): 153, 162.

28. See Michelle McKeegan, *Abortion Politics: Mutiny in the Ranks of the Right* (New York: Free Press, 1992), 136–37.

29. Edward Walsh, "Court Change Elevates Biden's Profile," *Washington Post,* 12 July 1987, A7.

30. *Public Papers of the Presidents of the United States: Ronald Reagan, 1984* (Washington, D.C.: Government Printing Office, 1987), 2:1230.

31. The White House Report: "Information on Judge Bork's Qualifications, Judicial Record, and Related Subjects," reprinted in *Cardozo Law Review* 9 (Jan. 1988): 187, 207.

32. Ibid., 209.

33. "The Biden Report," reprinted in *Cardozo Law Review* 9 (Jan. 1988): 219, 244.

34. Senate Judiciary Committee, *Nomination of Robert H. Bork to Be Associate Justice of the Supreme Court of the United States: Hearings before the Senate Committee on the Judiciary,* 100th Cong., 1st sess., 1987, S. Exec. Rept. no. 100-7, 114–17.

35. Quoted in Louis Fisher and Neal Devins, *Political Dynamics of Constitutional Law* (St. Paul, Minn.: West, 1992), 202.

36. Ibid.

37. Senate Judiciary Committee, *Nomination of Robert Bork,* 20.

38. *Cong. Rec.,* 100th Cong., 1st sess., 133, daily ed. (23 Oct. 1987): S14997 (statement of Sen. Robert Dole).

39. Robert H. Bork, *The Tempting of America* (New York: Free Press, 1990), 332. For an extended account of the Bork nomination, see Ethan Bronner, *Battle for Justice: How the Bork Nomination Shook America* (New York: Norton, 1989).

40. David M. O'Brien, "The Reagan Judges: His Most Enduring Legacy," in *The Reagan Legacy: Promise and Performance,* ed. Charles O. Jones (Chatham, N.J.: Chatham House, 1988), 63.

41. Eastland, *Energy in the Executive,* 146.

42. Richard P. Nathan, *The Administrative Presidency* (New York: Macmillan, 1983), 5.

43. George C. Eads and Michael Fix, *Relief or Reform: Reagan's Regulatory Dilemma* (Washington, D.C.: Urban Institute Press, 1984), 143.

44. Joseph A. Califano Jr., *Governing America* (New York: Simon and Schuster, 1981).

45. Ibid., 66.

46. Margaret "Midge" Costanza to the President, memorandum re staff and interest group reactions to president's abortion statements, 13 July 1977, obtained from Carter Presidential Library, Atlanta, Ga.

47. David Johnston, "Washington at Work: Reno's Popularity Rises from Ashes of Disaster," *New York Times,* 1 May 1993, A9; Ronald J. Ostrow, "Reno Confirmed as First Woman Attorney General," ibid., 12 Mar. 1993.

48. See David Garrow, *Liberty and Sexuality* (New York: Macmillan, 1994), 418, 465–80.

49. Charles Fried, *Order and Law: Arguing the Reagan Revolution—A Firsthand Account* (New York: Simon and Schuster, 1991), 33.

50. Ibid., 72.

51. Lincoln Caplan, *The Tenth Justice: The Solicitor General and the Rule of Law* (New York: Knopf, 1987), 146 (quoting Terry Eastland).

52. Fried, *Order and Law,* 33.

53. Brief for the United States as Amicus Curiae, 2–3, *City of Akron* v. *Akron Center for Reproductive Health,* 462 U.S. 416 (1983).

54. "No Friend of the Court," editorial, *New York Times,* 4 Aug. 1982, A22.

55. James McClellan, "A Lawyer Looks at Rex Lee," *Benchmark* 1, no. 2 (Mar.–Apr. 1984): 1.

56. Caplan, *Tenth Justice,* 107.

57. Brief for the United States as Amicus Curiae, 20, *Thornburgh* v. *College of Obstetricians and Gynecologists,* 476 U.S. 747 (1986).

58. Fried, *Order and Law,* 72, 34.

59. See Brief for the United States as Amicus Curiae, 7, *Webster* v. *Reproductive Health Services,* 109 S.Ct. 3040 (1989).

60. *Webster* v. *Reproductive Health Services,* 492 U.S. 490, 518 (1989).

61. Oral argument transcript, 7, Brief for the United States as Amicus Curiae, *Planned Parenthood of Southeastern Pennsylvania* v. *Casey,* 112 S.Ct. 2791 (1992).

62. See Joan Biskupic, "Justices Reject Challenges to Clinic-Access Law," *Washington Post,* 20 June 1995, A8.

63. *Rust* v. *Sullivan,* 111 S.Ct. 1759, 1767 (1991).

64. Richard Nixon, "Abortions at Military Hospitals," *Weekly Comp.* 7 (10 Apr. 1971): 598.

65. Ibid.

66. See Henry C. Cashen II to John Ehrlichman, "Eyes Only" memorandum, 7 Dec. 1971, in Devins, *Federal Abortion Politics,* vol. 2, pt. 1, p. 19.

67. Eva R. Rubin, *Abortion, Politics, and the Courts,* rev. ed. (New York: Greenwood Press, 1987), 151.

68. Gerald Ford to Caspar Weinberger, draft letter, 1975, in *Executive Initiatives,* ed. Neal Devins (New York: Garland, 1995), 2:58–59.

69. Califano, *Governing America,* 82.

70. Ibid., 84–85.

71. *U.S. Statutes at Large* 84 (1970): 1504, 1508.

72. *Program Guidelines for Project Grants for Family Planning Services,* pt. II, 8.6 (Rockville, Md.: U.S. Department of Health and Human Services, 1981), 13.

73. Ibid., 896, 898.

74. "Statutory Prohibition on Use of Appropriated Funds in Programs Where Abortion Is a Method of Family Planning," *Federal Register* 52 (1987): 33210, 33215.

75. Carole I. Chervin, "The Title X Family Planning Gag Rule: Can the Government Buy Up Constitutional Rights?" *Stanford Law Review* 41 (Jan. 1989): 401, 408.

76. Ibid.

77. *Rust* v. *Sullivan,* 111 S.Ct. 1759, 1772 (1991).

78. John Chafee, "Congress Should Remedy the Court's Decision," *Washington Post,* 7 June 1991, A23.

79. George Bush, "Memorandum of Disapproval for the Departments of Labor, Health and Human Services, and Education, and Related Agencies Appropriations Act," *Weekly Comp.* 27 (19 Nov. 1991): 1684.

80. *Cong. Rec.,* 102d Cong., 1st sess., 1991, 137, daily ed. (19 Nov. 1991): H10491–50.

81. Bill Clinton, "Memorandum for the Secretary of Health and Human Services on the Title X 'Gag Rule,'" *Weekly Comp.* 29 (22 Jan. 1993): 88.

82. *Planned Parenthood Federation of America* v. *Agency for International Development,* 915 F.2d 59 (2d Cir. 1990), *cert. denied,* 500 U.S. 952 (1991).

83. Bill Clinton, "Memorandum on the Mexico City Policy," *Weekly Comp.* 29 (22 Jan. 1993): 88.

84. Louis Sullivan to William Raub, acting NIH director, 2 Nov. 1989, in Devins, *Federal Abortion Politics,* vol. 2, pt. 2, p. 691.

85. *Cong. Rec.,* 102d Cong., 2d sess., 1992, 138, daily ed. (24 June 1992): H5091 (remarks of Rep. Jolene Unsoeld).

86. "FDA Import Alert 66047," in Devins, *Federal Abortion Politics*, vol. 2, pt. 2, p. 566.

87. *Benten* v. *Kessler*, 112 S.Ct. 2929 (1992).

88. Bill Clinton, "Memorandum on Importation of RU-486," *Weekly Comp.* 29 (22 Jan. 1993): 89.

89. "RU-486 Press Conference," reprinted in *Federal News Service*, 16 May 1994.

90. Eastland, *Energy in the Executive*, 306.

CHAPTER 8. WHAT THE ABORTION DEBATE TEACHES US ABOUT AMERICAN POLITICS

1. Owen M. Fiss, "Foreword: The Forms of Justice," *Harvard Law Review* 93 (Nov. 1979): 1, 10.

2. See *McRae* v. *Califano*, 491 F.Supp. 630 (E.D.N.Y.), *rev'd sub nom. Harris* v. *McRae*, 448 U.S. 297 (1980) (upholding Hyde Amendment); *Kendrick* v. *Bowen*, 657 F.Supp. 1547 (D.D.C. 1987), *rev'd*, 487 U.S. 589 (1988) (upholding AFLA).

3. See Senate Committee on Labor and Human Resources, *Oversight of Family Planning Programs, 1981: Hearings on Examination of the Role of the Federal Government in Birth Control, Abortion Referral, and Sex Education Programs before the Senate Committee on Labor and Human Resources*, 97th Cong., 1st sess., 1981.

4. See Senate Committee on Labor and Human Resources, *Adolescent Family Life*, 97th Cong., 1st sess., 1981, S. Rept. 97-161.

5. Senate Committee on Labor and Human Resources, *Reauthorization of the Adolescent Family Life Demonstration Projects Act of 1981: Hearings on an Overview of the Adolescent Pregnancy Problem and Reauthorization of Title XX of the Public Health Services Act before the Subcommittee on Family and Human Services*, 98th Cong., 2d sess., 1984, S. Hrg. 98-1209, 4. This approach reflects the tendency of nonlawyer members of Congress to pass constitutional questions along to the courts. See Donald G. Morgan, *Congress and the Constitution: A Study of Responsibility* (Cambridge: Harvard University Press, 1966), 336.

6. See *Cong. Rec.*, 94th Cong., 2d sess., 24 June 1976, 122, pt. 16:20410–12; ibid., 94th Cong., 2d sess., 24 June 1976, 122, pt. 24:30898; ibid., 94th Cong., 2d sess., 24 June 1976, 122, pt. 21:27672–75.

7. Brief for Jim Wright et al , *Harris* v. *McRae*, 448 U.S. 297.

8. See *Human Life Bill: Hearings on S. 158 before the Subcommittee on Separation of Powers of the Senate Committee on the Judiciary*, 97th Cong., 1st sess., 1981; *Report of the Committee on the Judiciary on S. J. Res. 110, Human Life Federalism Amendment*, 97th Cong., 2d sess., 1982, S. Rept. 465 (with minority views).

9. See Mark C. Miller, "Congress and the Constitution: A Tale of Two Committees," *Seton Hall Constitutional Law Journal* 3 (fall 1993): 317; Roger H. Davidson, "The Lawmaking Congress," *Law and Contemporary Problems* 56 (autumn 1993): 99.

10. Richard F. Fenno Jr., *Congressmen in Committees* (Boston: Little, Brown, 1973), 280; Miller, "Congress and the Constitution," 341–42.

11. Roger H. Davidson, "Procedure and Politics in Congress," in *The Abortion Dis-*

pute and the American System, ed. Gilbert Y. Steiner (Washington, D.C.: Brookings Institution, 1983), 36.

12. Frederick S. Jaffe, Barbara L. Lindheim, and Phillip R. Lee, *Abortion Politics: Private Morality and Public Policy* (New York: McGraw-Hill, 1981), 115.

13. See Senate Judiciary Committee, *Hearings before the Subcommittee on the Constitution of the Senate Judiciary Committee, Constitutional Amendments Relating to Abortion*, 97th Cong., 1st sess., 1981.

14. See Subcommittee on Separation of Powers of the Senate Committee on the Judiciary, *The Human Life Bill, S. 158: Report Together with Additional and Minority Views to the Committee on the Judiciary*, 97th Cong., 1st sess., 1981, S. Rept. 1, 7, 53–54.

15. George Bush, "Remarks to the National Association of Evangelists," *Weekly Comp.* 28 (3 Mar. 1992): 391.

16. Senate Committee on Labor and Human Resources, *The Freedom of Access to Clinic Entrances Act of 1993, Hearing before the Committee on Labor and Human Resources*, 103d Cong., 1st sess., 1993, S. Hrg. 103-138, 180 (joint statement of Michael Stokes Paulson and Michael W. McConnell).

17. Senator Edward Kennedy (D.-Mass.), for example, contended that there is "little merit to the argument that these terms would have been unconstitutionally vague or overboard." Senate Committee on Labor and Human Resources, *Freedom of Access to Clinics Act of 1993: Report*, 103d Cong., 1st sess., 1993, S. Rept. 103-117, 30.

18. Ibid., 39 (statement of Sen. David Durenberger).

19. Paul Brest, "Congress as Constitutional Decisionmaker and Its Power to Counter Judicial Doctrine," *Georgia Law Review* 21 (1986): 93, 97.

20. See William P. Barr, attorney general, to Edward Kennedy, chairman, Senate Committee on Labor and Human Resources, 1 July 1992, in *Federal Abortion Politics*, ed. Neal Devins (New York: Garland, 1995), vol. 1, pt. 2, p. 527.

21. Senate Committee on Labor and Human Resources, *Freedom of Choice Act of 1991, Hearing of the Committee on Labor and Human Resources*, 102d Cong., 2d sess., 1991, S. Hrg. 102-813, 16 (statement of John C. Harrison).

22. Senate Committee, *Freedom of Access*, 18 (statement of Janet Reno).

23. Ibid., 17 (Reno testimony).

24. Senate Committee, *Freedom of Choice*, 16 (Harrison testimony).

25. Charles Fried, *Order and Law: Arguing the Reagan Revolution—A Firsthand Account* (New York: Simon and Schuster, 1991), 72.

26. Stephen J. Markman, "Judicial Selection: The Reagan Years," in *Judicial Selection: Merit, Ideology, and Politics*, ed. Henry Abraham (Washington, D.C.: National Legal Center for the Public Interest, 1990), 33.

27. M. Jewell and S. Patterson, *The Legislative Process in the United States*, 3d ed. (New York: Random House, 1977), 454.

28. Senate Committee on Governmental Affairs, *Study on Federal Regulation: Congressional Oversight of Regulatory Agencies*, Comm. Print, 1977, S. Doc. 95-26, 31.

29. Gilbert Y. Steiner, ed., *The Abortion Dispute and the American System* (Washington, D.C.: Brookings Institute, 1983), 5.

30. See Barbara Hickson Craig and David M. O'Brien, *Abortion and American Politics* (Chatham, N.J.: Chatham House, 1993), 174–75.
31. See *Margaret S. v. Edwards*, 794 F.2d 994, 995–96 (5th Cir. 1986).
32. Quoted in *CNN Transcripts, Inside Politics*, 99-5, 30 June 1992, available in LEXIS, Nexis Library, CNN File; "Governor Clinton's Litmus Test," *Washington Post*, 9 July 1992, A22.
33. Stephen Labaton, "Senators See Easy Approval for the Nominee," *New York Times*, 16 June 1993, A22.
34. See Stephen Wermiel, "Reagan Names Friend to Become Solicitor General," *Wall Street Journal*, 26 Sept. 1985, 64.
35. Quoted in David Lauter and Ronald J. Ostrow, "Ways Sought to Improve the Confirmation Procedures," *Los Angeles Times*, 17 Oct. 1991, A1.
36. Quoted in Davidson, "Procedure and Politics in Congress," 44.
37. *Cong. Rec.*, 95th Cong., 1st sess., 17 June 1977, 123, pt. 16:19699.
38. Ibid., 19699. The chair noted that "the language in the bill addresses determinations by the Federal Government and is not limited by its terms determinations by individual physicians or by the respective States."
39. Ibid., 19699 (amendment offered by Rep. Henry Hyde).
40. Ibid., 19700 (amendment offered by Rep. Henry Hyde).
41. Ibid.
42. See generally Susan Behuniak-Long, "Friendly Fire: *Amici Curiae and Webster v. Reproductive Health Services*," *Judicature* 74 (Feb.–Mar. 1991): 261; Craig and O'Brien, *Abortion and American Politics*, 212–27.
43. *Webster v. Reproductive Health Service*, 492 U.S. 490, 535 (1989) (Scalia, J., concurring).
44. *Planned Parenthood of Southeastern Pennsylvania v. Casey*, 112 S.Ct. 2791, 1803 (1992).

CHAPTER 9. CONVERGING VALUES

1. David J. Garrow, *Liberty and Sexuality: The Right to Privacy and the Making of Roe v. Wade* (New York: Macmillan, 1994), 313.
2. Gerald N. Rosenberg, *The Hollow Hope: Can Courts Bring About Social Change?* (Chicago: University of Chicago, 1991), 173–265; Cass R. Sunstein, "Three Civil Rights Fallacies," *California Law Review* 79 (May 1991): 751, 766; Michael Kinsley, "The New Politics of Abortion," *Time* 134 (17 July 1989): 96.
3. Rosenberg, *Hollow Hope*, 178–80.
4. Peter H. Schuck, "Public Law Litigation and Social Reform," *Yale Law Journal* 102 (May 1993): 1763, 1778–79.
5. Rosenberg, *Hollow Hope*, 180.
6. See Jacqueline D. Forrest et al., "Abortion in the United States, 1976–1977," *Family Planning Perspective* 10 (1978): 271.
7. See Susan B. Hansen, "State Implementation of Supreme Court Decision: Abortion Rates since *Roe v. Wade*," *Journal of Politics* 42 (1980): 378.
8. See Jesse H. Choper, "Consequences of Supreme Court Decisions Upholding Individual Constitutional Rights," *Michigan Law Review* 83 (Oct. 1984): 1, 185–86.

9. Lawrence R. Berger, "Abortion in America: The Effects of Restrictive Funding," *New England Journal of Medicine* 298 (29 June 1978): 1474, 1476–77.

10. Rosenberg, *Hollow Hope*, 196.

11. Mark Cunningham, "The Abortion War: Political Controversy and Public Opinion," *National Review* 44 (2 Nov. 1992): 42.

12. Cynthia Gorney, "Abortion Providers Meet to Honor Their Peers," *Washington Post*, 9 May 1990, A6.

13. Cunningham, "Abortion War," 42.

14. Robert D. Tollison, "Public Choice and Legislation," *Virginia Law Review* 74 (Mar. 1988): 339–43.

15. Sunstein, "Three Civil Rights Fallacies," 767.

16. See generally, Glen Halva-Neubauer, "Abortion Policy in the Post-*Webster* Age," *Publius* 20 (1990): 32–40.

17. John Hart Ely, "The Wages of Crying Wolf: A Comment on *Roe v. Wade*," *Yale Law Journal* 82 (Apr. 1973): 947.

18. *Harris* v. *McRae*, 448 U.S. 297 (1980).

19. See generally William Michael Treanor and Gene B. Sperling, "Prospective Overruling and the Revival of 'Unconstitutional' Statutes," *Columbia Law Review* 93 (Dec. 1993): 1902.

20. Guido Calabresi, *A Common Law for the Age of Statutes* (Cambridge: Harvard University Press, 1982), 163.

21. Treanor and Sperling, "Prospective Overruling," 1931.

22. *Stare decisis* is the doctrine that disfavors the overruling of precedent. For an elaboration of the standards governing the application of *stare decisis*, see *Planned Parenthood of Southeastern Pennsylvania* v. *Casey*, 112 S.Ct. 2791, 2808 (1992).

23. Ibid., 2814.

24. Tom R. Tyler and Gregory Mitchell, "Legitimacy and the Empowerment of Discretionary Legal Authority: The United States Supreme Court and Abortion Rights," *Duke Law Journal* 43 (Feb. 1994): 703, 715.

25. *Planned Parenthood* v. *Casey*, 112 S.Ct. 2791, 2814.

26. Ibid., 2815.

27. Ibid., 2816.

28. Robert F. Nagel, "Disagreement and Interpretation," *Law and Contemporary Problems* 11 (autumn 1993): 17–18.

29. *Roe* v. *Wade*, 410 U.S. 113, 116 (1973).

30. *Planned Parenthood* v. *Casey*, 112 S.Ct. 2791, 2803.

CHAPTER 10. THE INTERACTIVE CONSTITUTION

1. Walter F. Murphy, "Who Shall Interpret? The Quest for the Ultimate Constitutional Interpreter," *Review of Politics* 48 (summer 1981): 401, 417.

2. Ibid., quoting Disraeli.

3. James B. Thayer, "The Origin and Scope of the American Doctrine of Constitutional Law," *Harvard Law Review* 7 (25 Oct. 1893): 129.

4. Benjamin Cardozo, *The Nature of the Judicial Process* (New Haven: Yale University Press, 1921), 168.

5. See Louis Fisher, *Constitutional Dialogues* (Princeton: Princeton University Press, 1988); Gerald Rosenberg, *The Hollow Hope: Can Courts Bring About Social Change?* (Chicago: University of Chicago Press, 1991); Barry Friedman, "Dialogue and Judicial Review," *Michigan Law Review* 91 (Feb. 1993): 577; Peter H. Schuck, "Public Law Litigation and Social Reform," *Yale Law Journal* 102 (May 1993): 1763; Neal Devins, ed., "Elected Branch Influences in Constitutional Decisionmaking," *Law and Contemporary Problems* 56 (autumn 1993): 1.

6. Quoted in Daniel Patrick Moynihan, "What Do You Do When the Supreme Court Is Wrong?" *Public Interest* 57 (1979): 3, 22.

7. *Brown* v. *Allen,* 344 U.S. 443, 540 (1953) (Jackson, J., concurring).

8. Robert G. McCloskey, *The American Supreme Court* (Chicago: University of Chicago Press, 1960), 224.

9. Richard Funston, "The Supreme Court and Critical Elections," *American Political Science Review* 69 (1975): 795, 796.

10. Fisher, *Constitutional Dialogues,* 228.

11. This episode is discussed in Neal Devins, "*Metro Broadcasting v FCC:* Requiem for a Heavyweight," *Texas Law Review* 69 (1990): 125.

12. Kathleen M. Sullivan, "Law's Labor," *New Republic,* 23 Mar. 1994, 42, 44.

13. For an extensive treatment of this question, see Hugh Davis Graham, *The Civil Rights Era: Origins and Development of National Policy, 1960–1972* (New York: Oxford University Press, 1990).

14. *The Religious Freedom Restoration Act,* 103d Cong., 1st sess., Public Law 103-141, 107 Stat. 1488 (1993).

15. Morris Raphael Cohen, *Law and Social Order* (New York: Harcourt, Brace, 1933), 380–81.

16. *Fair Labor Standards Amendments of 1985,* 99th Cong., 1st sess., Public Law 99-150, 99 Stat. 787 (1985).

17. Robert F. Nagel, "Disagreement and Interpretation," *Law and Contemporary Problems* 56 (autumn 1993): 11, 19.

18. *Planned Parenthood of Southeastern Pennsylvania* v. *Casey,* 112 S.Ct. 2791, 2815 (1992).

19. Alexander Hamilton, *The Federalist,* ed. Henry Cabot Lodge (New York: Putnam's Sons, 1895), 483.

20. Alexis de Toqueville, *Democracy in America,* ed. Phillip Bradley (New York: Knopf, 1945), 1:151–52.

21. Robert H. Jackson, "Maintaining Our Freedoms: The Role of the Judiciary," *Vital Speeches* 19 (1 Oct. 1953): 761.

22. Walter F. Murphy and Joseph Tannenhaus, "Publicity, Public Opinion, and the Court," *Northwestern University Law Review* 84 (spring/summer 1990): 985, 992.

23. See Robert A. Dahl, "Decision-Making in a Democracy: The Supreme Court as National Policy-Maker," *Journal of Public Law* 6 (fall 1957): 279; Funston, "Supreme Court and Critical Elections"; Beverly B. Cook, "Public Opinion and Federal Judicial Policy," *American Journal of Political Science* 21 (1977): 567.

24. Dahl, "Decision-Making in a Democracy," 286.

25. Ibid., 285.

26. Funston, "Supreme Court and Critical Elections," 796.

27. Ibid.
28. Robert J. Blendon, John Benson, and Karen Donelean, "The Public and the Controversy over Abortion," *JAMA*, 5 Dec. 1993.
29. *Lee* v. *Weisman*, 112 S.Ct. 2649, 2655 (1992).
30. Louis Fisher, "Social Influences on Constitutional Law," *Journal of Political Sciences* 15 (1987): 7, 8.
31. Jonathan D. Casper, "The Supreme Court and National Policy Making," *American Political Science Review* 70 (1976): 50, 63.
32. *Ohio* v. *Akron Center for Reproductive Health*, 497 U.S. 502, 520.
33. Robert Jackson, *The Struggle for Judicial Supremacy* (New York: Knopf, 1941), 291.
34. Alexander Bickel, *The Supreme Court and the Idea of Progress* (New York: Harper and Row, 1970), 99.
35. Paul Gewirtz, "Remedies and Resistance," *Yale Law Journal* 92 (1983): 585, 599.
36. *Board of Education* v. *Dowell*, 498 U.S. 237 (1991); *Freeman* v. *Pitts*, 112 S.Ct. 1430 (1992).
37. *Yonkers Board of Education* v. *United States*, 486 U.S. 1055 (1988); *Kansas City, Mo., School District* v. *Missouri*, 484 U.S. 816 (1987).
38. Barbara Hickson Craig and David M. O'Brien, *Abortion and American Politics* (Chatham, N.J.: Chatham House, 1993), 15.
39. Joan Biskupic, "Ginsburg Stresses Value of Incremental Change," *Washington Post*, 21 July 1993, A6.
40. John Agresto, *The Supreme Court and Constitutional Democracy* (Ithaca, N.Y.: Cornell University Press, 1984), 167.
41. Earl Warren, "The Bill of Rights and the Military," *New York University Law Review* 37 (1962): 181, 193.
42. Fisher, *Constitutional Dialogues*, 279.
43. Cass R. Sunstein, "Constitutional Politics and the Conservative Court," *American Prospect* 1 (spring 1990): 51.
44. James B. Thayer, *James Bradley Thayer, Oliver Wendell Holmes, and Felix Frankfurter on John Marshall* (Chicago: University of Chicago Press, 1967), 107. The Reagan administration borrowed this line in its *Webster* brief. Brief of the United States as Amicus Curiae Supporting Appellants, *Webster* v. *Reproductive Health Services*, 492 U.S. 490, 21 n. 15 (1989).
45. William Nelson, *On Justifying Democracy* (Boston: Routledge and Kegan Paul, 1980), 119.

Index

Library of Congress Cataloging-in-Publication Data

Devins, Neal E.
    Shaping constitutional values : elected government, the Supreme Court, and the abortion debate /
Neal Devins.
    p.   cm. — (Interpreting American politics)
Includes bibliographical references and index.
ISBN 0-8018-5284-6 (hc : alk. paper). — ISBN 0-8018-5285-4 (pbk. : alk. paper)
    1. Abortion—Law and legislation—United States.   2. United States—Constitutional law.   3. Law
and politics.   I. Title.   II. Series.
KF3771.D48   1996
342.73—dc20
[347.302]   95-39584